*The Older Woman
in Recent Fiction*

# The Older Woman in Recent Fiction

ZOE BRENNAN

McFarland & Company, Inc., Publishers
*Jefferson, North Carolina, and London*

LIBRARY OF CONGRESS CATALOGUING-IN-PUBLICATION DATA

Brennan, Zoe, 1971–
    The older woman in recent fiction / Zoe Brennan.
    p.    cm.
    Includes bibliographical references and index.

    **ISBN-13: 978-0-7864-1900-5**
    (softcover : 50# alkaline paper) ∞

    1. English fiction—Women authors—History and criticism.
2. Women and literature—English-speaking countries—
History—20th century.  3. English fiction—20th century—
History and criticism.  4. Older women in literature.
5. Old age in literature.  6. Aging in literature.  I. Title.
PR888.W6B74   2005
820.9'3522'09045—dc22                        2004024778

British Library cataloguing data are available

©2005 Zoe Brennan. All rights reserved

*No part of this book may be reproduced or transmitted in any form or by any means, electronic or mechanical, including photocopying or recording, or by any information storage and retrieval system, without permission in writing from the publisher.*

Cover photograph ©2004 Image Source

Manufactured in the United States of America

*McFarland & Company, Inc., Publishers*
  *Box 611, Jefferson, North Carolina 28640*
    *www.mcfarlandpub.com*

For my mother, Trish Brennan,
and Professor Kate Fulbrook,
without whom this book would
never have been completed

# Table of Contents

| | |
|---|---:|
| *Introduction* | 1 |
| 1. Paradigms of Aging and Ageism | 17 |
| 2. The Angry and Frustrated Older Woman | 46 |
| 3. The Passionate and Desiring Older Woman | 76 |
| 4. The Contented and Developing Older Woman | 110 |
| 5. The Wise and Archetypal Older Woman | 134 |
| *Conclusion* | 156 |
| *Notes* | 161 |
| *Selected Bibliography* | 175 |
| *Index* | 183 |

# *Introduction*

The central proposition of this book is that certain contemporary female novelists who choose to represent old women characters create alternative discourses of senescence to those that dominate late twentieth-century Western culture. Faith in fiction's potential to provide a space in which contentious issues such as aging can be explored is an axiom of many feminist studies of literature. This project differs from them in that it does not just rely on a gender-conscious perspective but more completely examines how age interacts with gender to affect the representation of the older female protagonist. When certain narratives are viewed from this angle, they clearly engage with and more importantly challenge society's axiomatic beliefs about old age in areas ranging from dependency to sexuality. Further, both the novels and my analysis of them refuse to deal solely in the language of stagnation and decline, an indiscriminate feature of many conventional discussions of senescence that reveals their inherent ageism.

Equally telling in terms of society's thinking about the senescent is what it chooses not to say about the old. Simone de Beauvoir rightly asserts in the introduction to her *j'accuse* style exposé *Old Age*, first published in 1970, that humankind evades "those aspects of it [the human condition] that distress them," adding that "above all they evade old age."[1] She writes that her aim is to "break the silence" that results from this anxiety and expresses itself in the literal and figurative banishment of those visible reminders that avoidance is not really an option. The writers I will be discussing similarly work toward countering the social marginalization of the old by placing them, and their concerns, at the center of their narratives. Underlying this decision is a conviction that older women are fully human and their lives are worthy of interest, which the reader will gradually learn is a more radical belief than it may initially appear.

The marked imaginative poverty of representations of the old reflects their social status as Other. Heavily reliant on stereotypes, popular portraits of aging suggest a very limited range of images and behaviors as appropriate to female senescence. Images are largely pejorative in nature, and one that appears endlessly in both fiction and the media is that of the demented and isolated woman, a "Miss Havisham" figure who lives in the past and cannot cope with the present, much less the idea of the future. Echoes of this Dickensian character vibrate throughout contemporary depictions of older women and perpetuate the assumption that the isolation of the senescent is acceptable and natural. This stereotype simultaneously appeals to common sense while cloaking the social construction of this position. However, as with all discourses that rely on stereotypes, there is some truth behind the prejudice and distortion. Many older men and women are indeed isolated and lonely, but this is more the result of attitudes that foreclose possibilities conducive to creating a fulfilled life rather than an inherent facet of old age. Conjuring up a more positive picture of aging is the character of the adored and adoring grandmother who, although on the sidelines, remains an integral member of the family. Yet this scenario cannot encompass a life for the matriarch away from her offspring and totally excludes single women.

The paradoxical portrayal of the old woman as grandmother/spinster is an extension of the virgin/whore dichotomy that recurs throughout Western culture. In old age, the virgin turns into the respectable and sexless grandmother, and because old age is constructed as a period devoid of an expressible sexuality, the whore transforms into the crone-like spinster. This label also encompasses a third figure who, in her youth, would have been a "bluestocking," troubling society because of its inability to make her fit into a dichotomous vision of femininity. However, she is finally made culturally intelligible by being transformed into the prim spinster, frightened of her sexuality and choosing to live alone. Just as the polarization of female roles affects younger women by reining in their potential, so the grandmother/spinster dualism impoverishes the life of their older sisters. While this binary opposition is gendered, it is worth stating that many representations and models of aging apply to both men and women. However, I am particularly interested in their effect upon and in discourses specific to older women and so have not spent time pointing out those paradigms that are relevant to individuals of either gender (unless this relevance is crucial to the discussion at hand).

Scattered throughout the following chapters are references to conventional representations of senescence and their often-destructive effects, which allow readers, among other things to measure how far the authors under discussion move away from using stereotypes. Novels that negotiate the path between the twin poles of misrepresentation and silence tread a relatively uncharted road. Yet, this is a familiar situation for female authors who often find themselves marching into a void and writing about aspects of women's lives that officially do not exist. Virginia Woolf's impassioned and witty treatise on women's writing, *A Room of One's Own* (1929), contains one of the most memorable twentieth-century examples of this type of investigation into a social silence. She uses the allegorical tale of Shakespeare's sister to answer the "perennial puzzle" of why women did not write in a period "when every other man, it seemed, was capable of song and sonnet."[2] Dreaming up the talented but socially powerless Judith allows Woolf to creatively explore the conditions that made it difficult for women to produce fiction, even as they were the subject of it, and challenge the idea that female authors do not possess genius. Contemporary authors who create unofficial narratives about the lives of older characters are part of the same tradition. For instance, the protagonist of Jenny Diski's *Happily Ever After* (1991), the irreverent Daphne Drummond, is represented as sexually active, adventurous and creative, all traits that are absent from conventional imaginings of the aged woman. She is akin to Woolf's Judith insofar as she is a socially trangressive figure, but unlike her predecessor she is rewarded with the "happily ever after" of the title.

Novels like Diski's represent scenes that are uncommon in fiction, or at least from perspectives that are unusual in fiction. To a degree, this is because older protagonists cannot always be appropriated for the same stories that drive narratives about younger characters. For example, an older woman could not be substituted for the hard-boiled P.I. Warshawski in Sara Paretsky's crime series, at least not without damaging the social reality claimed by the genre. As a consequence, texts about the aged explore less familiar sorts of stories, as illustrated by Doris Lessing's *The Diary of a Good Neighbour* (1983), which represents the struggles of the older protagonist with her deteriorating body. Although dependency and disability are not the sole province of the senescent, Lessing includes meditations on the aged that result in a different sort of novel then one based, for instance, on a seventeen-year-old character dealing with equally difficult physical problems. The theme might be similar, but its treatment will show as many disparities as equivalencies.

Feminist literary criticism has been as guilty as more conventional schools of thought in ignoring fictions of senescence and authors' confrontations with constructions of aging. This theoretical omission is indicative of a particular mindset that has repercussions for feminism outside of the literary arena. Failure to engage with old age, whether represented in fiction or by dominant rhetoric, perpetuates a paradigm noted by Bridget Hutter and Gillian Williams, in "Controlling Women: The Normal and the Deviant" (1981): "Old age is an element which is not seen as a characteristic of the 'normal woman.'"[3] If feminists do not pay more attention to the subject, we will continue to underestimate the variety of discourses that delineate the boundaries of gendered behavior and perpetuate the illogical, but pervasive, belief that senescence is an abnormal condition. Further, the feminist interest in theorizing differences between women, a trend that has become increasingly evident in the last two decades, runs the risk of being purely rhetorical for, like gender, age cuts across class, race, and sexuality. As it stands, most women reach old age and have to cope alone with the experience of being discursively situated as doubly Other.

Representations that do focus on female senescence add their weight to those voices that seek to prevent the premature foreclosure of the subject of contemporary constructions of femininity. Feminism is increasingly beginning to show signs of examining its own, and society's, attitudes toward older women due largely to the fact that the still vocal pioneers of the second wave have reached their sixties and incorporated issues of aging in their work. For instance, Germaine Greer's study of attitudes toward menopause, *The Change*, was published in 1991, and Betty Friedan has produced a comprehensive polemic about the American and British senescent entitled *The Fountain of Age* (1993). In terms of literary criticism, Barbara Frey Waxman's *From the Hearth to the Open Road* (1990) covers the same subject area as this project, although it remains the only full length study of this kind of which I am aware.

In support of the slowly increasing interest in senescence, I will be exploring the following three properties of novels that sensitively foreground the older female character: first, their creation of alternative images of old age; secondly, the extension these make to the category of "woman"; and finally, their treatment of subjects from perspectives uncommon in fiction.

In deciding upon which novels to focus, the primary criterion was that texts sympathetically and realistically represent older female protagonists and do not rely on debasing models of senescence. Other boundaries had to be set, and one of my initial decisions concerned the production of a working definition of old/older that resulted in characters over sixty being referred to as old. Despite the thought that went into this choice, it is still a relatively arbitrary figure based on the general opinion that sixty to sixty-five is the chronological age at which senescence begins.[4] The most aged character that I came across, at least as far as I could tell from explicit textual information, is the ninety-four-year-old Maudie from Lessing's *Diary of a Good Neighbour*. However, when a protagonist's precise age is not mentioned, I estimated it based upon time-scales mentioned within the narrative and/or familial relationships. (If a character has adolescent grandchildren, for instance, it is comparatively safe to assume that she is over sixty years of age.)[5]

While on the subject, it is worth mentioning that definitions of the term *old* are often inextricable from ageist discourses. Bill Bytheway summarizes the problem in his 1995 study, *Ageism*:

> Why not compare the life expectations of the thirteen-year-old and the twenty-three-year-old; or the seventy-eight-year-old and the eighty-eight-year-old? ... By comparing age nought years with age sixty-five years, we are fostering the ageist idea that old age is life in a different country, it's the life of a different species.[6]

Bytheway correctly emphasizes that this way of thinking about age reinforces a divisive notion of "them" and "us." It also results in the misconceived judgment that ageism only affects older generations, although it is fair to suggest that prejudiced discourses become more apparent as one grows older. Women who have faced menopause might realize this earlier than their male peers, for whom there is no equivalent event that is socially constituted as one of the first signs of encroaching old age.[7] However, I have chosen not to analyze the female climacteric in any detail, as I agree with Lilian S. Robinson in her critique of Greer's *The Change*: "Change of life is not the last change in life and the problems of the old in general, and women in particular, should not be minimised by assimilating them to those of the middle aged."[8]

In striving to maintain a balance between the general and the particular, I draw on North American and British fiction rather than presuming to write about older women on a wider geographical scale, and I focus on white characters because different ethnic groups have their own attitudes toward the aged. For example, in the African American community of Willow Springs, created by author Gloria Naylor and featured in *Mama Day* (1988), the old, particularly the eponymous protagonist, are accorded great respect. Further, traditional African images of older women feed Naylor's writing, as Dorothy Perry Thompson argues in "African Womanist Revision in Gloria Naylor's *Mama Day* and *Bailey's Café*," thus tapping into different discourses than those discussed in this study.[9]

On a temporal level, I focus largely on late twentieth-century novels (written after the 1950s). This is because I agree with Paulina Palmer who contends, in *Narrative Practice and Feminist Theory* (1989), that the politics specific to contemporary female-authored fiction are often overlooked because of feminist literary criticism's interest in novels written by earlier generations. While acknowledging the usefulness of this endeavor, it "results in the neglect of a significant area of female creativity. It also encourages a disregard for a set of topics and areas of experience of vital importance to women."[10] Palmer points out that the second wave of feminism will have affected contemporary authors who either possess an explicit knowledge of feminist ideas or have been afforded wider social opportunities than their predecessors. Therefore, their work will express some particular, as well as similar, concerns to those narratives produced in the earlier half of the twentieth century.

In terms of novels of senescence, the most notable development is the explicitness with which contemporary writers critique society's treatment of the old and the variety of older characters they represent. For instance, Fay Weldon produces more overtly radical texts than Agatha Christie, and this is partly because Weldon's work is clearly fed by and feeds into feminist debates and paradigms. She can achieve a wide-ranging polemic because both she and many of her readers are conversant in the same feminist shorthand. When the "Golden Age" crime writers, of whom Christie is one, started their careers in the 1930s, they did not have this vocabulary available to them. They still engaged with discourses of aging but had to use a different strategy to break the social silence surrounding the subject, basing their narratives on a socially acceptable type of older woman, hence the genteel, middle-class older female sleuth such as Christie's Miss Marple or Patricia Wentworth's Miss Silver.

Differences between texts produced before and after the second wave of feminism are further illustrated by a comparison of Pym's *Some Tame Gazelle* (1950), and *Quartet in Autumn* (1977). The latter text, written twenty-seven years after the former one, moves away from focusing on the albeit shabby women of "independent means" to depict lower-middle-class single women who must work to support themselves. As such, the more recent protagonists are less insulated from sexism and ageism than earlier ones, which allows Pym to comment on the inefficiency of social services and the superficiality of neighborly concern, particularly in relation to the terminally ill and unlovable character of Marcia (one of the "quartet" of the title). With this sort of change in representational practice in mind, I have, wherever possible, analyzed contemporary portraits of senescence and make it clear when I do touch upon pre–1960's texts.

It is worth addressing the opinion that the literary critical strategy of studying fictional images of women is a phase through which feminism has passed. As Shirley Neuman stresses in the introduction to *ReImagining Women: Representations of Women in Culture* (1993), "a more generous and just response might be that it grounds much that we have moved into. And a more politically aware response might urge that such work is more than ever strategically necessary."[11] This fact became increasingly apparent in the 1980s, with critics calling attention to female authors' negotiations with discourses of race, ethnicity, and sexuality, and insisting that these factors were as influential to one's subjectivity and relationship to power as gender. Gayle Rubin summarizes the impulse behind this enterprise when she writes that representations of women should be explored in order to identify both dominant discourses of femininity in their "endless variety and monotonous similarity," as well as those that can usefully be co-opted to question the norms of female behavior.[12]

## *Power, Subjectivity and the Female Author*

Rubin's comments can be read as touching upon the connection between discourse, power and norms, areas that are important to my interpretative perspective. I now want to spend some time discussing these relationships more fully, starting with a consideration of Foucault, who writes extensively about them in his work. I will then go on to detail my understanding of identity and its connection to representational practices for, as Sally Robinson rightly points out in *Engendering the Subject* (1991), "representation and subjectivity are two terms and concepts which cannot be separated."[13] To finish making explicit the theoretical underpinnings of my analysis, I turn to the figure of the female author and explain why I have chosen to focus on women's writing, followed by a brief summary of the succeeding chapters.

Foucault's work has made a noticeable impression on modern cultural criticism, including the field of literary studies. Although I will not be offering a strictly Foucauldian analysis of novels featuring older female characters, his ideas have influenced, for example, the framework of this study, as might be noted from the fact that it lies at the intersection of discourses of literary criticism, age studies, and feminism. This epistemological move corresponds to the Foucauldian formulation that discourses about a particular subject radiate from numerous localized sources and thus are best analyzed from a perspective that acknowledges this multidirectional dynamic.

I decided to use Foucault only up to a point because he does not consider gender when analyzing power. Consequently, he fails to note the masculine bias of much dominant discourse, although as M. E. Bailey states in "Foucauldian Feminism" (1994), his "analysis of power ... does not deny the possibility of understanding gender relations as serving specific, interlocking interests. Thus it allows an understanding of social formulations as masculinist."[14] However, feminism's commitment to social change means that it must consider the reasons why certain discourses are dominant, rather than contenting itself with exposing the internal mechanisms that allow them such success.

Nonetheless, elements of Foucauldian theory are valuable as tools for dismantling complex discourses, such as those involved in the production of truths about senescence. Therefore, I am going to briefly discuss his insights into norms, their relationship to self-censorship and power, and the means by which certain discourses dominate others as expressed, for the most part, in *Discipline and Punish: The Birth of the Prison* (1975) and *The History of Sexuality* (three volumes, the first of which was published in 1976, and the last in 1984).[15] This will allow readers to sense Foucault's implicit influence in subsequent chapters.

Most significantly for this study, Foucault believes that discourse is inextricably linked to power in a relationship of mutual reinforcement: An individual cannot understand power unless she studies the way in which it works to produce discourses that manipulate the very bodies that make up a population. This is not as straightforward as it initially may seem. In the first volume of *The History of Sexuality*, Foucault feels the need to establish how power does *not* operate, proposing that power is not monolithic and wielded by a privileged few, even if in "political thought and analysis, we still have not cut off the head of the king."[16] He argues that although hierarchies of power exist in all relationships, there is no polarized opposition between rulers and ruled: Someone who is strong in relation to one institution can occupy a weaker position in regard to another. Thus power arises from localized centers and works in far more subtle ways than is conventionally recognized. The authors of the fiction I will be analyzing reflect this mutability by consistently refusing to portray their protagonists as purely victims of, or unscathed by, a callous society.

Accepting that power is not a static oppressive structure, it cannot be characterized as primarily functioning using practices associated with this earlier model. Although systems of taboo, censorship and interdiction are employed by institutions to prevent certain kinds of behavior, they are peripheral to the functioning of modern social control, which is driven by the creation of knowledge or "truths" about a subject. This knowledge is subsequently employed to produce definitions of the normal and abnormal. Individuals usually try to remain within the boundaries that delineate the normal within their culture, fearful of being labeled strange, criminal or insane because of the social implications connected to these labels. Surveillance, in its broadest sense, is undertaken by a myriad of connected institutions, such as schools, surgeries, courts, and churches, sustaining this often unconscious self-censorship and creating the panoptical culture of the twentieth and twenty-first century.

Individuals not only attempt to comply with norms through fear or shame but because of the particular pleasures involved in behaving as they "should." Sandra Bartky, in *Femininity and Domination: Studies in the Phenomenology of Oppression* (1990), details the feeling of competency that arises when people believe they are fulfilling a social expectation even when it is regulatory.[17] The idea that women collude in their own oppression is a concern that weaves throughout feminist theory.[18] As this is not a point I consider elsewhere in any depth, it is useful to expand upon it here in a reading of one of Pym's novels in which the subject is central, *Quartet in Autumn*.

The text portrays the daily lives and routines of four single office workers who are in their sixties, and covers the months around their retirement. As is customary with Pym's protagonists, they are very aware of social norms, and the author paints amusing portraits of the amount of time they spend worrying about social etiquette. Letty, the most self-conscious of the quartet, tries the hardest to behave appropriately. She meets her erstwhile colleagues for lunch in her first week of retirement, and in response to their inquiries about what she does with her days replies: "I seem to fill my time quite pleasantly." The omniscient narrator undercuts the sincerity of this statement by adding: "She must never give the slightest hint of loneliness or boredom, the sense of time hanging heavy."[19] There is no discourse that Letty can appropriate to express her emotions, as retirement is constructed as a wholly positive event. Her only reward for playing the role of happy retiree is a sense of gratification that her colleagues approve of her sensible demeanor. However, toward the end of the text, Letty finally becomes more self-aware and realizes that her rigid adherence to social norms is preventing her from doing what she wants. Although her circumstances do not radically alter, her perspective does, and it is convincing when she muses optimistically that "life still held infinite possibilities for change."[20] Pym represents this as a victory for her protagonist who no longer colludes with her, albeit subtle, victimization.

A Foucauldian analysis would suggest that Letty's change of heart is possible because although discourses arise from multiple sources and are adaptable and culturally specific, or "tactically polyvalent," they simultaneously create spaces for resistance because there is no "comprehensive system" to prevent localized disruptions.[21] Foucault writes that there are a "plurality of resistances," some "that are possible, necessary, improbable; others that are spontaneous, savage, solitary, concerted, rampant or violent; still others that are quick to compromise, interested or sacrificial...."[22] The novels featured in the following chapters fictionalize such actions and represent characters who seize the opportunities for rebellion against narrow discourses of female aging that their situations allow.

The texts not only depict subversive acts, but also themselves are reverse discourses that challenge, and perhaps supplant, more dominant and restrictive models of senescence.[23] Foucault warns though, that the mainstream can swiftly accommodate and distort reverse discourse out of recognition. For example, arguments about the older woman's theoretical right to express her sexuality can be twisted to suggest that it is necessary for her to be sexually active within a normative and heterosexual framework, which would seem a backward step. With this in mind, it is helpful to accept that theorists and authors cannot control the ways in which their work is interpreted: There is no such thing as a "pure" subversive text that is beyond assimilation. However, as I will continue to argue, it is still possible and useful to strategically recognize and label some works as radical or dissident.

Moving on to models of subjectivity, in the same way that Foucault recognizes the spaces for maneuver that are created by discourse, he notes similar "gaps" in the construction of identity. Bailey, in "Foucauldian Feminism," summarizes his attitude towards socialization—it:

> ...is never complete, because competing interests and identities create conflicts. In arbitrating between identities [formed through various discourses], the power-knowledge of identity allows a limited self-definition and self-determination, which perhaps we could term "agency."[24]

He suggests (in volumes 2 and 3 of *The History of Sexuality*) that the individual can model himself into the sort of person they desire to be through various self-reflexive "technologies of the self," because the discourses that construct the individual are never fully "concretised." Although he focuses upon classical Greek and Roman culture, he does not discount the idea that modern subjects can follow a similar process to find a certain amount of autonomy.

Foucault died before he could fully develop the work on subjectivity he began in these volumes. However, theorists such as Madan Sarup have used what he did produce as a starting point for their own paradigms. Sarup concurs, in *Identity, Culture and the Postmodern World* (1996), that identity is a process rather than a static construct and usefully discusses individuals as "processual subjects" with identities that are never entirely determined.[25] He usefully extends Foucault's work by framing the relationship between subjectivity and larger discourses as one that involves processes of identification and counter-identification, and stressing that individuals do not have a "homogenous identity" but are perpetually mobile in their subjectivity.

Isabella Paoletti, in *Being an Older Woman: A Study in the Social Production of Identity* (1998), charts this ongoing project specifically in the context of the senescent. She describes how particular individuals experience "being an older woman" in various social contexts and so provides a relevant illustration of the way in which identity is under constant negotiation. The group under observation participated in the Italian

Older Woman's Action Project, forming various committees to plan events for the program. Paoletti, for some of the study, describes the varying subject positions that the women assume in the course of different meetings. One woman, for instance, feels tongue-tied when discussing the nature of the choir with the larger group while another feels empowered. The latter individual, however, is deferential toward a representative of the local government and silenced when trying to negotiate a rehearsal room for her group at the male-dominated general meeting of the Center. The variety of identities taken up within the group helps to dispel the myth of homogeneity within a membership category, but also the myth that one person occupies a static subject position.[26]

So far, I have taken for granted that readers accept that identity is constructed, although early in the twentieth century this would have been a more problematic assumption. Feminism's skepticism about the paradigm of the subject as a stable, unified entity arose, predominantly, from the recognition that female and male subjectivity were not characterized in the same way. Virginia Woolf in *A Room of One's Own* (1929), and Simone de Beauvoir in *The Second Sex* (first published in France in 1949), argue that female identity has traditionally been defined in reference to male identity.[27] The relationship is not one of equality but is quantifiable as one of lack, with women featuring in conventional philosophical thought as the negative Other against which the positive figure of man is positioned.

Belief in the universal, unitary self was further eroded by postmodernists. However, while both groups share many of the same attitudes toward the subject, feminists cannot afford to unquestioningly embrace their approach. This is because if we embrace the fragmentation of the category of "women" without adding certain conditions, it potentially undermines the possibility of fighting for "women's rights." Susan Bordo, in *Unbearable Weight: Feminism, Western Culture and the Body* (1993), characterizes the dilemma created for feminists by the rise of the deconstructive impulse in Western theory:

> Feminist knowledge and the knowledges born of racial experience and consciousness were allotted the historical equivalent of approximately ten minutes to stake a claim on the conscience of our culture before the processes of their deconstruction—not only by academic theory, but also in the popular and aesthetic imagination—began.[28]

Agreeing with this observation, I have opted to take what might seem like the middle road and view identity as something far more provisional and strategic than traditionally perceived but still able to strategically claim a position in social networks of power.

The processual subject is a very useful figure to hold onto when interpreting representations of older women. It allows readers to accept and notice the sometimes-subtle changes that characters undergo during the course of a narrative, countering any thoughts about life stopping after a certain age. Although all the novels I discuss reflect the mobility of subject positions in senescence, it is an issue foregrounded in Fay Weldon's *Rhode Island Blues* (2000). The text tells the story of the eighty-three-year-old Felicity's voluntary entry into and subsequent escape from, the "Golden Bowl Complex for Creative Retirement." The narrative is divided between an omniscient narrator and Felicity's granddaughter Sophia, a film editor who imagines everyday life in cinematic terms. This allows Weldon to comment explicitly on the ways in which life differs from its popular representation. About halfway through the text, after the younger protagonist uncovers some information about her grandmother's past, she believes that the story of Felicity's life is complete. Retrospectively she muses: "That Miss Felicity's life wasn't finished yet did not occur to me. One tends to write off women in their mid-eighties as simply hanging around until death carries them away." Weldon undercuts this common perspective by adding, "One is wrong," and representing the older woman embarking on an intimate and sexually fulfilling relationship.[29] Throughout Weldon's literary career she has challenged commonplaces about women's lives, and in *Rhode Island Blues* she squares-up to the myth of psychological stasis that is often mistaken as the whole story of senescence.

This strategy of "re-presentation" is obviously not unique to Weldon. Women's writing, and specifically feminist narratives, can be seen as entering the discursive battle for individual subjectivity and working to denaturalize entrenched ageist and sexist beliefs. I have chosen to focus on novels written by women for this reason, which I want to expand upon here.

The first point to make is that the figure of the female author can be co-opted to support destructive patriarchal discourses in the same way as can the processual subject. Christine Battersby, in *Gender and Genius: Towards a Female Aesthetic* (1989), writes that the poststructuralist proclamation of "the death of the author" is premature when women have never been conceived of possessing either subjectivity or a female aesthetic.[30] This analysis prompts Battersby to write that the idea of a "fissured ego is by no means the same as the egolessness celebrated (in different but disturbingly similar ways) by the later Romantics, the Lacanians and by other postmodernists."[31]

Sally Robinson, in *Engendering the Subject* (1991), presents a similar argument about the "fissured" subject's continued ability to speak and represent subjectivity in terms of the difference between Woman "a singular, often metaphorical conceptualisation of feminine difference" and women, "a plural and heterogeneous" category.³² The latter term signals individuals who exist within a specific historic and cultural situation but share with other women a position within the social structure which "lacks power and mobility and requires change."³³ She continues by stating that rather than seeking closure or reconciliation between the terms "Woman" and "women," female subjectivity should be seen as formed through negotiation with these positions. She writes of this movement:

> To become Woman means to place oneself in a position that is sanctioned by, and guarantees, masculinist structures of representation.... Woman is spoken by discursive and social practices; she does not speak. On the other hand, to become a woman means to de-naturalise gender and its representations.³⁴

That female authors can work toward this denaturalization by producing unstereotypical fictive representations of older women is a proposition that lies at the heart of this project. So, too, is the fact that, in the case of the older woman, normative representations often fail to "speak her," which can be partially explained by Robinson's definition of Woman as "a discursive figure most often constructed to the logic of male desire."³⁵ Dominant attitudes toward women posit her primarily as a lover and mother, and when she cannot satisfactorily fulfill these roles and is not an object of male desire, she is no longer regarded as a woman. Her continued existence, however, does not trouble the dominant description of what it is to be female, creating an impasse against which discussions of aging can often find themselves.

Foucault opens up the possibility of theoretically reading silences, as he regarded them as equally informative about a subject as discourse: "There is no binary division to be made between what one says and what one does not say.... There are not one but many silences, and they are an integral part of the strategies that underline and permeate discourses."³⁶ Foucault explores this idea of there being "many silences" within a discursive arena in *The History of Sexuality*. He states that he is interested in "what one says and what one does not say," questioning "how those who can and those who cannot speak about them are distributed, which type of discourse is authorised, or which form of discretion is required."³⁷

Authorized discourses about senescence have a tendency to portray aged female characters in a very limited number of roles and to misrepresent the diversity of older women's lives. However, there still exists a social and psychological pressure on real women to conform to these subject positions. Shirley Neuman, in *ReImagining Women*, quotes Nicole Brossard on this point:

> Until now reality has been for most women a fiction, that is, the fruit of an imagination which is not their own and to which they do not *actually* succeed in adapting.... On the other hand, we can also say that women's reality has been perceived as fiction ... maternity, rape, prostitution, chronic fatigue.[38]

Our increasing cultural invisibility as we age could be added to the list but is ignored because it is widely underestimated as an element that can negatively impact upon and divide women. However, Brossard's observation insightfully reminds us that certain aspects of female existence are liable to be treated to a damaging cultural "discretion."

Pym, in *Quartet in Autumn*, demonstrates an acute awareness of the model whereby socially sanctioned fictions hide elements of women's lives that would benefit from discursive attention. She literally uses the idea of fictions hiding, for example, experiences of aging, in the first few pages of the novel when she describes Letty's search for a book in the library:

> She had always been an unashamed reader of novels, but if she hoped to find one which reflected her own sort of life she had come to realise that the position of an unmarried, unattached, ageing woman is of no interest whatever to the writer of the modern novel.[39]

As well as being a just appraisal of contemporary fiction, in a wider context it points to the fact that society does not offer the older woman support in taking up any subject position that strays from the norm. This situation is part of a process mentioned earlier whereby, as Chris Weedon states in *Feminist Practice and Poststructuralist Theory* (1987), "the power of all forms of subjectivity relies on the marginalisation and repression of historically specific alternatives."[40] Representation constitutes one discursive area where the struggle for identity can be traced and alternative subjectivities focused on, as confirmed by the texts explored in this study.

## *Structure of the Study*

The first chapter, "Paradigms of Aging and Ageism," surveys a variety of hypotheses about senescence from a number of disciplines including gerontology, psychology and feminism. I have presumed that, because relatively few literary studies consider representations of older women from a feminist perspective, the reader may be unfamiliar with the discourses relevant to such an endeavor. Therefore I have been conscious not only to detail my theoretical approach, but also to provide a sense of the debates about old age that take place both inside and outside the confines of literary criticism.

The four chapters that follow consist of age- and gender-conscious readings of texts written by contemporary female authors such as May Sarton, Angela Carter, and Doris Lessing. Each chapter focuses on particular characteristics of the older protagonists that are not usually associated with the senescent (such as passion and desire) and are foregrounded by the novels themselves.

Chapter 2, "The Angry and Frustrated Older Woman," considers the portrayal of physically dependent characters and how their anger is framed as a sane response to society's treatment of them and the difficulties caused by a failing body. This chapter is placed before the others in order to foreground embodiment so as to avoid further marginalizing the disabled old.

Chapter 3, "The Passionate and Desiring Older Woman," discusses how paradigms of female sexuality are constructed in such a way as to discursively exclude the possibility of older women being sexually craved and craving. The narratives in this section demonstrate that desire is too fluid to be contained within such theoretical boundaries and represents characters as possessing an active sexuality (even if, for some, it is only expressible in their fantasies).

"The Contented and Developing Older Woman," chapter 4, analyzes novels that focus on the prosaic from which characters produce a contented daily life. Referring to the theories of Michel de Certeau (developed from Foucault's model of power), I argue that these texts reappropriate a space created by dismissive discourses that suggest nothing happens to the older person and revalue smaller tragedies and triumphs (of the sort experienced by individuals of all ages).

The final chapter, "The Wise and Archetypal Older Woman," discusses the older female detective's role in ratiocinative fiction. Approaching the genre from an age-conscious perspective reveals in it more radical discourses than are usually noted. A consideration of references to female archetypes helps to explain the older sleuth's presence as a stock figure in the genre, which makes her a literary anomaly.

To reiterate my expectations for this piece of work: I hope it will provide a sense that contemporary literature possesses the ability to move discourses of female senescence beyond their predominately ageist and sexist concerns. The texts that are treated create memorable older female characters who possess a continually developing identity and cope with old age in the face of social neglect and marginalization. On a more pragmatic final note, I would also like to think that I will successfully manage to convey both the thought-provoking and entertaining sides of the novels and so inspire readers to search out those with which they are not familiar and develop their own engagement with narratives of aging.

# 1
# *Paradigms of Aging and Ageism*

## *Introduction*

The novels I will be exploring reveal a status quo that grounds contemporary Western society—one that is age-sensitive and rewards youth while penalizing old age. While this not a modern circumstance (one need only consider the ridiculous or unpleasant older secondary characters who appear in the work of authors as diverse as Moliére, Austen, and Dickens to appreciate this fact), it has become more pervasive in the twentieth century. For instance, this period sees the creation of the phenomenon of the teenager and a subsequent fascination with youth culture, spawning novels from Jack Kerouac's romantic depiction of the beatniks in *On the Road* (1957) to the more recent, and disaffected, view of the "slacker" generation provided by Douglas Coupland's *Generation X* (1991). In tandem with this foregrounding of youth are admonishments to older individuals urging them to extend theirs, or at least the appearance of theirs, for as long as possible, and technologies are constantly being developed to help people achieve this aim. Science fiction extrapolates the consequences of such developments with its continuing interest in artificial body parts, cyborgs and "ghosts in the machine," with consciousness that is not tied to a continually deteriorating body (a heavenly or hellish state, depending on your viewpoint).

These brief examples point to just a few of the ways in which age is an important concern to society and fiction. This chapter develops this discussion by considering a variety of discourses of aging, some of which are more useful in interpreting fictions of senescence than others. The less relevant ones are featured in the first section of the chapter in relation to the popular representations of the aged that they spawn (which are, on the whole, depressingly narrow and familiar). Moving on, I range over some of the more insightful gerontological theories, such as the "mask of ageing," followed by a discussion of feminist paradigms of senescence. These are particularly important as they expose, and attempt to fill, the silences that more conventional approaches demonstrate with regard to gender, and provide one way of interpreting the fictional worlds inhabited by the older female protagonist. However, as I have argued, feminism is not blameless in its relationship with the older woman, and so I will explore the roots of ageism against women, by women, as it appears in feminist rhetoric. To round off the survey of attitudes toward ageing and foreground its literary aspect, the final part of this chapter examines critical responses to stories of senescence.

## *Popular Views of Senescence*

Europe has a rapidly aging population: In Britain, during the 1990s, one in five people were over the age of sixty-five, and it is predicted that this proportion will increase to one in four by the year 2020.[1] It would be reasonable to expect a heightened awareness of the senescent because of the sheer increase in their numbers, but popular representations of the old do not reflect this fact. The same relatively unvaried and unrealistic stereotypes appear relentlessly in Western culture. We can take our pick from the cheerful grandparents, an extension of the supposedly solid nuclear family, selflessly caring for their grandchildren; the lonely spinster, worrying about whether or not she can afford to turn on the gas heater to warm her drab home; the impotent old man making lecherous comments about the women who cross his path; the interfering mother-in-law who ceaselessly passes on unwanted pieces of advice; or the old man sitting in a nursing home, unsure of his whereabouts and as helpless as a child. Images such as these appear within many different contexts: soap operas, news reports, advertisements, photographs and political speeches. Each of the following chapters will refer to these often paradoxical stereotypes in more detail. At this point, it is sufficient to emphasize that they share a dehumanizing tendency, creating two-dimensional images that perpetuate the ghettoization of the aged and eradicate the complexity of their lives.

Popular culture supports a climate in which a bumper sticker proclaiming "I hate old people 'cos they smell of pee" is regarded by some as humorous.[2] This statement instantly becomes intolerable if *women* or *blacks* is substituted for the words *old people*, because of the increased social awareness of the guises of sexism and racism. As it stands, this sticker demonstrates that the recognition of ageism is not as common and that the old are characterized as a homogenous mass, incapable of controlling their bodies or caring for themselves. Even the best scenarios tend to characterize elderly individuals as smiling token matriarchs and patriarchs, with no passions outside of the family but no real influence within it.

The Canadian writer Margaret Laurence engages with such facile depictions of the older woman in *The Stone Angel* (1964), which traces the final weeks and reminiscences of its protagonist, Hagar Shipley. Hagar is indeed a matriarch who lives with her son, Marvin, and his wife, but there the resemblance to the popular portrayal of the figure ends. Although she has no institutional power, she manipulates her family and is certainly not a benign presence. She says of her criticisms of the put-upon Marvin: "To carp like this—it's my only enjoyment, that and the cigarettes, a habit I acquired only ten years ago out of boredom. Marvin thinks it's disgraceful of me to smoke, at my age, ninety."[3] She is certainly not portrayed sentimentally by Laurence, but neither is she vilified. Hagar might possess a proud, often unfeeling personality, but through the narrative's sympathetic representation of her current dependency on others, interspersed with flashbacks to her earlier life, the reader learns why she clings so fiercely to her independence. Sara Maitland, in the afterword to the Virago Modern Classic edition of the book, calls her an "everywoman" and writes: "We fear Hagar Shipley even as we empathise with her ... I hate her because she is frighteningly like I am—not at my worst or at my best, but at my daily-est."[4] The fact that Laurence can create a character that elicits such a response is remarkable in view of the received wisdom that older people are not like everyone else but distinctly Other. As such, she shares a talent with the majority of authors in this study who portray complex, three-dimensional and ultimately human protagonists, defying the divisive and simplistic sketches of the senescent that normally circulate.

While dominant representations could be dismissed as simplistic or harmless, feminist theory has alerted us to the very real consequences that they have in restricting the lives of those being stereotyped. To demonstrate this point I will analyze some of the issues involved in the expectation that women in Britain will retire at sixty and men at sixty-five.[5] This supposed exit from the workforce is dependent upon chronological age rather than on whether or not a worker can still carry out assigned duties, or obtain the same result s/he did the year previously. Although the gendering of retirement is highly relevant to my critical approach, what I want to emphasize here is that governmental policy promotes the idea that individuals over a certain age are of no value to a capitalist society. While these guidelines could be viewed as an effort to guarantee an individual's "peaceful old age," companies actually manipulate them to maintain a youthful workforce—arguably to avoid paying for the extra experience that an older worker might possess.

Bill Bytheway analyzes the relationship between individual and organization in his thought-provoking study, *Ageism* (1995). He suggests that the idea of an older person "stepping aside" for a younger colleague is part of the mentality of both employer and employee, and one that should be challenged as ageist. He goes on to argue that although ageism may superficially seem to be a problem between individuals, it is actually built into many state policies.[6] The recognition of links between prejudices held at a micro- and macro-level complements a Foucauldian analysis of power that asserts discourses from localized sources join up to produce seemingly monolithic social norms. In this case, the widespread belief that older people are inherently frail and unable to cope with new technology is translated, at state level, into a blanket retirement age.[7] This government policy also highlights the two influential aspects of Western society mentioned at the very start of this chapter: that it is youth-oriented and age-specific.

Bytheway writes of our age-specific society that, "we all have learned to be age sensitive while not necessarily being age-conscious."[8] He persuasively argues that chronological age plays an important part in the creation of the norms that manipulate the individual into compliance with certain kinds of behavior. Some examples of age-related norms that illustrate his suggestion include the fact that an individual in Britain cannot vote or consume alcohol until the age of eighteen; that the age of a protagonist is seen as worthy of mention within media stories; and that our date of birth is necessary on applications for bank accounts, driver's licenses, and so forth.

Age-sensitive behavior is also exemplified by the unspoken rules that govern the asking of the seemingly straightforward question, "How old are you?" A Foucauldian-inspired reading of this inquiry would lead to the observation that it is not usually demanded of someone who is middle-aged or older. Perhaps this is because aging is widely regarded as an unpleasant experience and reminding people of the fact that they are old has no place in polite conversation. The dividing line between the question being acceptable and unacceptable is not measured chronologically. Instead, it is judged by the physical age of the interrogatee (how old the person appears) or by relational age (the number of years between the interrogator and interrogatee's ages), highlighting two of the different ways in which age can be measured. As this is a literary critical piece of work, there is no need to expand on these classifications (Bytheway cites six categories in all, such as "biographical"), but it is useful to realize that there are several.[9]

In everyday life, the age of a person is not consciously troubling, but it is a judgment that demands to be made subconsciously (in the same way as we assign a gender to those with whom we come in contact). This process is exemplified in the pronouncement that some women over a certain age are "mutton dressed as lamb": a declaration driven by a consensus with informal age-related restrictions. Commenting censoriously about those in one's social milieu is a habit that exists on the same axis as self-censorship. The discourses that manipulate individuals into judging themselves also work to encourage Foucault's panoptical society. People regulate their neighbors who, in turn, regulate themselves, and vice versa. In *The Stone Angel*, Hagar's daughter-in-law uses this phrase to attempt to shame Hagar into behaving in a socially appropriate way. Hagar writes of the episode: "How annoyed she was with me when I bought this dress. Unsuitable, she sighed and sniffed. Look at that style—mutton dressed as lamb. Let her talk. I like it, and will wear it on weekdays now, perhaps as well."[10] In keeping with the older protagonist's attempts to live life on her own terms, she seizes this opportunity to enact a mini-rebellion. However, she does not always possess the confidence to ignore judgments about normal behavior and is frightened, for example, of being thought senile when she temporarily forgets the name of her destination on boarding a bus.

The phrase "mutton dressed as lamb" not only speaks of age-related norms but also of the glorification of all things youthful whereby older people are ridiculed for wearing clothes that are solely meant for the young. The fashion and beauty industry, although by no means the sole offender, is the most visible supporter of a hierarchy of generational groups that places young adults at the top of the scale. Beauty is equated with youth, particularly of a thin adolescent kind, and, although this seems mainly relevant to women, the growing male cosmetic industry indicates that men are also being harried into maintaining a youthful face and figure.[11] While there is nothing wrong in wanting to play with one's appearance, it is worrying that individuals may feel it is imperative in order to disguise their age.

The relationship between paradigms of beauty and ageist norms demonstrates the cultural prevalence of, what Germaine Greer terms in *The Change* (1992), "youthism." This social bias is not confined to discourses about appearance but affects a multitude of other areas such as medicine, psychology, social policy, and education. The strengths and weaknesses of adults before they reach middle age are counted as representative of adults of all ages (similar to the way in which men are often theoretically taken to represent the whole of humankind). Betty Friedan writes extensively about this insidious attitude in *The Fountain of Age*. She is convincing in her argument that, for example, the medical profession's focus on curing illness (unarguably an admirable goal) is based primarily on the needs of the younger adult and has resulted in a scarcity of research concerned with improving the daily functioning of the older patient.[12] The age-as-disease paradigm is also described as the medicalization of old age by theorists such as Sarah Harper in "Constructing Later Life/Constructing the Body: Some Thoughts from Feminist Theory" (1997). Like Friedan, Harper points out that depression, and other illnesses in senescence, are often overlooked because they are seen as a normal part of old age, regardless of whether or not there is a reason for the problem, such as the death of a spouse. Conversely, but arising from the same conceptual framework, is the prevalent attitude that gradual physiological decline is a disease rather than a natural part of the aging process. Friedan writes of how a holistic approach to illness, which aims to maximize a patient's potential and help maintain their autonomy in the face of a deteriorating body, is sadly missing from much of mainstream medicine.

At an individual level, the age-as-disease mentality may result in an older person being prescribed a variety of drugs that, if taken indiscriminately, can cause as many problems as they cure. On a larger scale, this attitude reinforces ageist attitudes and labels older people as helpless victims of a treacherous body (whereas the body can prove problematic throughout life for a variety of reasons). These examples illustrate some of the ways in which the complementary attitudes of youthism/ageism can affect the senescent in real and harmful ways. In the next section, I consider contemporary gerontological material that provides a deeper insight into how this prevalent dual perspective contributes to the construction of old age.

## *Contemporary Theories About Aging and Ageism*

Anne Jamieson and Christina Victor, in the introduction to *Critical Approaches to Ageing and Later Life*, suggest that contemporary gerontology is becoming more multidisciplinary in nature and fed by fields outside of medicine and sociology (such as literary criticism). The proliferation of theoretical thinking about old age has stepped up debates about the validity of previous analysis. One influential hypothesis that has come under scrutiny is the disengagement theory, forwarded by Cumming and Henry in their book *Growing Old: The Process of Disengagement*, published in 1961. Friedan succinctly summarizes their argument: "They hypothesised that it is 'functional' for both society and the individual for older people to voluntarily retire, retreat, 'disengage' from active involvement in society."[13]

This scenario, which represents old age as a time of waiting to die, has been attacked by gerontologists, such as Sarah Arber and Jay Ginn, as deeply ageist. It presumes that older people have no place in society and that their disengagement from the community is unconnected to external cultural pressure. Margaret Drabble, in *The Witch of Exmoor* (1997), adds a twist to the supposed withdrawal of the aged in her representation of the opinionated older protagonist, Frieda Haxby. Frieda takes herself off to a remote gothic mansion, much to her pretentious children's chagrin, but does so because she finds contemporary society dreary and superficial. Cumming and Henry would not have considered this possibility, and further, they did not take into account issues of gender, class and race that would disrupt their conclusions.[14] Friedan points out that it is because of such problems that the disengagement theory was one of the last influential hypotheses to have faith in its ability to make generalizations about later life. Contemporary theories, although they may recognize far-reaching trends, focus on the relationships between older individuals and specific institutions, the "local centers" that Foucault discusses as crucial to understanding how power prevails over populations.

Mike Featherstone and Mike Hepworth write extensively about this idea in their essay entitled "The Mask of Ageing and the Postmodern Life Course" (1991). They argue that postmodern change has resulted in gerontologists moving away from universalism and favoring instead local knowledge, and that the life course is becoming deinstitutionalized insofar as it is becoming more difficult to delineate lives into age-specific stages. They stress, though, that this direction is currently an emerging cultural trend rather than commonplace.

Later within the same essay, Featherstone and Hepworth discuss "the mask of ageing," a phrase they use to describe the process whereby the older individual sees physical indications of aging as hiding a more youthful self. Featherstone and Hepworth believe that the mask "alerts us to the possibility that a distance or tension exists between the external appearance of the face and body and their functional capacities, and the internal or subjective sense or experience of personal identity which is likely to become prominent in our consciousness as we grow older."[15] They view the mask as one of the major barriers to successful aging but believe that, since World War II, traditional images of old age are being destabilized and so at some point in the future the mask will become redundant.

Simon Biggs, in "Choosing Not to Be Old? Masks, Bodies and Identity Management in Later Life" (1997), responds to the earlier essay by adding that the mask is not only an impediment to the old but also to postmodern theories of the body: "Ageing as a mask ... becomes a nightmare for the postmodern dream ... producing a contradiction between the fixedness of the body and the fluidity of social images."[16] He suggests that this "nightmare" is not totally resolvable with the terminally and chronically ill demonstrating a point past which the body is no longer fluid.

Paul Thompson reads the distancing of the self from the body in a more positive light in his essay, "I Don't Feel Old: Subjective Ageing and the Search for Meaning in Later Life," published in 1992. He considers the statement contained within the title, which was constantly repeated by his interviewees, as a constructive response to the aging process. "So far from implying passivity, it demands an exceptional ability to respond imaginatively to change.... Denial of old age is a defiance of spoiled identity."[17]

While this optimistic interpretation contains some truth, Barbara Macdonald and Cynthia Rich, in *Look Me in the Eye*, write worriedly about the process of distancing oneself from one's appearance and all it stands for. They call the technique "passing": a term they borrow from discussions of race to describe the strategy of a black person's adopting the identity of a white person. (This is just one of many examples of theorists who want to talk about age adapting arguments from already established discussions of race.) Rich and Macdonald are quite specific about the strategy on which they are commenting: the attempt to "disguise" oneself as a younger individual, a ruse particularly used by older women to counter the hostile reactions with which their undisguised body would be greeted. They warn of the dangers inherent to this project, explaining that the individual who attempts it must constantly be on guard lest they betray their façade. This involves suppressing anything that might make them appear old. Macdonald and Rich are not suggesting that the individual can never represent to the world some sort of true inner image; their concern revolves around the pressures of trying to maintain a singular coherent image, particularly if, as Rich points out, it results in a sense of alienation every time they look in the mirror.[18]

Passing, the mask of ageing and the assertion "I don't feel old" are strategies (albeit risky ones) evolved by older individuals to cope with ageist discourses that do not speak realistically about them or their lives. Fiction, with its attention to emotion and the management of identity, can and does dramatize this experience. For example, scenes in which the older protagonist looks in the mirror recur throughout narratives of aging and act as a shorthand way of communicating their feelings about the process. For example, Doris Lessing's protagonist in *Love, Again* (1996), internalizes prejudice about old age and grows dismayed when she catches its physical signs reflected in the mirror. The feisty Felicity, from Weldon's *Rhode Island Blues*, has a more ambivalent attitude toward aging, as her reaction to her reflection indicates: "Look in the mirror and you always saw something different; sometimes you saw the spirit of yourself, perfectly fresh and youthful: sometimes you saw corrupted flesh."[19] Although she succeeds in seizing the possibilities that exist in old age, even she cannot manage to embrace her "old" reflection and its pejorative connotations. So, while she may challenge the staff at the retirement complex, she does not change their deep-seated and negative beliefs about the senescent, and is forced to seek refuge at her lover's woodland retreat in order to escape their disapproval of her relationship (an ending that is reminiscent to that of Charlotte Brontë's *Jane Eyre* [1847], insofar as the equally convention-flouting union of Jane and Rochester can only flourish if they retreat to Ferndean and separate themselves from society).

However, both the denial and acceptance of the categorization of old bring with them certain dangers both in fiction and real life. Judith Butler writes about the dilemma involved in claiming group affiliation in "Imitation and Gender Subordination," published in 1991. She makes the Foucauldian assessment that "identity categories tend to be instruments of regulatory regimes, whether as the normalising categories of oppressive structures or as the rallying points for a liberatory contestation of that very oppression."[20] Butler then discusses her ambivalence about saying "I am a lesbian," because of the fear that she will foreclose her options by identifying herself with a particular category that has been inscribed with a finite number of possibilities. She believes that any grouping should be contestable and open to change, yet she realizes that oppression can work by silencing or refusing to name a subject, constituting "a domain of unviable (un)subjects—*abjects*, we might call them—who are neither named nor prohibited within the economy of the law."[21] Therefore, Butler writes that she will continue to use the label "lesbian" but realizes the dangers in doing so. The same perils exist in using the category "old," both individually and by those who wish to raise the profile of a marginalized group. However, awareness that all identities are necessarily provisional and temporary will help to prevent the foreclosure with which Butler is rightly concerned.

At the level of language, gerontologists tend to use the terms *aged* or, more recently, *older*. The latter term is seen as relational, destroying a linguistic barrier that posits the youthful on one side and the old on the other. Therefore, I have followed suit and tended toward the term *older* rather than *elderly*, *senior citizen* or *old-aged pensioner*, which, although once seen as progressive, are now largely considered patronizing. There is also a persuasive argument for employing the word *old* as part of a strategy of reclaiming language by subverting the familiar connotations of this description and using it in a combative and positive sense. Shevy Healey, one of the creators of the American Old Lesbians Organizing for Change Group, writes in "Confronting Ageism" (1993):

> We are neither "older" (than whom?) ... nor "elder" ... nor "senior." We name and proclaim ourselves as OLD for we no longer wish to collude in our own oppression by accommodating to language that implies in any way that old means inferior, ugly or awful.[22]

The strength inherent in this statement is something that I wish to capture, and because contesting prejudices at the level of language is a successful strategy, I have also decided to use the word *old* to describe protagonists. The context in which the term is used, in an analysis of non-stereotypical representations of older women, will hopefully prevent ageist associations from being foregrounded in the reader's mind.

Having discussed ageism within popular culture and some gerontological perspectives on senescence, it is worth mentioning one view of the progressiveness of governmental thinking about old age. Alan Walker and Tony Maltby wrote *Ageing Europe* in 1997, to discuss data collected by the European Observatory on Aging and Older People between 1991 and 1993. In the conclusion, they write:

> It is possible to witness already a "policy deficit" between, on the one hand, the needs and demands of older people ... and, on the other, the social and economic policies of governments. In a few extreme cases the contrast is glaring between the obsessive concern of some politicians with the economic "burden" of societal ageing and the increase in poverty among older people or the increased inequality between elder and younger people.[23]

Walker and Maltby's conclusions suggest that, unfortunately, ageist attitudes will continue to permeate governmental policy in the near future, although they add that if older people are more fully integrated within society, this situation is contestable. They stress that this is only likely, however, if older people demand change for themselves.

Hopefully, the renowned political awareness of the "baby boomers" will expand to encompass activism over issues of senescence. There are clues that this is beginning to take place as second-wave theorists, such as Greer and Friedan, have added their voices to debates about aging, and authors who emerged at the same time, such as Fay Weldon, are paying more attention to the older female character. Further, although Walker and Maltby do not consider this option, the proliferation of non-prejudicial studies into the aging experience will allow useful alliances to emerge between the young and old.

## Feminist Explanations of Aging

One such alliance, necessary to the prevention of the cultural marginalization of older women, occurs between feminism and gerontology.

So far in this chapter I have underplayed gender issues in order to discuss some of the cultural discourses that apply to both older men and women (although I have been using feminist material to do so). Nonetheless, as a feminist who believes that gender affects all stages of life, it has been difficult not to emphasize the impact that it has upon the aging process. On the contrary, traditional gerontology, which has professed to theorize about older people of both sexes, actively used a male-as-norm model. The senescent were generally treated as homogenous, with gender, race, ethnicity, sexuality and class barely affecting the so-called "universal" paradigms of aging (as mentioned in relation to disengagement theory). Julie McMullin in "Theorising Age and Gender Relations" (1995) points out that some attempts were made to address the situation by, for example, adding on gender as a variable of sociological inquiry. Nonetheless, she explains why this was an inadequate gesture:

> A central goal in "add on" approaches is to compare women to men, and older to younger people, with men and the young often serving as ideal referents. However, if gender and age relations simultaneously structure social life, examining differences between these groups is like comparing apples and oranges.[24]

McMullin correctly believes that unless women are the focus of study, very little will be discovered about their lives. Using a framework that is based around youthful and/or male concerns results in inappropriate inquiries being made of the older woman, and the silences with which she answers contribute to her continued marginalization.[25]

Feminism has begun to refuse to rely on mainstream theory to successfully provide explanations of female aging, although this is not an entirely recent phenomenon. For example, in Simone de Beauvoir's *The Second Sex*, published in 1949, she devoted a chapter to the older woman, "From Maturity to Old Age," in which she described the ways in which society forces women to experience old age as a tragedy.[26] Her analysis of aging is tied to her belief in a transcendental theory of selfhood. Mature adults are seen as "advancing" their lives (a positive action) when they "transcend" their past by carrying out "projects" (tasks that range from creating a work of art to building up an estate). Patriarchal strategies force women into immanence by defining them as Other and expecting them to provide support for men and their projects. Beauvoir believes, however, that the older woman is no longer conceived as useful in this role of nurturing men, and therefore society loosens some of its prescriptive hold. Germaine Greer in *The Change* echoes this conviction and frames this as a positive result of the aging process, whereas Beauvoir believes that this freedom comes too late for the older woman. She is envisaged as rarely possessing any ongoing projects and as feeling that she has run out of time to start anything of worth.

Greer and Beauvoir's difference in attitude can partly be put down to the times in which the two texts were written, but also to Beauvoir's definition of "projects." She seems to exclude ventures that are not all-consuming and socially important, and so overlooks many of the more prosaic pursuits that can sustain an individual.[27]

Yet this does not invalidate the majority of her opinions about senescence, which she develops in *Old Age*, published when she was aged sixty-two and twenty-one years after *The Second Sex*. Interestingly, as Kathleen Woodward notes in "Tribute to the Older Woman" (1995), feminists have paid little attention to this "second great book," a result of the lack of theoretical interest in senescence.[28] Beauvoir would not have been surprised by this reception, as one of the axioms of her study was that the senescent are marginalized. She developed her ideas to suggest that the old are viewed as unable to contribute to society and that this lack of expectation is internalized (positioning both men and women in a state of immanence). She further links their casting out to their perceived proximity to death, which continues to be a taboo subject and one that generates social anxiety.[29] Old age then becomes too unseemly to mention (illustrating a Foucauldian discursive silence) and results in the old being treated as a different species. "From Maturity to Old Age" and *Old Age* thus paint a bleak portrait of this period of life, particularly for older women who are depicted as trapped in stultifying immanence that, in existentialist philosophy, is an individual's worst fate.[30]

It is interesting to note how Beauvoir's long short story, "The Age of Discretion," published in 1967 alongside two others in her last fictional work *The Woman Destroyed*, dramatizes the ideas about aging that she expresses in *The Second Sex* and reveals the seeds of her thinking for *Old Age*. The story is about the narrator's realization that, on a personal and social level, she is considered an old woman. At the start of the story, she hardly notices her age, comparing the breakfast she takes with her husband, André, to earlier and future ones: "We should do so again tomorrow, and in a year's time.... That moment possessed the sweet gentleness of a memory and the gaiety of a promise. Were we thirty or were we sixty?"[31] She is optimistic about the future and the book she is working on about Rousseau and Montesquieu (an example of the sort of task that Beauvoir "counts" as a project).

The text then proceeds to demonstrate the dangers of denying age: an attitude that has been discussed as precarious because society will, sooner or later, thrust its pejorative view of senescence upon the individual. After the idyllic breakfast scene, the narrator goes to market and sees a "little old lady" doing her shopping. She muses: "In earlier days I never used to worry about old people; I looked upon them as the dead whose legs keep moving. Now I see them—men and women: only a little older than myself."[32] Her previous attitude is indicative of the social marginalization with which Beauvoir engages in *Old Age*. Further, the character's realization that she has nearly become one of "them," someone who in her opinion is just marking time, signals her imminent downfall.

Several events bring home to the narrator the transition she is being forced to undergo. Her son, to whom she had previously been close, neglects her for his wife, whom she dislikes intensely, and demonstrates a disregard for her politics that she takes as a personal slight. André fails to understand her distress, and this causes a rift between them that she could not have foreseen at the start of the text. Perhaps her biggest disappointment comes when the book on which she has been working receives lukewarm reviews—praised for its competence but not its innovation. Toward the end of the story, she reaches an uneasy truce with herself, making up with her husband and aiming to accept her son's life as it is. In terms of her project, she is sustained by her decision to continue to write but states that she "has seen her limits." This disturbing note of limitation and precariousness is repeated in the last paragraph, in which the narrator muses on the future:

> Should I be able to work or not? ... Would the dread of ageing take hold of me again? Do not look too far ahead. Ahead there was the horror of death and farewells: it was false teeth, sciatica, infirmity, intellectual barrenness, loneliness in a strange world that we could no longer understand and that would carry on without us. Shall I succeed in not lifting my eyes to those horizons? ... Let us hope so. We have no choice in the matter.[33]

As this passage demonstrates, Beauvoir was convinced that the ordinary person is not supported in negotiating the "horrors" of the aging process, which are worsened by a society that leaves them to fend for themselves. The narrator is represented as reasonable for dreading old age in such a climate, and she cannot move beyond the nullifying expectations and judgment of others.

Although this story is an exposé, as is most of Beauvoir's work, it expresses an especially nihilistic view of senescence, which is accounted for by Toril Moi in *Simone de Beauvoir: The Making of an Intellectual Woman* (1994). She writes that Beauvoir primarily equated old age with a loss of love and sexual attractiveness, and that she projected these fears onto her paradigms of aging. If we accept Moi's account, which I do, it can help explain some of Beauvoir's more problematic beliefs. For example, she dismisses the possibility that an older woman could continue to be found attractive, yet she is ready to believe that an old man could be found sexually appealing (if only by a partner who is awed by his social standing). She does not entertain the concept that a woman, if viewed from a different perspective, could still be considered physically engaging. This is reflected in "The Age of Discretion" by the narrator's distancing from her sexual body and her conception of it as "an old friend" that she looks after with "bored conscientiousness": an attitude that the narrative does not question.[34]

Again, the eruption of Beauvoir's personal anxieties into her work does not hugely detract from its continued relevance. She achieves her explicit aim in *Old Age* of raising the cultural profile of the senescent, and her earlier piece of fiction works toward the same end. By emphasizing the problematic aspects of being old, particularly for women, she effectively shocks the reader into noticing the cultural omnipresence of discrimination. Furthermore, she is writing about society as it is and not how it could be, as she believes that dehumanized old age is an ideological rather than natural construct: "Every society creates its own values; and it is in the social context that the word *decline*, takes on an exact meaning."[35] The aging process is mediated by responses that are external to the individual, and in a more just society, they would consist of appreciation and acceptance. Instead, Beauvoir writes that the predominance of ageist attitudes, and their conception of decline in relation to senescence, actually "exposes the failure of our entire civilisation": a dramatic but just condemnation.[36]

Beauvoir's portrayal of women as doubly disadvantaged by the interrelated discourses of ageism and sexism is a recurrent theme in feminist theory. While this perspective can be criticized for its tendency to portray older women purely as scapegoats, a point discussed later in the chapter, it is a hypothesis that does need to be made explicit. Susan Sontag wrote her renowned essay "The Double Standard of Ageing" in 1972, two years after *Old Age* was published, and she states in one of the opening paragraphs that getting older is "less profoundly wounding for a man." She goes on to argue that society "is much more permissive about ageing in men, as it is tolerant of the sexual infidelities of husbands. Men are 'allowed' to age, without penalty, in several ways that women are not."[37]

Sontag believes that women are most drastically penalized for showing physical signs of aging because they are highly prized for their fertility, which is linked to youth, whereas men, who can produce children for longer, are socially appreciated for other qualities. This may seem a simplistic analysis, but Sontag is convincing in her explanation of the pervasiveness of this fact and the stress that it subsequently induces in aging women. Their bodies, every day, move farther away from the social ideal, and even if they constantly monitor their appearance, they will eventually be defeated.[38]

Fay Weldon makes similar links between nature, fertility and attitudes toward the old in *Rhode Island Blues*. The feminist suspicion that society uses discourses of the natural to support its construction of gendered norms appears throughout her work. The eponymous heroine of Weldon's *Praxis*, published in 1978, explicitly addresses this strategy in one of the chapters where she addresses her metaphorical "sisters":

> It is nature, they say, that makes us get married. Nature, they say, that makes us crave to have babies.... It seems to me we must fight Nature tooth and claw. Once we are past child-bearing age, this Nature ... disposes of us.... Nature does not know best; for the birds, for the bees, for the cows; for men, perhaps. But your interests and Nature's do not coincide.[39]

Weldon repeats this assertion in *Rhode Island Blues*, written twenty-two years after *Praxis*, but this time she loses her ambivalence about whether or not discourses of the natural work for men, indicating that they work for young men but not the more institutionally powerless older man. For instance, the sympathetic Dr. Bronstein is skeptical about the chief nurse's explanation that the food Felicity is eating makes her ill because it is natural and she is used to eating processed foods. He rightly suspects that it is drugged with sedatives and makes a similar argument to Praxis about the deployment of the term *natural*, but extends it to include old men:

> It's an illusion to believe that because something is natural, it's good for us. Nature doesn't care whether we live or die. Nature's only purpose is to get us to procreative age in one piece, by whatever slipshod manner she can contrive. Once we're past that she has no interest in us at all.... It behoves us oldsters to treat nature as an enemy and not a friend.[40]

As this quotation illustrates, Weldon extends her gender-aware social critique to suggest that older men are as susceptible to the treacheries of the body and as prey to socially manipulative discourses of the natural as their female peers.

However, Weldon's humane representation of older men does not contradict Praxis' assertion that women are thrown on the "scrap heap" far earlier than their male counterparts. As such, *Rhode Island Blues* as much as *Praxis*, supports the statement made by Gari Lesnoff-Caravaglia in "Double Stigmata: Female and Old" (1984), that the "dominant response called for by society with respect to women is a biological one."[41]

Like Sontag, Lesnoff-Caravaglia believes that ageism against women arises partially from the value placed upon female youth and fertility, but he also believes that this pressure is compounded by the increasing importance given to technology by capitalist societies: "Human beings have become expendable.... Younger and newer are seen as equivalent for better. Wives, particularly older ones, are seen as expendable.... We have become a throwaway culture in terms of people, as well as goods."[42] This viewpoint serves as a further counterargument against discourses that suggest older people, within an increasingly consumer culture, will be able to buy lifestyle choices that will afford them a citizenship they are currently denied.

Paul Higgs, in "Citizen Theory and Old Age," published in 1997, discusses this viewpoint from a Foucauldian perspective, stressing the idea that these, what might be considered "technologies of the self," are possible in Western society, but only within a limited framework. Older consumers, particularly those whom gerontologists term the *old-old* (the oldest generation), face boundaries insofar as frailty and "dependency are not ideal circumstances from which to exercise consumer sovereignty. Power imbalances and real physical limitations are just two impediments."[43] Regarding these power imbalances from a gendered perspective, a further impediment to "consumer citizenship" would stem from the fact that many old women do not possess the wealth to make this a viable option.[44] Primarily this is because the majority of people in the West are working class (and globally, the poor still outnumber the rich). More specifically, the current generation of older women has experienced different career patterns from their male peers. Women's employment histories tend to be characterized by both fragmentation, due to childbirth and marriage, and relatively low wages, due to working part-time, being employed in relatively junior positions or simply because female wages are proportionally lower than male ones (as discussed by Friedan, Arber and Ginn, among others). Although female working patterns are changing, a remedy for the feminization of poverty seems unlikely within the near future, and thus so does the likelihood of women being able to purchase an improved way of life.

Pat Barker's *Union Street* (1982) is a useful text to mention at this juncture, as it graphically depicts the effects that being both old and poor can have upon the individual and serves as a useful counterpoint to rosy visions of life in a consumer society. The novel is divided into seven chapters, each one representing a different female character, ranging from eleven-year-old Kelly Brown to the ancient Alice Bell, who live on the industrial and poverty-stricken street of the title. The chapter focusing on the oldest character depicts her attempts to deal with the debilitating effects of a stroke while alone and in the face of an uncaring son who wants to put her, much to her dismay, in an institution. The opening passages capture the unshrinking quality of Barker's novel and the tone of Alice's existence:

> It was January now. Alice Bell spent her days in bed: it was her solution to the price of coal. Whenever she moved newspapers rustled all around her. The bed was full of them. She had read somewhere that newspapers were as good as blankets, and the house was cold.
> There wasn't a lot of fat on her to keep warm. Her thighs were folds of creased skin, hanging from the bone. Yet beside her on the bed was a black handbag with £100 inside. She had saved it out of her social security money: the "pancrack" as she contemptuously called it. What she got was barely adequate for heating and food....[45]

The remainder of her story traces her fight to keep for herself the conditions of a human life to the point where Alice realizes that, despite her struggles, she will be made to leave her home. She then decides that "what she wanted was simple. She wanted to die with dignity.... She would not be waiting here when they came."[46] Her walk to the local park in the freezing dead of a winter's night is represented as allowing her to fulfill her wish, but Barker's narrative laments the fact that this is the only option that society allows her.

*Union Street*, with its commitment to women of all ages, engages with the stereotype of the poverty-stricken older woman and demonstrates that this figure is the result of a lifetime of social deprivation. As such, Alice's story acts as a cautionary tale; Barker's refusal to Other her reminds the reader that her fate could be her own unless society radically changes its attitude toward age and gender.

Before leaving *Union Street*, it is worth pointing out that although the specter of the penniless older woman recurs in the popular imagination, literature tends to shy away from the subject. Apart from Doris Lessing's *The Diary of a Good Neighbour*, the texts I explore focus on middle-class characters.[47] This is because, as Beauvoir notes in *Old Age*, the poor are marginalized in literary discourse, and so to be female, old and impoverished renders you even more invisible and less likely a participant in representational practices.

Betty Friedan, in *The Fountain of Age*, analyzes various types of strategies that older individuals have used to more successfully negotiate ageist discourses, alongside a consideration of the larger social structures that need to change, or are transforming, to accommodate this goal. Her message is a positive one that stresses continued development in later life; subsequently, many of the hypotheses that she presents are absent from analysis that frames old age solely as an era of decline. Although Friedan does not focus specifically upon women, as might have been anticipated from the author of *The Feminine Mystique* (1963), she is gender-aware and suggests that, as women live longer than men, society could learn from their responses to aging.

These methods of coping with senescence are constantly touched upon in the novels I discuss in this study, but it is worth briefly mentioning the two main factors that Friedan believes contribute to female longevity. The first revolves around the fact that women expend more energy than men do in forming close relationships outside of a primary partnership. Friedan cites this continued intimacy, in direct opposition to disengagement theory, as one of the keys to successful aging, and sisters, daughters and female friends do seem to populate the novels that I analyze. Secondly, she argues that because of the discontinuity in women's lives, they are forced to develop the skills necessary to adapt to changes in social status. She asks, rhetorically, "Could the very discontinuity ... that has taken place in women's roles over a lifetime—their continual practice in retirement and disengagement, shift and re-engagements—account for their greater flexibility and resilience in age?"[48] The discontinuity upon which this female skill of adapting is based could be seen as a very questionable asset, at least in vocational and ultimately economic terms, but like Beauvoir, Friedan is discussing society as it is, rather than as it might be.

Friedan simultaneously picks up on the suggestion that gender-prescribed behaviors become less demarcated as one ages. She analyzes studies that suggest that a gender-crossover of the characteristics conventionally associated with masculinity and femininity takes place: with women, for example, becoming more assertive and men tending to become more expressive of their emotions. In the essay "'I'm the Eyes and She's the Arms': Changes in Gender Roles in Advanced Old Age" (1995), Gail Wilson nods to this idea and suggests that in the future,

> a socially approved life stage may develop which older people can accept as their own, rather than having to construct their lives without any positive models. Women's values would likely to be more dominant than they are at an earlier age, if only because their numbers would be greater.[49]

Wilson sees the gender-crossover as a nominally one-way process, with feminine traits overwhelming conventionally masculine ones. It is impossible to know which paradigm is more accurate in its predictions because, as Wilson hints, old age is a relatively uncharted territory, at least in terms of what it may mean to age productively. This is one of the points at which literature can intervene in the discursive construction of aging: to use Foucault's phraseology, "fictioning" the possibilities of senescence for both individuals and society more generally.

Problems can arise, however, if the focus of reverse discourse is only on those who age successfully, the most insidious of which permeates Friedan's work. Foucauldian approaches to liberatory discourses ask which groups are being sidelined, often unintentionally. In this case, the actions of those who are able-bodied are valorized at the expense of those who are dependent and/or disabled in some way. Friedan seems unaware that her study marginalizes the most vulnerable sectors of the senescent. For example, she discusses how studies have shown that inhabitants of retirement homes who are allowed a relative amount of independence remain physically and psychologically healthier than those who are not allowed to make decisions about their environment or daily timetable.[50] In order to stress the positive, Friedan underplays the prohibitive nature of the fact that many individuals have no hope of leaving institutions. She ignores the correlation between economic security, dependency and successful aging; while having sufficient wealth does not guarantee a good old age, it undeniably helps in many situations. Those whom Friedan considers to have aged with style are often wealthy, educated, and healthy enough to make choices that are not available to other individuals (including characters such as Barker's Alice Bell). With this oversight, she acquiesces with the creation of an aged minority, the fourth age. These are individuals who have passed through the third age where a middle-aged style of life, in terms of health and resources, is prolonged (i.e., the consumer citizens talked about by Featherstone). Bill Bytheway warns that in promoting the concept of a third age that differs only slightly from middle-age, the "labelling problem [defining old age] is pushed onto even older and more defenceless people."[51]

Neither Friedan nor Bytheway specifically mention the disabled old (although perhaps they are those to whom Bytheway euphemistically refers as "more defenceless"). This gap recurs in theories of aging but also in society more generally as the disability activist Jenny Morris discusses in her article "Feminism and Disability" (1993). She writes that those "people whose physical characteristics mean they require some kind of help (whether this need is actually created by the physical environment or not) have no place in the public world."[52] What is surprising is that theorists of senescence actually help to prove this statement correct, particularly in light of the statistic that two-thirds of the disabled in Britain are over age sixty.[53]

Turning her attention to feminism, Morris writes that part of its silence about disability, and thus, to a certain extent, old age, stems from its insistence on the personal as political. She acknowledges that this is a useful strategy for women in politicizing their daily reality, but feels that it may prevent women, who exist in a multitude of different social and physical conditions, from imaginatively reaching beyond their own specific situations. This initially seems a paradoxical argument, because it arises from a politicizing of the differences between women and then it seemingly attempts to eradicate them. However, Morris is really discussing degrees of empathy, and she is correct to highlight the ease with which people can overlook troubles and joys that do not touch directly upon their lives. She tends, however, to overestimate the strength of this conceptual barrier, seeming not to take into account the fact that feminists often use empathic approaches to reach outside of their own social circumstances.[54]

Maureen Cain discusses this dynamic in "Foucault, Feminism and Feeling," published in 1994, and analyzes how contemporary feminists are approaching questions of difference and essentialism. She argues that Foucauldian-influenced theory has provided a language to define methodologies that are already developed within feminist practices and which she describes as "standpoint politics," where feminists:

> make strategic decisions about differences: both as to which are relevant at a particular conjecture, as to useful alliances and their limits, and as to how the discourse of difference itself may be developed and deployed. Feminists do not all share a site, a place in the field of relations, but they may, if they choose, all share standpoints.[55]

Colette V. Browne also uses this idea in *Women, Feminism and Aging*, urging for "coalition-building" within feminism, which, if not automatic, can be achieved through the "moral reasoning" that underpins the feminist project and its battles against "-isms"; be they sexism, racism, or ageism.[56]

## *Ageism Within Feminism*

Despite this potential for politically and personally connecting with others in a dissimilar situation, it is not always easily achieved, as illustrated by feminism's tendency to ignore the older woman: the most familiar guise of ageism within the movement. I have already mentioned this subject in passing, and it is convincingly demonstrated by Barbara Macdonald in *Look Me in the Eye*, who uses her experience, as a sixty-five-year-old woman, of taking part in a "Reclaim the Night" demonstration in the early 1980s to comment upon youthist attitudes. She was shocked to find that its organizers automatically doubted her ability to keep pace with the other women and, further, that they directed questions about her health to her younger partner.

This event caused Macdonald to consider hierarchization within feminism and led her to the disturbing, but valid, conclusion that "youth is bonded with patriarchy in the enslavement of the older woman."[57] She contextualizes this statement by considering the history of the movement, beginning with its first wave (in the late nineteenth and early twentieth century). She refers to the fact that its chief protagonists were middle-aged and older, as they were less socially constricted in their roles of wife and mother than their younger counterparts. In contrast, it was younger feminists who, having gained a certain amount of social freedom due to the efforts of earlier ones, directed the second wave of the 1960s. Macdonald believes that this demographic is reflected in the concerns that it prioritized, such as motherhood, contraception and careers. Subjects that pertained to the older woman did not, and still often do not, reach feminism's political agenda. Macdonald personalizes this problem and writes humorously:

> If an old woman talks about arthritis or cataracts, don't think old women are constantly complaining. We are just trying to get a word in edgewise while you talk and write about abortions, contraception, pre-menstrual syndromes, toxic shock, or turkey basters.[58]

Not only does this extract comment on the ageism that underlies the choice of subjects deemed suitable for discussion, but it also comments on the attitudes that prevent older women from articulating aspects of their reality.

Germaine Greer, in *The Change*, agrees with Macdonald's charge that younger women are often ageist: "Youth in women is prized by men, and therefore, by women themselves."[59] Anophobia (the dislike and fear of older women) is internalized and results in the aging process being conceptualized by many women purely in terms of the tragic. Greer also develops Macdonald's concept of the divide-and-conquer technique of patriarchal discourses by adding that not only do younger women cooperate with ageist strategies that trivialize senescence, but the situation is also worsened because older women seize the limited opportunities they have to manipulate younger women: "It is a permanent aspect of all kinds of oppression among human groups that the oppressed are forced to act out institutionalized oppression and exact pressure on those immediately beneath them in the power structure."[60] As Foucault explains, power relations between an individual and institutions are not static, and a person can be powerful in one relationship and weak within another: An older manager may wield power over a junior, but the younger woman can use ageist discourse to ridicule her boss. Despite this instance of the fluidity of power relations, it is generally the fate of older women to be discursively portrayed as deviant.

Within feminism, the process of Othering the senescent, besides seeming to forget that most Western women will become old, prevents scholars from accurately analyzing patriarchal controls across the life course. This oversight results in older women facing the task of aging alone and reliant upon their own survival strategies rather than receiving help from an established body of knowledge. The following quote from Audre Lorde, in "Age, Race, Class and Sex: Women Redefining Difference" (1980), connects the two results of ageism within feminism:

> If the younger members of a community view the older members as contemptible or suspect or excess, they will never be able to join hands and examine the living memories of the community, nor ask the all important question: "Why?" This gives rise to historical amnesia that keeps us working to invent the wheel every time we have to go to the store for bread.[61]

Lorde is correct to judge that if the generation gap is left intact, the knowledge possessed by old people will remain hidden, and the oppression they face on a daily basis will continue unchallenged. Failure to achieve a successful old age will remain a personal defeat, and while we cannot always evade individual responsibility, the effectiveness of agency must be assessed within the wider framework of dominant discourses that define acceptable or deviant behavior.

## *Literary Critical Approaches to Representations of Old Age*

Ageist attitudes are equally apparent in the field of literary criticism. Relatively little critical attention is paid to fictions of aging in comparison to that paid texts about other stages of life. Undoubtedly, part of the reason for this is that there are comparatively few narratives on which studies could be based, although the following comments by Kate Soper, from "Productive Contradictions" (1993), places this point in context:

> The fate of oppressed groups is not decided simply at the level of competing discourses. What is critical to their advancement is the specific economic and political climate in which they are expressing their resistance, and this can be more or less favourable to their reception.[62]

For example, a conventional approach to authors such as Barbara Pym and Gladys Mitchell might not respond to their narrative engagements with discourses of gender, while feminist readings highlight their presence but often fail to note their commentary about aging. More explicitly polemical writers such as Fay Weldon and Angela Carter's dissections of old age are overlooked by an approach that focuses on gender but fails to take age into account. However, investigations into representations of aging are gradually becoming more commonplace because of society's increasing interest in senescence, and I want to consider a range of theoretical approaches here.

Richard Fallis, in "Grow Old Along with Me: Images of Older People in British and American Literature," published in 1989, disputes the idea that fiction contains little about the old. He believes that readers can gain valuable insights into experiences of aging from works as varied as Chaucer's *Canterbury Tales* to Miller's *Death of a Salesman*. While the sentiment is sound, he actually focuses upon stories in which older protagonists are portrayed in very narrow terms as the social Other. He seems to ignore fiction's role in perpetuating and reinforcing norms by treating the texts under analysis as mere reflections of society. Therefore, his readers may share his view that the texts under discussion "tell the whole story" of old age, but only if they, too, accept as a *fait accompli* the paradigm of older people as outsiders.

However, Fallis is perceptive in recognizing that authorial hostility toward the old can arise because writers are often "younger than the aged characters they create; and older people are a threat to the young, or they seem so, as they try to control their lives, or more subtly, they come to symbolise an inevitability the young would prefer to ignore."[63] He does not expand upon these points, but they complement a sentiment attributed to André Gide, who put down the lack of older protagonists in literature to the "fact" that creativity is the province of younger people who are uninterested in representing the senescent.[64]

While these perspectives are insightful, they are based on the belief that only the young write fiction. Without offering a comprehensive list of older authors, it is worth mentioning some female writers who help to undermine the equation of old age with creative stagnation. May Sarton, for example, produced fiction, poetry and autobiographical works throughout her life, including the subtle, and self-explanatory, *Endgame: A Journal of the Seventy-Ninth Year* (1993). A British and more popular (at least in terms of sales) author, Mary Wesley, had her first novel, *Jumping the Queue*, published during the 1980s when she was aged seventy, and she has since written numerous bestsellers. In terms of texts in this book Molly Keane wrote *Time After Time* (1983) when she was eighty; Sarton wrote *As We Are Now* (1973) in her late seventies; Weldon was sixty-eight when *Rhode Island Blues* was published, and so forth. Further, writers are under no obligation to only represent their own demographic when creating characters, and the younger authors I have come across appear as interested in discourses of aging as their older counterparts.

Fallis's essay might be considered more useful by a reader who is interested in older male protagonists, although the author himself does not note that the narratives he considers predominately represent masculine experiences of aging. As would be expected, Beauvoir does not duplicate this gender-blindness in *Old Age*. The text produces its "history" of senescence using literary sources ranging from the Bible, through Emile Zola's *La Terre*, to twentieth-century drama (focusing, for the greater part, on Western works), and Beauvoir introduces her survey with the facetious comment, "what we have here is a man's problem."[65] She explains that depictions of older women are rare and links this representational gap to the fact that the most visible struggles for power take place among males. On a literary level, this dynamic is recognizable as driving the "revolt-against-the-father" genre, of which there is no female equivalent. On a historical level, Beauvoir makes the now common observation that most of its chronicles are written by powerful men (or, at least, commissioned by them).

As well as deciding that detailed narratives about old age, whether fictional or biographical, center on male experiences, Beauvoir reaches a number of other important conclusions. Although I made similar points in the introduction, they are worth reiterating because of their relevance. For example, she states that representations of the aged are consistently based on negative stereotypes. Older characters throughout the ages are either depicted as figures of fun because of their social ineptitude and inappropriate desires, or punished by narratives for being interfering and outdated in their attitudes. (Older generations are viewed as behind the times, regardless of the period in which a text is written). Beauvoir sees contemporary literature as continuing to rely upon these stereotypes and "inherited clichés."

Nonetheless, she is hopeful that social ideas about aging will become "richer," and that this will be reflected in a greater, and more varied, number of fictional texts on the subject. Her hopes seem to have been fulfilled to a certain extent: As I have suggested, there does appear to be an increasing number of female authors interested in discrediting the myths of senescence. Unfortunately, Beauvoir made her comments thirty years ago. As there has not been a startling increase in the number of narratives about old age during this time, my recognition of a gradually expanding genre should be read in the cautious way in which it is offered. Beauvoir's faith in change was possibly rooted in the fact that she had already practically contributed to the field of fiction about aging with "The Age of Discretion."

Celeste Loughman, in "Novels of Senescence: A New Naturalism" (1977), believes, even more optimistically, that fiction has already reached a point where its interest in old age is obvious. Loughman pinpoints

Muriel Spark's *Memento Mori*, published in 1958, as heralding the start of a literary trend in which entire works are populated by older protagonists. She discusses texts such as Saul Bellow's *Mr. Sammler's Planet* (1970) and Junichiro Tanizaki's *Diary of a Mad Old Man* (1965), believing they fuse:

> the subject of senescence with a literary naturalism rooted in biological determinism, focusing on man as a dying animal at a point close to extinction, his personality and behaviour determined to a large degree by the inevitable process of degeneration and decay, and by the realisation that he must die.[66]

Although it is not clear from this extract, she is actually praising the authors' representations of old age. What is disturbing is not that she believes individuals are subject to physiological change (which is incontrovertible), but that she ignores the possibility that they may cope with this eventuality and that she considers senescence purely in terms of physical degeneration.

Loughman thus finds the narrative focus on the "isolation," "impotence," and "decay intrinsic to the ageing process" a balanced approach. The sole positive theme that she identifies as running throughout the novels is an insistence on sexuality as a normal aspect of old age. This authorial obsession contradicts the usual view of old age and sexual desire, even if the fantasies of the characters remain unfulfilled because of their physical inability to carry them out.

It is this point about sexuality in old age that Emily M. Nett, in "The Naked Soul Comes Closer to the Surface: Old Age in the Gender Mirror of Contemporary Novels" (1990), uses to question the universality of Loughman's reading. Nett suggests that the reason Loughman finds her chosen novels concerned largely with loss of various sorts is that she mainly focuses on texts by, and about, men. Nett argues that male identity is partially constructed around an ability to perform sexually and that a youthful/penetrative model acts as a benchmark for normal sexuality. The authors project this onto their male protagonists, who are represented as failures because of their inability to function within this restrictive paradigm, and they find that "the tragedy of being old is a decline of potency—sexual power above all."[67]

Conversely, Nett believes that women writers, such as Elizabeth Taylor in *Mrs. Palfrey at the Claremont* (1971) and Margaret Laurence in *The Stone Angel* (1964), represent older female protagonists as freed from the restrictive subject positions of their youth (defined by patriarchal discourse). These characters are then able to embark on a "journey to the realm of inherited female power."[68] This spiritual rebirth is achieved through "memory and reflection" and is seen as a process that can disrupt the lives of other protagonists, including the male ones. Furthermore, Nett suggests that this "transcendental movement" is a feminine rather than exclusively female experience and so it is one that older men can achieve in order to live to a "good" old age (as does Friedan in *The Fountain of Age*).

However, Nett's article, while persuasive, contains some problematic assumptions. It connects women to spirituality and men to sexuality, thus reinforcing, rather than questioning, a dichotomous conception of social behavior as structured by gender. As such, it also supports a paradigm of subjectivity as inherent rather than constructed. Further, Nett expresses the idea that discussions of the older woman enrich "feminist literary theory greatly by going beyond the theme of female eroticism."[69] While this statement contains some truth, it largely underestimates the range of topics in which feminist literary theory is interested.

The differences between the two essays illustrate a broad shift within the field of literary gerontology. The growing influence of feminist theory (in both literature and gerontology) can be traced in Nett's gender-conscious readings and is representative of the fact that "old age in literature" is no longer underscored by a male-as-norm analysis, based upon the illusion that the elderly are a homogenous group unaffected by gender (as presumed by Fallis and Loughman).

Barbara Frey Waxman's study, *From the Hearth to the Open Road: A Feminist Study of Aging in Contemporary Literature*, was published in 1990, the same year as Nett's essay, and it also foregrounds a female aesthetic. In fact, she identifies a new genre produced by female authors and representing the older woman: "I call this genre, in a feminist literary critic's act of naming, the *Reifungsroman*, or novel of ripening—opposing its central tenet to the usual notion of deterioration in old age."[70] She believes that the novels that belong to the genre break down "Western culture's binary opposition between youth and age, with all positive attributes on the side of youth, and instead ... create positive associations with age."[71] To deconstruct the polarization of youth and age, the *Reifungsroman* asserts the older protagonist's "futurity": their continued development and humanity.[72] She feels *Reifungsroman* can act as a "springboard for subversive thought," helping women to name, and therefore celebrate or lament, their experiences of aging.[73] The idea that fictional scenarios can play a didactic role is not new, nor is the belief that that which cannot be articulated is marginalized. In fact, these are principles that drive feminist critics to search for texts that represent a variety of ways of being a woman.

I find Waxman's recognition of authors' refusal to characterize old age as a time of immanence particularly attractive and pertinent. Many of the texts considered by this study fall within the parameters of the *Reifungsroman*, and indeed, Waxman analyzes Sarton's *As We Are Now* and Lessing's *The Diary of a Good Neighbour* as do I. Notwithstanding, the approaches to the texts are not identical due to the difference in theoretical underpinnings. One example of the way in which my work follows a different path than Waxman's is demonstrated by my decision to investigate crime fiction's older female sleuth. The potential of novels from this genre to challenge static notions of old age is similar to that of *Reifungsroman*, but the generic techniques employed to achieve this goal are not.

## Conclusion

As I have been arguing, both popular and academic paradigms of aging need to move beyond their current obsessions with regard to the way they represent and interpret senescence. There is a need for explanations of this stage of life to balance, what Wayne Booth terms in *The Art of Growing Older* (1992), "losses, fears and lamentations" with "cures, consolations and celebrations."[74] Kathleen Woodward, in "Age-Work in American Culture" (1994), stresses that currently there is a tendency to focus upon the negative abstractions at the expense of the positive ones. All stages of life contain a variety of experiences, and yet dominant representations of youth and middle age do not dwell exclusively on their problematic aspects, as happens when senescence enters the picture. Woodward writes that understanding and "making meaning of the experience of ageing would seem to require that we think through" both sets of Booth's oppositions.[75] She stresses the need for theorists to realistically expect that an older individual will lead a life in which lamentations and celebrations coexist, and then reflect this in their analysis.

This guideline is one to which I have attempted to adhere; a task that is made easier because it is blatant that the authors I consider write with this equilibrium in mind. They contest naturalized views of aging by producing representations of older women that explode complacent notions of senescence. Those who choose to emphasize the more positive aspects of aging still consider its more problematic sides. Even if they had glossed over its difficulties, there is truth in the argument Isabella Paoletti puts forward in *Being an Older Woman*. She nods to the risks inherent to celebrating old age but continues, "I don't believe that they are greater than those in negative constructions of elderliness, with their danger of a self-fulfilling prophecy."[76] Authors who do focus on the difficulties of aging still refuse to fall back on negative constructions of senescence. Instead, they emphasize that many of the problems experienced by the characters are the result of social constructions of old age and are therefore contestable.

Novels that contain this sentiment can be regarded as part of a radical project that exposes the fluidity of the supposedly static boundaries that separate the old from the rest of humanity. In doing so, they fulfill one of the functions of literature suggested by Foucault:

> It seems to me that the possibility exists for fiction to function in truth for a fictional discourse to induce effects of truth, and for bringing it about that a true discourse engenders or "manufactures" something that does not yet exist, that is, "fictions it."[77]

Although Susan Bordo, in *Unbearable Weight* (1983), is right to insist that norms are easier to resist in texts than in reality, it does not nullify fiction's ability to help create alternative truths about a subject.[78] Jana Sawicki warns that women must not participate in self-refusal (constantly questioning one's relationship to various discourses) to the extent that they become timid in sharing their experiences with others through fear of their particularity. Fictions though, because they are not bound to represent a particular version of the truth, can sidestep this predicament and freely explore non-reductive ways of being.

However, a text is open to both normative and subversive readings: The discursive arena in which it is received significantly affects its polemical content, as mentioned earlier. Waxman makes a similar point when she discusses the creation of a theoretical culture in which representations of older women are central: "I give priority to age ... to compensate for other literary critics and theorists' neglect of it; we critics need to raise readers' awareness of ageism and the harm it does before we can enlist their aid in diminishing its strength."[79]

The suggestion that feminist literary gerontology is still in its infancy, and so needs to assert its validity and raise awareness of the issues involved in such an endeavor, explains why I have been so precise in detailing the theoretical underpinnings of this piece. To this end, I want to reiterate the several functions that I see my chosen novels as performing. Primarily, they emphasize that old age, like gender, is socially constructed and that the meanings attributed to this period are filtered through ageist attitudes and discourse. Authors unveil this status quo by conversely refusing to Other the older woman and making her the subject of the narrative rather than a marginal figure. In doing so, they insist that her outsider status is a myth (although with very real effects) and show the "generation gap" to be a divisive construction that prevents feminism from recognizing the ways in which oppressive discourses envelop women from birth to death. Finally, because the novels avoid the normal stereotypical depictions of older women, the texts expand the horizons of what it is possible for female characters to "do" within literature. Authors recognize the different experiences that senescence may bring but refuse to portray them as alien or abnormal.

This final authorial strategy is used extensively in the next chapter, which analyzes representations of dependent older women. Fictional characters who are physically dependent rarely appear as central protagonists because disability and terminal illness is a taboo subject. The authors within the chapter conclude that this type of social reticence, and consequent absence of concern, intensifies the problems inherent to the older body that is not functioning "perfectly."

# 2

# The Angry and Frustrated Older Woman

## Introduction

Discourses that aim to move discussions of aging away from questions of decline can inadvertently do so at the expense of the physically challenged fourth age. In order not to replicate this stance, I intend to focus first on narratives that portray characters dealing, both directly and indirectly, with the deteriorating body and increasing dependency. Many of the images that appear in these texts of older women without friends or money, exiled to a retirement home and unable to care for themselves, haunt the popular imagination, where they are treated as if they represent the full spectrum of experiences open to the senescent.

In order to quickly banish this specter, I am going to briefly review some statistical material on the frequency, and types, of dependency in senescence. For example, Betty Friedan, in the *Fountain of Age* (1993), states that only three percent of people in the United Kingdom aged over sixty-five live in residential care.[1] In one British survey carried out in 1964 and referred to by clinical psychologist Graham Stokes in *On Being Old: The Psychology of Later Life* (1992), only four percent of those analyzed were disability-free. Yet of those who were disabled, only nine-and-a-half percent were "bedridden, immobile, or capable of limited outdoor mobility" (in other words, wholly dependent).[2] These figures are not cited to undercut the importance of representations that engage with anxieties about dependency, but to negate the conception that it is the only possible outcome of senescence. Further, the statistics provided by Stokes suggest that even individuals who receive assistance can continue living with disabilities and a degree of autonomy: Whether or not the necessary help is readily available is one of the subjects considered by the authors in this chapter.

Loughman's "Novels of Senescence" and Nett's response, "The Naked Soul Comes Closer to the Surface," represent opposing critical viewpoints about fictional treatments of the dependent old. As a reminder, Loughman concludes that the texts she considers produce a "naturalistic treatment of old age—the isolation, the impotence, and the decay which are intrinsic to the ageing process."[3] She feels the misery focused on by the authors is a wholly accurate reflection of experiences of aging. Nett, taking issue with this "unlovely picture of old age," convincingly argues that it is a result of Loughman's focus on male authors who construct sexual potency as central to masculinity and its loss as responsible for their male characters' bitterness. Nett goes on to locate an alternative female vision of senescence, which, without a preoccupation with virility, tends to represent characters who, "despite the trials and tribulations of ageing ... sample triumph at the end in some important way."[4]

This pattern is frequently apparent in fictions of aging, and can be traced in the last text discussed in this chapter, May Sarton's *The Reckoning* (1984). However, it is not the only type of polemical narrative structure open to writers who focus on dependency. Some texts are more recognizable as the type about which Loughman comments, representing the older woman as helpless and frustrated by her body's inability to accomplish simple tasks. Yet, contrary to Loughman's perspective, the authors treated in this chapter do not suggest relentless misery is the sole and natural result of a deteriorating body. Instead, they employ a maneuver common to the creation of feminist discourse in other areas, concerned with both fiction and theory, and unravel the part external circumstances play in women's allegedly personal problems. The texts in question are *The Diary of a Good Neighbour* by Doris Lessing (1984), and *As We Are Now* (1973) and *The Reckoning* by May Sarton.[5] I will also be referring extensively to Margaret Laurence's *The Stone Angel* (1964) and Margaret Forster's *Have the Men Had Enough?* (1989), and mentioning, among others, Ellen Newton's autobiographical text, *This Bed My Centre* (1980).

All of the older protagonists in these texts, at some point, express their anger at society's lack of interest in their circumstances. Barbara Frey Waxman, in *From the Hearth to the Open Road*, writes that such rage is "central to *Reifungsroman* about dependent elders" and that it is a "good antidote" to the "despair and fragmentation" that constantly worry their efforts to cope bereft of social support.[6] The result of this type of representation is a reclamation of the stereotypical traits of anger and frustration that are often attributed to the senescent. Popular culture paints them as moaning about "nothing," while here their agitation is recontextualized as a valid response to trying circumstances. Waxman rightly believes that narratives that frame strong emotions in such a way are "a reaction against patriarchal society's fear of old women and impulse to deny, curb or trivialize their anger," and provide a "forum for the anger so that other women can read about it."[7]

Engaging with society's trivialization of the older woman is a trait common to many of the novels investigated in this study, but *The Diary of a Good Neighbour* and *As We Are Now* seem particularly explicit in their political critique. Conversely, *The Reckoning*'s radicalism tends only to become visible when read in relation to these other texts. It represents an idealized scenario, at least in terms of the control that the terminally ill, sixty-year-old protagonist, Laura Spelman, can exert on her surroundings and care she receives. Nonetheless, when it is contrasted with Sarton's earlier text, *As We Are Now*, readers are forced to agree with one of the axiomatic principles of Jenny Morris' *Pride Against Prejudice: Transforming Attitudes to Disability* (1991): "To put it simply, it is not an inability to walk which disables someone but the steps into the building."[8] Sarton represents Laura as retaining a degree of autonomy that allows her to focus on spiritual growth, whereas Caro, the narrator of *As We Are Now*, must struggle with the mundane, bullied and neglected by those paid to care for her until she is eventually robbed of both her optimism and identity.

Caro suffers from other characters' prejudice against the old, the frail and the disabled, biases that also exist in the sphere of representation. Morris is explicit in stating that negative attitudes toward the disabled, of whatever age, is reflected in the paucity of fiction about their lives. The cultural erasure of a section of society viewed as deviant in some way is a dynamic familiar to this study, and the following quote from Morris emphasizes, once again, why stigmatization occurs: "It is fear and denial of the frailty, vulnerability, mortality and *arbitrariness* of human experience that deters us from confronting such realities. Fear and denial prompt the isolation of those who are disabled, ill or old as 'other,' as 'not like us.'"[9] She laments the fact that fiction, with its ability to provide "points of reference with which to make sense of our reality," tends to shy away from the task.[10] The following texts are in many ways exceptions that prove the rule: They meld anger, triumph, frustration, friendship, spirituality and death to represent indomitable, older female, dependent protagonists.

## *Female Friendship and Social Abandonment in* The Diary of a Good Neighbour[11]

Doris Lessing's *The Diary of a Good Neighbour* is primarily about the relationship that develops between the middle-aged narrator, Janna, and the ninety-four-year-old Maudie Fowler. They are represented as accidentally meeting when the younger woman helps the older to decipher a prescription. What begins as an occasional cup of tea progresses, over a couple of years, to a point where Janna visits Maudie twice a day to help her bathe and buy her food. This care continues until Maudie is hospitalized due to the worsening effects of cancer and dies a few weeks later.

Lessing depicts the older character's life before Janna as overwhelmingly lonely. The reader learns over the course of the text that she had been briefly married until her husband had left, taking their son with him. Her deteriorating health threatens the independence she had worked hard for all of her life. She becomes consumed by the fear that she will lose her rented flat if she betrays any sign of her increasing physical frailty and therefore carefully guards her solitude. Janna informs the reader that, before the beginning of her "diary," she had lost her older husband to cancer and readily admits she gave him little support. After his death, she continued her career as the editor of a successful woman's magazine and throughout the text discusses her love for the job. Her conception of herself, before she grows close to Maudie, is as the efficient and bright "boss" of a creative environment. Yet the subtext of her autobiography reveals her as the inhabitant of an emotionally cold world characterized by office politics and solitary grooming rituals.

Lessing represents their burgeoning friendship as one of mutual affection and benefit. Maudie finally finds someone who can offer emotional, as well as practical, support and Janna finds that the contact with the older woman causes her to reassess her life and values. Gayle Greene, in *Doris Lessing: The Poetics of Change* (1994), stresses the importance of the fact that the relationship is between women from different generations and social backgrounds. Greene argues that the protagonists' unlikely friendship crosses, and thus questions, the stability of boundaries of age and class, offering instead a "right relationship between youth and age, an exchange based on reciprocity."[12] This dynamic is reinforced by Lessing's inclusion of a third generation in the shape of Janna's teenage niece who invites herself to stay with her aunt. She also chips away at the narrator's emotional isolation, and although she initially indulges in teenage acts of rebellion, the niece learns to temper her excess of feelings by observing her aunt's self-possession and discipline. This less-central relationship contributes towards Lessing's creation of a community of female characters that also includes Janna's work colleagues, other older characters with whom she makes contact, and social workers. No male protagonists of any import appear in the text, which focuses on the women who weave in and out of each other's lives, proffering help and learning lessons from one another. (Lessing appears to be commenting on the fact that caring is a gendered role, a point developed later in the chapter.)

Although the roles of nurturer and nurtured are often represented as fluid within female friendships between peers, it is less common for this formula to be applied to relationships between different generations, particularly when one character is physically dependent on the other. Not only does Lessing challenge this model, but she does so in a surprisingly unsentimental fashion. She includes commentaries, for instance, about the work that it takes for Janna and Maudie to maintain their intimacy and about the nuances in emotional tone that characterize their meetings, after one of which Janna writes:

> The trouble with a summing-up afterwards ... is that you leave out the grit and grind of a meeting. I could say, she was cross to begin with, then got her temper back, and we had a nice time drinking tea... But what about all the shifts of liking, anger, irritation—oh, so much anger, in both of us.[13]

As the text progresses, the reader learns that the protagonists' anger and irritation comes from a variety of sources. They both have to work to cross a generational and class divide, and this shows itself most obviously in their mastering of the art of giving and receiving assistance graciously. Maudie's suspicions about the outside world initially make her loath to accept help. Janna, at first, cannot grasp the importance that the older character places on her independence and cannot hide her irritation at what she thinks is just false pride. However, the two characters grow beyond these misunderstandings, and at no point does Lessing represent Janna as facing a thankless task or Maudie as possessing a "chip on her shoulder" (a common way of nullifying the anger expressed by older generations). The protagonists' frustrations are framed as valid and are represented as an accepted part of their relationship rather than something that destroys it.

Lessing's realism, and deviation from the usual way of representing the dependent old, is hardly surprising, as she is known as an author unafraid to experiment with form and content in her work. Besides producing fiction such as *The Diary of a Good Neighbour*, and *The Grass Is Singing* (1949), she has written plays, an autobiography, and the critically acclaimed science-fiction series *The Canopus in Argos: Archives* sequence.[14] Further, *The Diary of a Good Neighbour* is not the first novel in which Lessing demonstrates an interest in aging: *The Summer Before the Dark* was published in 1973 and depicts a middle-aged female character's coming-to-terms with growing older; and Lessing continues her exploration of the subject in *Love, Again*, published in 1986.

Lessing's general political awareness shows itself in the preface to *The Diaries of Jane Somers* (a volume that contains both *The Diary of a Good Neighbour* and its sequel *If the Old Could...*), when she explains why she used a pseudonym when contacting publishers about, and initially publishing, the novels.[15] The first reason she provides is that she wished to avoid reviewers and readers precociously labeling the novel because of their expectations about her work; the second is that she wanted to expose the difficulties faced by new authors in getting their material published. (Two publishers turned the novel down before Michael Joseph accepted it). One rather ungracious response to these stated aims is to suggest that they are excuses for what was really a simple publicity stunt.[16] Yet even if this is the "real" reason for the deceit, it does not detract from Lessing's successful exposure of the mechanisms of the publishing world.

Lessing also demonstrates her mindfulness of the social construction of aging when she writes of how the content of *The Diary of a Good Neighbour* contributed to its "unpublishable" status. She states that one scathing review acted as "a nasty little reminder of how many people reach instinctively for the revolvers at the mention of something they don't like."[17] She does not need to expand on what the "something" is because it is self-evident: depictions of the poor and physically dependent old.

Lessing's insights into the social constructions of class and age can be linked to her early interest in Marxism (although she later lost faith in it as an ideology and became interested in the Moslem philosophy of Sufism).[18] Certainly, elements of the novel fictionalize earlier arguments made by Simone de Beauvoir in the anti-capitalist study *Old Age*. For instance, Beauvoir's belief that the marginalization of the aged is a result of capitalism's lack of interest in those who do not contribute to the economy is mirrored in *The Diary of a Good Neighbour*. At the beginning of the text, Janna possesses a typically bourgeois mindset and admits, after a few meetings with Maudie, that the number of older women she had begun to notice surprised her. "I looked up and down the streets and saw—old women. Old men too, but mostly old women.... I had not seen them."[19]

It is Janna's equation of social and self-worth with participation in the workforce that results in the senescent being literally, as well as discursively, out of sight to her. The narrator's recognition of this blindspot is represented as exceptional rather than normal in scenes where Janna comes into contact with an electrician she has arranged to rewire Maudie's home, barely habitable by late twentieth-century standards. When Janna pays him, he blurts out, "What's the good of people that old?" Lessing creates this opening to allow the narrator to explicitly muse about his attitude: "What he said was what people do say. *Why aren't they in a Home? Get them out of the way, out of sight, where young healthy people can't see them, can't have them on their minds!*"[20] Janna understands his thoughts because previously they would have been hers.

Over the course of the text, the younger protagonist questions the priorities of a society that abandons workers when they are no longer economically productive. In tandem with her immersion in a female community, she relinquishes her belief that her career can only be successful if she abandons the prospect of a personal life (a perspective that is traditionally regarded as masculine). This change of heart, coupled with the realization that older individuals are not rewarded by society for working hard, encourages her to spend less time in the office and pursue her passion for writing: Her first successful novel is a knowingly romanticized version of Maudie's time as a milliner. It is very much to the point that her new choice of career, as well as moving her away from masculine work patterns, has no "sell-by" date attached; the character could hypothetically be writing when she is Maudie's age. In reality, not all women would be economically secure enough to pursue this romantic dream of "becoming," which is further limited by talent and demand. However, Lessing appears interested in representing a less patriarchal way of earning a living and demonstrating how the young, if they overcome their anophobia, can learn from the old.

Lessing's portrayal of the senescent as still able to contribute to society is part of her refusal to Other the old. For the same reason, she exposes the distancing mechanisms that society uses in its dealings with older women, tracing Janna's discovery of the processes by which "we" become "they."[21] When she first visits Maudie's home, she unconsciously wrinkles her nose at the dirt on the teacup and the general squalor of the place. After a couple of weeks of occasionally visiting, the grubbiness of the flat and unwanted feelings of responsibility cause Janna to write, "I went to bed that night saying I had made a contribution to Mrs. Fowler's welfare and that was more than she can possibly expect. And that it was enough. I simply would not go near her again."[22] Lessing represents this as an empty threat caused by tiredness, as the narrator cannot return to her former blindness and ignore the old. Nonetheless, throughout the novel Lessing inserts scenes that show the younger protagonist having to face her fears and prejudices about aging. There is no sudden or magical change in Janna's attitude from the previous statement to the point where it becomes routine to clean the flat and anticipate Maudie's emotional and more pragmatic needs, such as attending to her bathing and chamber pot.[23]

Lessing marks the disintegration of Janna's preconceived notions about the old by including passages in which the narrator imagines a day from Maudie's standpoint. The technique of shifting perspectives is found more frequently in Lessing's science fiction work, as Moira Monteith notes in the essay "Doris Lessing and the Politics of Violence."[24] The purpose of the strategy, though, is similar in both types of writing:

to emphasize the disparate experiences of various characters. In *The Diary of a Good Neighbour*, the extracts serve simultaneously to depict the growth of Janna's empathy and to shift the focus of the narrative onto Maudie, thus allowing the character a voice. These sections also ensure that the novel's interest in the senescent, and their standing in society, is not overpowered by its treatment of middle age.

Lessing represents the difficulties faced by the physically weak Maudie when, for example, she has to go to the store because she runs out of toilet paper and cat food, and when she allows the flat to become cold because of worries about high electricity bills. Moira Monteith notes that the author's "ability to report what she perceives" provides her work with a sense of authenticity, to the extent that it "has often been used as a documentary source."[25] In *The Diary of a Good Neighbour*, this gift of recognizing telling detail is illustrated in Lessing's sympathetic presentation of the everyday scheduling needed to cope with an "unruly" body. She is unafraid to represent even its more taboo aspects, discussing, for example, how Maudie's bowel movements dictate much of her daily routine: "A general planning campaign could not use more cleverness than Maudie does, as she outwits her weakness and her terrible tiredness. She is already at the back door: the toilet is five steps away; if she goes now it will save a journey later."[26] The explanation of how the older protagonist times and limits her intake of food and drink around her visits to the toilet, fearful of wetting herself, is full of pathos. Lessing gradually builds up a picture of the effects that even mild incontinence can have on someone of limited mobility who lives alone. Another passage that works to this end describes the thoughts of the older character as she wakes:

> She hears the cat moving about and knows she is alive. And warm ... and in bed.... Oh, oh, she says aloud, I must go to the toilet or I'll wet the bed again. Panic! Have I wet the bed already? ... She mutters, Dreadful, dreadful, dreadful.[27]

Maudie's distress is the result of her awareness of the discourses that establish the boundaries of the normal body. Individuals sense when they have crossed these lines and aspects of their physicality have become "unacceptable." Scott and Morgan, in *Body Matters* (1993), succinctly explain the way in which the body, self and society are connected: "Bodily discipline is intrinsic to the competent social agent ... active control is integral for the very nature of agency."[28] Conventional definitions of independence are very much tied to being in charge of one's body, and Maudie's cries of "dreadful" signal to the reader her anguish at the loss of this control. The repetition of the phrase shows how her physical difficulties are literally becoming too much for her to articulate, or "unspeakable."

That the demands of the body are represented as central to her life is not unusual when positioned in the wider context of feminist theory, which often points to the connections between the female body and social control. However, Lessing is explicit in elaborating on the ways that the claims of the body are experienced differently by older and younger women. Before her relationship with Maudie, Janna is represented as devoting whole evenings to grooming: painting her nails, soaking in the bath, and tidying her clothes for the coming week. These rituals are represented as essential to her sense of identity and through them she manufactures an image with which she is happy to greet the world. Eventually the energy she expends in her relationship with Maudie means that she cannot spend so long on what she comes to realize was maintenance: "I maintained and polished my beautiful perfect clothes, maintained and polished me, and now I don't, I can't. It is too much for me."[29] The younger protagonist's idea of physical care is in clear contrast to Maudie's struggles to deal with basic bodily functions.

The contrast between two sorts of embodiment questions the position of the body in postmodern ideology and is discussed by Mike Featherstone in both "The Body in Consumer Culture," published in 1982, and "Ageing and Inequality: Consumer Culture and the New Middle Age" (published in the same year, and co-authored with Mike Hepworth). He argues that in a society where the appearance of youth is held at a premium, the "inner" body is primarily viewed as something to be maintained in order to keep the "outer" body looking as young as possible.[30] Lessing, through forcing the reader to note the differences between Maudie's and Janna's physicality, could be understood as commenting on the fallacy that the individual can fully control their body through exercise, diet, cosmetics and even surgery, as do Featherstone and Hepworth in the following statement:

> The current survivalist concern with health and longevity is caught on a fundamental contradiction. The body inevitably deteriorates over time and even those who try to stay young at heart are constantly reminded of their decline and inevitable death by wrinkles, sagging flesh and unpleasant odours.[31]

More importantly, Lessing's novel emphasizes that it is not particularly wrinkles that challenge the malleability of the body, but the effort required to deal with cancer and other diseases of the inner body, such as strokes, arthritis, and dementia. The maintenance of the body as a perfect "machine" is only viable to a certain point, as the older characters discussed in this chapter demonstrate.

Nonetheless, society relies on visual clues to signal those who should be avoided, and the eschewal of those who remind others of the frailty of the body is not just a phenomenon that occurs between different generations. Bridget Hutter and Gillian Williams, in *Controlling Women: The Normal and the Deviant* (1981), contend that "she who is stigmatised in one regard nicely exhibits all the normal prejudices held towards those who are stigmatised in another regard."[32] Lessing shows that although "normal" women are culturally framed as premenopausal and older women learn that with senescence comes the label of "deviant," this does not necessarily prevent them from ostracizing one another. For example, Maudie explains to Janna that she does not go to the day center for the old because, when she once attended, her peers made her feel that she was not "good enough" for them.[33] With this comment, Lessing again brings issues of class to the forefront of the text. In addition, Maudie is described as looking unkempt and frail, and her ostracism at the hands of other older women reflects their fear of this fate, suggesting that the dependent old are the bogeymen of the independent old. Lessing makes this point more explicit in her representation of the relationship between two other older women whom Janna befriends, Eliza and Annie. When the narrator asks Eliza why there is antipathy between the pair, she responds that Annie "let herself go ... let the dirt accumulate."[34] Although this comment is partly born of snobbery, it also reflects her anxiety about becoming like Annie, particularly in the light of her later comments about needing to keep busy in order to keep ennui at bay.

An earlier passage in the novel prompts this reading, showing Janna pondering the ease with which disorder can quickly become the norm. She thinks about how one day Maudie probably felt too unwell to tidy the front room, "then she left it and left it; going in sometimes, thinking, well, it's not so bad. Meanwhile she was keeping the back room and kitchen spotless."[35] Janna imagines a further bout of illness striking and the cleaning becoming less thorough, eventually leading to a situation whereby it would take too much effort to return the rooms to a pristine state.

Being unable to keep a house clean causes such anxiety to the older characters in *The Diary of a Good Neighbour* because they fear that it will be read as a sign that they can no longer care for themselves (which Lessing suggests is often true). Maudie, for example, refuses doctor's visits in case the state of her house gives away the extent of her frailty. It is only Janna's support and encouragement that persuades her to receive some of the help to which she is entitled, such as Meals-on-Wheels, although the older character never loses her apprehension about those in authority. As Lessing generally portrays them as lacking either the time or inclination to get to know individuals, Maudie is vindicated in feeling that they would only see her as a problem waiting to be solved. Chris Phillipson, in "Women in Later Life: Patterns of Control and Subordination" (1981), examines the ways in which such feelings need to be negotiated by those working with the old. She calls for an increased awareness of gender-specific characteristics and their consequences, such as the increased worth that a home might have to the self-image of older women. As a result of a lifelong ideology that links women with the domestic sphere, "the shock and grief connected with having to give up one's home and possessions is often insufficiently stressed by those concerned with the care of the elderly."[36]

Lessing is not the only author to dramatize this situation: Margaret Laurence, in *The Stone Angel*, starkly represents the sense of anguish that Hagar feels when she learns of her son's plans to put her in a home. She "thunders" at him: "If you make me go there you're only signing my death warrant, I hope that's clear to you. I'd not last a month, not a week, I tell you _." [*sic*][37] She is represented as feeling, like Maudie, that as long as she remains in her own home, she retains the vestiges of adulthood. Her need to try and exert some control over circumstance is so strong that she runs away when she learns she is to go to the nursing home a week later. (Marvin finds her after two nights and takes her to the hospital where she dies after a few weeks.)

Laurence does not oversimplify the situation. While the older protagonist is given a voice to passionately speak of her attachment to her home and all it symbolizes, the author still manages to represent Marvin as a sympathetic character. He clearly wants to do what is best for both his mother and wife, Doris (who is in her sixties and finding it difficult to cope with the increasing levels of care required by Hagar). The older character's death provides an "answer" to a problem that is ultimately unresolvable in terms of finding a solution that would have been acceptable to all those involved.

Staying with this dilemma, Margaret Forster's *Have the Men Had Enough?* (1989) represents a similar scenario when some of the increasingly demented Mrs. McKay's family feel that she is becoming too much to handle without professional help. Her seventeen-year-old granddaughter, Hannah, and daughter-in-law, Jenny, share the narration of the novel. Forster uses this technique to allow the situation to be framed in different ways: Hannah, who carries less responsibility, reports the older protagonist's quirks and reminiscences; while Jenny, who provides a great deal of the care, discusses the trauma of trying to decide what is best for the family as a whole. One of the subjects that constantly perplexes the younger narrator concerns the quality of her grandmother's life. She reports a conversation in which Jenny had said, "...so long as the damage caused to other people's lives does not get too high a price to pay, then grandma's own life [outside of an institution] should not be brought to a close." Hannah undermines the seemingly reasonable nature of this statement by asking, who "judges what the damage is? Who sets the price?"[38]

The younger narrator then creates a list of the pleasures in Mrs. McKay's life, featuring such pluses as "love" and "fresh air." She compares this against one she compiles covering the "damage" caused to her mother, which includes "fifteen hours a week in time normally (but things are rarely normal)" and the "responsibility of shopping."[39] These inventories underscore that objective assessment is virtually impossible; how can the affection received by Mrs. McKay be measured against the worry the situation causes Jenny? But this is the sort of decision that caretakers must make, and Forster, even though not as political a writer as Lessing, represents how the process is complicated by the lack of outside assistance, which posits the care of the dependent old as a purely private, family matter.

Jenny Morris, in *Pride Against Prejudice*, considers a further common assumption that comes into play when such choices are being made. She argues that older people, particularly if disabled or dependent, are conceived of as possessing lives that are not worth living. Morris, who herself is paralyzed from the waist down, describes the attitude as driven by the assumption that "a body which behaves in a different way, means an incomplete body and this means that our very selves are similarly incomplete."[40] This equivalence affects situations as diverse as media coverage of disability, commiserations to the disabled such as "Oh, how awful, there's no cure for that, is there?" to the decision-making processes of Forster's fictional family.[41] Morris's reaction to such perspectives is understandably strong: "As a society we cannot, and should not, make judgements about the quality of other people's lives... Any assessment of whether someone else's life is worth living can only be based on what their lives mean to us, not on what it means to them."[42] This is the reverse of what is usually assumed, but Forster's text, particularly Hannah's segments, show that Morris has actually captured the essence of the verdict.

Morris's pronouncement is also reflected toward the end of *The Diary of a Good Neighbour*, when Janna attends Maudie's funeral. As the day progresses, Janna becomes increasingly furious with her friend's family and their shows of grief. She realizes that the mourners had "simply written Maudie off years ago," and that labeling her "impossible" had allowed them to wash their hands of her.[43] However, the obverse of Morris's statement is also apparent in the text, insofar as the older character meant immeasurable amounts to Janna, who did all she could for her until the very end. In this context, Lessing's sympathetic representation of an intimate inter-generational relationship between two strong women becomes even more unusual insofar as, despite Maudie's problems, at no point does she insinuate that her life was not worth living or fighting to improve.

## Mistreatment and Resistance in As We Are Now

May Sarton's *As We Are Now* takes a different approach to representing dependency: depicting a worst-case scenario in terms of the mistreatment of the aged; and consequently it is as angry a text as Beauvoir's *Old Age*. The harrowing novel is about the narrator, Caro Spencer's, stay and eventual suicide in the residential home "Twin Elms," which is run by the domineering Harriet Hatfield, aided by her daughter Rose. The isolated farmhouse houses fourteen older residents who, apart from Caro, are all male. They are discouraged from mixing and offered no facilities with which to entertain themselves (such as access to books, a television or radio).[44] The Hatfields treat Caro's infrequent visitors with suspicion and even regard the journal she keeps, which the reader is supposedly reading, with distrust. The narrator explains that she had briefly lived with her brother and sister-in-law before her arrival in what she describes, after only two weeks, as a "concentration camp for the old, a place where people dump their parents or relatives exactly as though it were an ash can."[45] The familial arrangement was a consequence of an earlier heart attack that had left Caro too weak to live alone and had become untenable due to the animosity with which she was treated by her sister-in-law.

Sarton depicts Caro as disliking Twin Elms from the start but determined to use her time constructively: "I intend to make myself whole here in this Hell. It is the thing that is set before me to do. So, in a way, this path inward and back into the past is like a map, the map of my world."[46] Caro, in Beauvoir's terms, creates a project of sorts upon which to work but is denied the support she needs to fulfill the task. Instead, the novel charts the protagonist's psychological fragmentation, caused by the interdictions that prevent her from producing a narrative of her life and by her increasing rage at the mean-spiritedness of her caretakers. The tragedy of the text can be expressed in terms of the waste and loss involved in the disintegration of Caro's individuality.

Sarton is careful to detail the cumulative effect that a variety of acts of spite and neglect has upon the character's sense of worth. One damaging rule that leads directly to the dramatic denouement of the novel is that Caro cannot secure her door. On the surface, the lack of a lock might seem a relatively small problem, but as Foucault argues in *Discipline and Punishment*, even the possibility that one may be under surveillance is enough to keep an individual "in line." Caro is aware of the Hatfields' panoptical tactics but is powerless to take steps to improve the situation, and toward the end of the text, discovers Harriet in her room, reading her journal. The furious narrator attacks her, rescuing her diary in the process, and bolts herself in the bathroom from which she emerges at night to successfully burn down the home and kill all its inhabitants (including herself and the Hatfields).

In an interview with Karen Saum, first published in *The Paris Review* (1983), Sarton said that *As We Are Now* is one of the novels with which she has the most affinity.[47] When asked why, she answered:

> I think I did succeed in making the reader identify with Caro, the old woman who is stuffed into a ghastly rural nursing home and who is trying to stay alive emotionally. I look at *As We Are Now* as a descent into hell in which there are different steps down. The first is the person being captured, so to speak, and put in jail.[48]

The author clearly wrote the novel to protest the incarceration of the old, and she manipulates the reader's potentially empathic relationship with a first person narrator to place the older subjectivity at the center of the narrative. The link that Sarton creates between the protagonist and reader successfully destroys any boundaries that might exist between old/young and dependent/independent, creating a more emotive connection than would a factual protest. Further, many of the "events" that happen in this novel are internal, concerning Caro's psychological struggles, and have more impact for the reader if they are allowed to trace them and the effect they have on the story she tells.

Laurence uses a first-person narrator in *The Stone Angel* for similar reasons. Although Hagar does actively run from her home, her flight would not seem as dramatic if described by another character. Even an omniscient narrator would distance readers from the tension that they share with Hagar when, for example, she gets on the bus to escape and guiltily feels that the driver might guess her intention: "He looks at me, even after I've managed to sit down in the nearest seat. What is it? Will he make me go back? Are others staring?"[49] The extent to which prosaic acts, such as traveling on public transport, are both physically and mentally demanding for the terminally ill, ninety-year-old character is revealed in this way. Laurence also draws readers closer to Hagar by allowing them to participate in her sense of relief when she manages such tasks; feel her shame when she realizes, too late, that she has spoken her thoughts aloud; and trace the connections she makes between past and present as she daydreams about her youth.

The empathy Hagar and Caro elicit from the reader is a far cry from the emotions they evoke in their caretakers. In *As We Are Now*, Harriet and Rose dislike their charges, and the enforced segregation that exists in Twin Elms between Caro and the outside world exacerbates her sense of alienation. She makes a comment about the pragmatic effects of this Othering when she observes that "this would be a far kinder and better place altogether if anyone concerned with us took the trouble to look around, to sense things to observe, and to keep an outsider's eyes on our keepers. But initiative of this sort does not appear to exist."[50] For a short time she is allowed two visitors, a local reverend called Richard Thornhill and his daughter, but they are watched intently by the Hatfields whenever they visit. Consequently, the narrator is afraid to express her anger or voice her dissent for fear of retribution. Sarton stresses that these are not Caro's delusional imaginings; when she does seize the opportunity to talk to Thornhill about the mistreatment of the residents, he informs the inspectors and she is punished for speaking out. The Hatfields' retaliation consists of ignoring Caro and, worse, undermining her hold on reality by pretending, for instance, to have no knowledge of visitors she had heard being turned away. Caro also overhears Harriet saying to a relative of one of the other inmates, "Poor Miss Spencer … she means well, but she is quite cuckoo. We have to warn people against anything her deluded mind makes her invent against us."[51] These asides effectively prevent Caro from making any further attempts to communicate her anger and unhappiness to the outside world, and her diary becomes her sole source of expression.

The importance Caro places on her journal is consistently emphasized in *As We Are Now* and dramatizes the need that individuals have to project their own voices in situations where they are being systematically silenced. After one written outburst, she states, "How *expression* relieves the mind! I feel quite lively and myself because I have managed to write two pages of dissent about old age! Among all the deprivations here we are deprived of *expression*."[52] In a wider context, Caro's need to create an un-sanctioned narrative is evocative of that which drives female authors to represent women in the face of dominant cultural misrepresentation. Sarton's novel fictionalizes Caro working from the space that exists between Women (the sanctioned Other) and women (who exceed the official label in all respects).

Even before Caro's arrival at Twin Elms, she realizes, due to her understanding of dominant paradigms of female senescence, that she must be cautious in expressing her feelings too openly. The tearfulness that she says gripped her after leaving the hospital irritated her brother because only "children are permitted tears."[53] Moreover, even behavior that is acceptable for adults is disallowed for the senescent. For instance, she states: "My anger, because I am old, is considered a sign of madness or senility. Is this not cruel? Are we to be deprived even of righteous anger? Is even irritability to be treated as a 'symptom'?"[54] Her outbursts are negated by discourses of aging that read passionate emotions as a signal of instability and allows those who express such feelings to be ostracized without scruple.

Sarton, for most of the text, represents Caro's grief, despair, and finally, over-riding anger as an indication of her sanity. Critics, such as Barbara Frey Waxman, question whether or not Caro actually goes "mad" at the end of the novel, and Sarton has commented that destroying the nursing home "isn't quite sane."[55] But the author's ambivalence encapsulates the sense that any individual in Caro's situation would experience similar emotions and anger. If the old character is mad at the finish of the novel, it is because she has been driven so by circumstance.

Nonetheless, popular anxieties about the loss of mental coherence in senescence would probably lead to Caro's actions being interpreted as markers of physiological decay rather than responses to her environment. This approach affects judgments about the competency of older individuals even though it is based on the fallacy that dementia is a natural part of the aging process. Graham Stokes, who specializes in researching mental illness in elderly patients, explicitly places his discussion of the causes of dementia in a section of *On Being Old* (1992) tellingly entitled "Abnormal Ageing." He states that "senility is abnormal, not normal and thus the causes are pathological and not the inevitable consequence of biological ageing."[56] He explains that recent research into the area "moves away from the conceptualization as the brain as either diseased or not.... As a consequence, in old age, development may be placed on a continuum from normal ageing to dementia of the Alzheimer type."[57]

Without wanting to minimize the seriousness of dementia and its effects on older people and their caretakers, as represented, for example, by Forster in *Have the Men Had Enough?*, popular notions of aging ignore the relatively low incident rate of severe dementia. In aged adults, the proportion of cases of "severe general [mental] impairment" is estimated at between 1.3 percent and 6.2 percent.[58] The portrayal of the majority of older people as likely victims of this pathology contributes to patronizing paradigms that equate senescence with infancy and supports the homogenization of older people. Ellen Newton, in the autobiographical *This Bed My Centre*, explicitly addresses the dire results of such attitudes in the context of the six years she spent as a patient in nursing homes in Sydney due to recurring attacks of angina.

The reason for *This Bed My Centre*'s inclusion in this chapter is that it parallels Sarton's novel in terms of its format and the issues it raises. Reading the texts alongside each other proves a useful reminder of the astuteness of the authors considered in this study. Although they create fictional representations, they engage with very real discourses about senescence and provide realistic insights into the multitude of ways of being an older woman. Barbara Frey Waxman, in *To Live in the Center of the Moment: Literary Autobiographies of Aging* (1997), also comments on the relationship between fiction and autobiography. She suggests that they both can potentially provide "views of age" that "challenge the mainstream cultural assumption that entry into old age means the end of vital engagement with life."[59]

This is certainly true of both *As We Are Now* and *This Bed My Centre*. The most striking point of comparison between the narrators is their sense of isolation and horror at how things have turned out for them. Responding to a situation caused partly by assumptions about the inherent nature of dementia in old age, Newton writes dramatically:

> I wonder if the time will come when families and physicians can understand the torture of the spirit that must be lived through in places like this.... Different, but not less, than the pain of a scald, or a crushed or twisted limb. And it must happen to any man or woman when terminal illnesses sentences them to life in a so-called geriatric hospital alongside the mentally ill.[60]

These comments are the result of a series of sleepless nights caused by the loud midnight protests of a disturbed resident in an adjoining room to Newton. Not one of the four institutions in which she finds herself makes separate provisions for those with dementia, despite the fact that these residents are disruptive to those who are solely physically dependent. The management's lack of insight is symptomatic of widespread indifference toward the old and, particularly, the dependent old. The concept that abusive behaviors are perpetuated by the very organization of institutions is mentioned by several authors in a collection entitled *The Abuse of Care in Residential Institutions* (1996), edited by Roger Clough. Evelyn McEwen explains, in "What's Special About Being Old?" that negative assessments of senescence result in the acceptance of low standards of care for older people in institutions and that, consequently, neglectful practices are normalized.[61]

Even Newton, who, unlike her fictional counterpart, is visited regularly by her sister and a multitude of friends, feels that she lacks human contact on an everyday basis. The majority of other residents are withdrawn and uncommunicative (for a variety of reasons), and the caretakers, although not unkind, rarely have enough time to spend with her. There are, of course, even more vicious kinds of maltreatment such as those based on physical injury, and while this type of abuse is obviously far more serious than the purely emotional sort, it is only an extreme manifestation of the disrespect meted out to the old on a daily basis.[62]

Newton speaks of how the treatment she receives dehumanizes the inmates, and encapsulates the crux of issues of neglect and abuse when she states: "No human being wants to be regimented. Some small part of every man and woman longs to be treated as a person."[63]

On one level, Newton's text is more affecting than Sarton's because she is careful to explain that she is financially secure, stays at respectable institutions, and receives support from family and friends. The bare facts of Newton's case would not suggest that she suffered inhumane treatment. However, her subjective impression of the period undermines this conclusion. Her autobiography consists of an edited version of her diary and attests to her daily struggles to maintain a sense of identity, like Caro, in face of the stultifying and repressive regimes. What makes this interpretation even more compelling is that, as soon as Newton realizes she can discharge herself, she moves into a flat of her own.[64]

Sarton, as a writer of fiction, dramatizes events and one of the points at which she clearly does so is in her representation of the caretakers. In *This Bed My Centre*, the staff of the homes are, at worst, neglectful, whereas Sarton polarizes the characters: Harriet and Rose are represented as entirely malicious, and halfway through the text, she introduces a foil in the shape of Anna Close, who is described by Caro as a "miracle." Arriving at Twin Elms to cover for Harriet when she takes a holiday, Anna's attitude toward the residents contrasts sharply with that of her predecessor. What makes her relationship with Caro so poignant is that the younger character does very little in order to immeasurably improve the older one's quality of life. Anna thoroughly cleans Caro's room, takes time to sit and listen to her (even if only for ten minutes) and places a flower on the invalid's meal tray. These small acts of kindness are represented as having a profound effect upon the narrator: "People have remissions from cancer when for a time they feel quite well. I am being given a remission from despair and decline."[65]

In reality, this level of care would cost more to those who manage institutions because of the necessary increase in staff. Yet if residents were envisaged as possessing more humanity, their quality of life would become a higher priority. Gerontological studies also stress that caretakers need increased support and training for what is, undeniably, a stressful job. For instance, Ewers, in "Care or Custody?" makes the point that the predominance of females in the profession creates a gendered dynamic that needs to be recognized.[66] She explains that there is "a dilemma arising from the patient as an image of the nurses' future self, engendering conflicting responses of total rejection, and provision of care to the best of the nurse's ability."[67] Nurses tend to negotiate this schism by using stereotypical labels for female patients in order to create a buttress between themselves and their charges. Male patients are less likely to be rejected in this way as the difference in gender precludes too close an identification between caretaker and cared-for.

This structure is visible at work in *As We Are Now* where the male residents of Twin Elms relate to their caretakers as either maternal or sexual figures, a relationship that suits both parties. Caro notices this and writes of the Hatfields: "They are both grossly fat. When they make the beds and their enormous breasts jiggle, the old men leer and wink at each other."[68] Harriet and Rose find this acceptable and trade on their sexuality to keep the male patients peaceful. On a different occasion, Caro writes disdainfully that the "old men in the other room have given up or become totally passive.... Ice cream brings a clatter of spoons and toothless smiles."[69] Sarton intentionally conjures up images of children's parties with the Hatfields, this time, taking on the role of mother and the old men that of children.

The caretakers do not know how to respond to Caro, who is not appeased by the sight of flesh or willing to be treated as a child and rewarded with party food, and so they push her away. Sarton brings the idea of class into the relationship with Caro's refinement, widening the rift between herself and the Hatfields: "'How are you feeling this morning, dear?' Harriet may ask, but she never waits to hear my answer. With me she is subservient in a nasty way, never rude, but she has, of course, many ways to humiliate me. Thank Heavens I can wash myself and am not bedridden!"[70] Caro's lucidity, initially at least, also sets her apart from most of the other residents who are represented as deteriorating mentally. These factors combine so that any comment she makes is treated as a challenge to the Hatfields' authority.

Sarton's portrayal of a tense and repressive relationship between female characters serves to remind the reader that anophobia is not a gendered phenomenon. Female protagonists who collude with dominant norms and act as jailers to other female characters appear sporadically in feminist fiction, including Charlotte Perkins Gilman's classic short story, "The Yellow Wall-paper" (1890). While not a contemporary text, I refer to it here because Gilman and Sarton's representation of a socially powerless woman is remarkably similar. Moreover, a comparison of the texts reveals that the Victorian habit of treating women as if they were children has not vanished but transferred itself, in the late twentieth century, to society's treatment of aged women.

The nameless narrator of "The Yellow Wall-paper" is suffering from a "nervous weakness" (that recent critics interpret as postnatal depression) and is incarcerated in a nursery of a remote country house by her overprotective physician husband, John.[71] During the day she is guarded by his sister, Jenny, who is described as the "perfect and enthusiastic housekeeper," "who hopes for no better profession."[72] Jenny fulfills the socially acceptable role of the "angel in the house" and unconditionally accepts John's opinions about how they are to cure her sister-in-law. He forbids the narrator from mixing with others and discourages her from keeping her journal, which she hides from Jenny through fear of punishment.[73] The siblings regard the narrator's descent into madness as a symptom of her inherent instability rather than a reaction to their treatment. Likewise, Caro, as mentioned earlier, is aware that her anger is interpreted as an indication of senility rather than a protest against her isolation. Gilman wanted to expose how the stereotype of the neurotic female was damaging to real women. She stated in an article entitled "Why I Wrote 'The Yellow Wall-paper'" (1913) that the story "was not intended to drive people crazy, but to save people from being driven crazy."[74] Sarton has much the same goal but updates it to protest against contemporary society's mistreatment of older women.

Sarton's representation of the Hatfields also provides the reader with an alternative vision of the caring relationship to that found in *The Diary of a Good Neighbour* and, within the text itself, to Caro and Anna's friendship. Sarton stresses that there is nothing life-affirming about Caro's association with Harriet and Rose. Their motivation for "caring" is not compassion but economic, and as a way of grasping back some of the power denied to them as working-class women. Forster's *Have the Men Had Enough?* similarly depicts a variety of characters who exhibit different reasons for looking after the older, dependent protagonist. Bridget, Mrs. McKay's daughter, unconditionally loves her mother and is largely willing to forego a personal life to ensure that she is happy, whereas Jenny primarily "supervises" her mother-in-law out of a combination of duty and guilt.

Without wanting to marginalize the dependent old by concentrating on their caretakers, it is worth acknowledging the fact that Forster represents women as responsible for nurturing men, children and the senescent. *Have the Men Had Enough?* genders the "injunction to care" by, for example, showing the female characters involved in the physical aspects of tending Mrs. McKay while Charlie, her son, is content to pay the bills. Jenny spends much of the narrative defending her husband's attitude, but as her comments are supposedly written in her diary, the question arises of who it is she is really trying to convince. The fact that she is not blind to Charlie's laziness is made explicit when a care-assistant is hired in Bridget's absence, and Jenny writes about her sister-in-law:

> I think she was looking forward to Charlie having to do what she does week in and week out, just so that he would appreciate her more. If so, she is very silly. If Charlie had to do four or five nights a week with his mother, the effect would be to make him rapidly overcome

those scruples he still has—he would have Grandma in some kind of institution within a week. He would refuse to endure the kind of tyranny I know.[75]

The difference between the male and female protagonists' attitudes is made very clear in this passage. The discursive construction of female nature means that Jenny continues to play a role that she feels "tyrannized" into adopting: Charlie would refuse and, what is more, social norms would support his decision. Further, Jenny's sense of entrapment is clearly aggravated by her husband's lack of appreciation, which duplicates, on a larger scale, society's attitude toward the dependent old and their caretakers.

Returning to *As We Are Now*, the narrator's relationship with Harriet and Rose is depicted as suffering a marked decline after Anna leaves, and they find a letter to her in which Caro expresses her gratitude and love. The Hatfields seize upon this affection as a weakness that they can exploit. Bringing in the narrator's lunch, Harriet states, "'I didn't know you were a dirty old woman.'" Caro responds, "'It's not filthy to love Anna.... She's a beautiful person.' 'And she kisses you, no doubt, and she clasps your hand.' The sneers fell like stones, well aimed. Every one found its mark."[76] Harriet threatens to have her committed to a state hospital if she tries to contact Anna, and Caro is overwhelmed by grief and guilt. Sarton, in the interview with Karen Saum, says that this is the point at which the ending becomes inevitable: "When genuine love is defiled. That's when everything goes. There is nothing left. Then she is in hell."[77] Soon after these events, Caro levels Twin Elms. This is heartbreaking for the reader, not the least because at the beginning of the novel the narrator writes: "I still believe in life as a process and would not wish to end the process by unnatural means. Old-fashioned of me, I suppose. Then I suspect that suicide is a kind of murder, an act of rage. I want to keep my soul from that sort of corroding impurity."[78]

Despite these sentiments, the torching of Twin Elms has been read as an expression of "one woman's indomitable spirit which turns her nightmare into triumphant freedom."[79] This seems a viable reading only in one very narrow sense. Suicides in a fictional context are often interpreted as a type of dramatic freedom for women who have no other means of protest, yet, as this quotation demonstrates, Caro's spirit becomes distorted beyond recognition during her final months. The fact that Sarton directs her readers into seeing Caro's actions, as, in many ways, sane, does not mean that turning into a murderer should be seen as an appropriate end for a sympathetic and courageous character. Waxman makes the more useful observation that Caro's action can be read as a protest that reaches beyond individual circumstance: "In cleansing the place, she also acts as a social critic, sounding the clarion against society's cruel treatment of the dependent elderly."[80] This viewpoint is supported textually by the care Caro takes to place her journals in the fireproof fridge. Her triumph lies in her ability to retain her passion and finally direct her justifiable rage outside of herself, leaving behind a "record" of the experiences that forced her to take such extreme action against cultural indifference to the old. In Foucauldian terms, this is resistance of the savage and sudden sort. The next text under discussion, also by Sarton, reflects a different way in which an older character resists the corner into which dominant discourses would paint her.

## *"Connections" and the Lived Body in* The Reckoning

*The Reckoning* tells the story of the last months, and eventual death from lung cancer, of the widowed narrator, Laura Spelman. Sarton depicts her as approaching this period of life as an adventure and one that she possesses the necessary support to undertake on her own terms. Although Waxman does not specifically discuss the novel in *From the Hearth to the Open Road*, it fits her description of *Reifungsroman* with their "commitment to ... personal authenticity" and representing "more philosophical deaths."[81] The reader gains a sense of its philosophical and spiritual tone very early in the text when Laura is told there is little hope of a remission for her illness. Following her initial sensation of fear, she is surprised to feel exhilaration, but "she told herself, we meet every great experience in ignorance ... being born, falling in love, bearing a first child ... always there is terror first."[82] Sarton frames death as part of the continuum of life. In doing so, she makes an effort to place its "unknowableness" into some sort of context by comparing it to other initially unknowable events that readers may have experienced. Throughout the novel she discusses Laura's trials using metaphors and similes from nature, reinforcing her vision of death as a natural event. She is not trying to suggest that all experiences fit this pattern: One need only consider her representation of Caro's angry suicide to illustrate her awareness that there are multitudes of ways of facing death and unnatural ways of dying. Yet she represents Laura as "lucky" enough to be able to manage to die on her own terms and so able to deal with the process as part of a natural, universal cycle.

Although feminism is wary of arguments that rely on the natural, at a point where death becomes inevitable and medical technology can no longer intervene, it provides one way to discuss a subject that, like old age, is normally characterized by a discursive silence. Moreover, exposing a taboo to scrutiny can make it less frightening, if no less monumental. This is reflected in the uses, that Sarton informs Karen Saum, to which *The Reckoning* has been put: "It's used in the hospices and nursing homes, and often read by people who are dealing with the dying. It has been useful, there is no doubt, and that is a wonderful feeling."[83] As well as commenting on the novel, this quote reinforces the two-way connection between fiction and reality and the importance of representing a variety of female characters who can "speak" to women about whatever situation they may find themselves in.

Laura decides her final months will provide a time of "reckoning," when she can assess her life and discover the "real connections": an ambition that sustains her throughout her subsequent good and bad days.[84] Sarton, in an interview with Kay Bonnetti carried out in 1982 (and published in *Conversations with May Sarton*, 1991), states:

> What I'm saying in *The Reckoning* is that we've got to live as if we are dying all the time. That is, we've got to think about the priorities and real connections. That's the lesson of the book, and some people feel it deeply. And it's only when Laura is dying that she begins to live her real life.[85]

To Saum, Sarton explains that the seeds for the novel were sown at a time prior to her own mastectomy, when she mistakenly thought she had cancer. At that time she felt that she was being presented with the opportunity to "simply live and look at the world ... look at the sun rise and not do anything that I ought to do."[86] This sentiment is central to her representation of Laura. For example, after a draining visit from her youngest daughter, Daisy, she thinks: "Only the present moment can have any real substance—so she looked again at the azalea ... and felt that this looking, this still intense joy in a flower, was her way of praising God."[87]

The introspective side of negotiating disability and illness is an aspect of dependency that I have sidelined in order to concentrate on novels that foreground society's failure to offer support to the disabled old. *The Reckoning* places more emphasis on the esoteric aspects of senescence; nonetheless, I want briefly to focus on its more pragmatic side by contrasting it to *As We Are Now*. At moments like the one in which, for example, Laura gazes at the flower, she finds an inner calm that was denied Caro. The crux of the difference between the two fictional scenarios can be reduced to the economic. Laura's finances make it possible for her to avoid spending any length of time in a hospital and enable her to employ an experienced companion, the compassionate Mary O'Brien, to help her at home when she becomes physically weak. Further, her family supports her efforts to retain a degree of autonomy, and she remains coherent enough to express her wishes lucidly. As mentioned in the introduction to this chapter, *The Reckoning* plays its part alongside the previous two texts in suggesting that dependency is a state that can be either aided or abetted by the environment in which characters find themselves

The anger that Laura feels is therefore not directed at society's inhumanity, from which she is insulated, but at the treachery of her body. When she briefly visits the hospital for pain-relief treatment, Sarton writes: "Now it was coming, what she had feared most all along, what she had to learn to accept, total dependence. Anger at the slide of a tear down her cheek, at her weakness, made her sit up."[88] Laurence, in *The Stone Angel*, portrays Hagar as being seized by rage from a comparable source, when she learns from her daughter-in-law that she had been unknowingly wetting the bed. The older character is frustrated at both her incontinence and lack of awareness. It is a mixture of self-reproach and shame that is reflected in her questions: "How is it that all these years I fancied violation meant an attack on the flesh? How is it that I never knew about the sheets? How could I have not noticed?"[89] Even though Hagar needs her family's help, she feels violated that her intimate bodily functions are common knowledge. Laurence's genius, as mentioned earlier, is that despite using a first-person narrator, the reader feels pity for both Doris and Hagar, although the gradual erosion of the older protagonist's autonomy is, undoubtedly, the most poignant aspect of the text.

Sarton's choice of conditions for Laura allows the protagonist the space, and time, to come to terms with her anger and the new behavior of her body. Her decision to create a personal narrative of her life, in which she recognizes the importance of certain relationships, is portrayed as crucial to this process. Annis Pratt's assertion, in *Archetypal Patterns in Women's Fiction* (1982), that the older woman's journey is spiritual rather than social, helps to explain the flavor of the narrative.[90] Sarton intersperses Laura's practical worries with reflections on her relationship with her overbearing mother and best friend of early adulthood, Ella.

The connection between the "hermeneutic" and the pragmatic is discussed in Simon J. Williams's essay, "The Vicissitudes of Embodiment Across the Chronic Illness Trajectory" (1996). Williams centralizes the lived body and provides a phenomenological perspective on the strategies individuals use to cope with illness on a day-to-day basis, alongside their attempts to find an answer to the rhetorical query, "What purpose does it serve?"[91] The impulse to assess one's life is seen by Williams as part of an "imaginative endeavour" that looks for "not only possible points of connection between antecedent factors and the disease, but also narrative points of reference between the individual and society in an unfolding process."[92]

Williams is mentioned here because he provides a gloss to the efforts of Sarton's fictional character, and while not denying that pain can act as a "catalyst" for "spiritual achievement," he usefully stresses that it can alternatively act as a "negation of all meaning," dependent on the individual and their circumstances.[93] This adds to an understanding of the differing stories of Caro and Laura and provides an additional qualifier to Sarton's optimism in *The Reckoning* (if any is needed after the discussion of *As We Are Now*).

Although couched in different terms, the "imaginative endeavors" that are recognized by Williams are the equivalent of the "spiritual journeys" talked about by Annis Pratt. She comments that novels that represent this process use a constant flux between "then and now" to structure their narratives.[94] Inarguably, a constant drifting between the past and present is a feature of many fictions that place the older character at the center of the text and is a technique that produces a myriad of effects. On one level, this strategy creates suspense, with readers working to piece together fragments of a protagonist's early life: in Laura's case, about what happened in her relationship with Ella and her mother. In novels in which conventionally dramatic events are notably absent, this is a useful way of creating pace. More importantly, learning about the decisions and paths that lead a character, whether ill or not, to her situation in the "now" demands that readers regard them as individuals, reminding us, as the epigraph of Sarton's *As We Are Now* states: "As you are now, so once was I..."[95]

Laura's retrospective musings allow her to decide that her "connections" with women have been the most influential and important aspect of her life (a word used repeatedly by both Sarton and Williams), mirroring the conclusion that is drawn in *The Diary of a Good Neighbour*. Whereas Lessing makes this point subtly, Sarton foregrounds the bonds between women and how they, and their relationships, are undervalued by society. Laura expresses this opinion to her harassed daughter-in-law in terms of the myriad roles a woman is expected to successfully undertake: "If a 'woman' marries and has children, she is going to give up a large part of life, perhaps a third, to child-rearing, to homemaking, and this is simply not true for a man, so all emphasis today on 'becoming oneself' only adds to the inescapable conflict."[96] In this scene, Laura shares with the younger character the fruits her learning, hoping to help her daughter-in-law. Sarton's insistence on such kinship between women, and across time, is very persuasive, particularly as the narrative shows its existence in both the "then" and "now" of the text. However, the author manages to avoid idealizing female relationships, as, for example, Laura comes to terms with her mother and finally forgives her overbearing nature, but never feels any great warmth towards her.

## 2. The Angry and Frustrated Older Woman

Narratives that weave together the past and present can focus more exclusively on this type of idiosyncratic conclusion, as does *The Stone Angel*. Hagar's reminiscences mainly allow the reader insight into the character's continuing emotional development: Any wisdom that she gains is largely pertinent to herself (although one could implicitly learn lessons about how to live a life, as with any text). Like Laura, Hagar thinks about particular passages in her past, and her memories show her as a snobbish and highly judgmental character who believed, for a long time, that she married beneath herself. Pondering over events, she begins to accept some responsibility for the breakdown of her marriage, reliving a multitude of pivotal moments when she could have reached out to show comfort or acceptance to another character but decided against it. Laurence represents her as learning from her mistakes when she forgives a man whom she briefly meets when sleeping rough as a "runaway." He contacts Hagar's son after he had shared a bottle of wine and discussed his family with the older character. She feels betrayed and is surprised to note that the stranger wants to be "pardoned" and, even more extraordinarily, that she grants him his wish: "Impulsively, hardly knowing what I'm doing, I reach and touch his wrist. 'I didn't mean to speak crossly. I—I'm sorry about your boy.' Having spoken so, I feel lightened and eased. He looks surprised and shaken, yet somehow restored."[97]

The meeting of past and present in this poignant exchange stresses that although both *The Stone Angel* and *The Reckoning* recall the older character's past, they do not dwell there exclusively. Hagar, who describes herself as "rampant with memory," states dogmatically: "Some people will tell you the old live in the past—that's nonsense. Each day, so worthless really, has a rarity for me lately. I could put it in a vase and admire it, like the first dandelions ... and marvel that they were there at all."[98]

Laura learns the skill of "living in the moment" as she becomes increasingly ill and attempts to find ways to deal with her body. At first, it does not make itself felt, and she spends time talking with her loved ones, getting into a routine with Mary O'Brien, and following the prompting of her memory. This continues until one morning, when she "had to admit that she felt really ill for the first time:"

> Until now she had been busy living and getting ready in her mind for whatever was to come that she had not felt fear. Now she was terribly afraid, not of death as much as dying, of getting more and more ill, of pain. She could feel the beads of sweat on her forehead.... Fear, she supposed, was as much a part of all this as a fit of coughing.[99]

The pain that had been minimal to this point forces its way into the forefront of consciousness, destroying the barrier that usually keeps suffering, as Williams describes it, a distant possibility "or the plight of others."[100] Her new situation means that she must surrender to the demands of the body rather than those of the social world, as she appreciates after a visit from her sister:

> Laura realized that this visit, dear as it had been, had left her now strangely defenceless. Once her solitude was impinged upon, she lost ground. Or rather the deep current on which she had floated ... was closed off. Instead of floating she felt imprisoned in a sick body.[101]

The journey she is taking is progressively one that she must manage alone (although, paradoxically, the level of physical care she requires increases). Other characters, however well-intentioned, drain her of energy she needs to cope with her body and find the meditative state in which she can "float." The next passage proceeds from her sudden sense of imprisonment and develops in more depth the state of mind she attempts to cultivate:

> "How can I accept this?" and then she remembered—what an angel memory can be!—their father's old friend Owen Paine, who had been crippled by arthritis and in the last years lived in a wheelchair. He used to say, "Sister Pain is very near and dear to me." At the time it had seemed just a little precious ... now she began to understand. I must try to think of everything on that plane ... a mysterious friend to whom I am more intimately connected than with any human being.[102]

This metaphor of pain as a "dear" companion provides an answer to her own question about acceptance: She cannot separate from her body until the end and in the meantime must live with its demands. She takes solace from a spiritual discourse that frames all things as connected and part of a benign, preordained plan.

In the penultimate chapter, Laura's faith is represented as helping her to abandon the "human web." Her family and their problems have loosened their hold on her, and she realizes that she is nearly "ready to leave them all."[103] Yet, it is not until her friend, Ella, arrives from England, that Laura is represented as completing the jigsaw that she had made of her life. The protagonist is then described as feeling that there "is nothing now, no silent thread to hold her back. She had only to let go, let the tide gently bear her away. She felt light, light as a leaf on a strong current."[104] Sarton deliberately uses language with spiritual overtones when talking about death, and it is in such a context that Laura eventually "lets go."

The final word can go to Laurence's Hagar who experiences a very different sort of death. Despite her growing humanity, Hagar never reaches the somewhat lofty heights of Laura's spirituality or acceptance. After a period of reminiscing, Hagar thinks: "I can't change what's happened to me in my life, or make what's not occurred take place. But I can't say I like it, or accept it, or believe it's for the best. I don't and I never shall, not even if I'm damned for it."[105] This defiant quality, that has both helped and hindered her throughout her life, asserts itself at the very end. She dies in the midst of insisting to a nurse that she can hold her own cup but not before she acknowledges, "I only defeat myself by not accepting her.... But I can't help it—it's my nature."[106] Her fidelity to her own, albeit belligerent, self prevents her death from being tragic, and she dies as she lived: fighting to have her opinion counted and demanding not to be ignored. She, like Caro, would have pleased the narrator of Dylan Thomas's poem, "Do not go gentle into that good night," who states that: "Old age should burn and rave at the close of day; / Rage, rage against the dying of the light."[107]

## *Conclusion*

The novels in this chapter represent older characters who are, theoretically, at the "bottom rung" of a hierarchy of senescence. While wary of talking about female victimization, these protagonists are dependent on an ageist and sexist society, which is a worrying situation. The authors' collective message is not particularly comforting: Until society responds to dependency with improved services and environments, rather than seeing it as indicative of a life not worth living, older women's attempts to come to terms with their failing bodies will be hindered by more mundane concerns, such as being sent to a poorly managed institution. The texts I have been discussing engage with a society that frames senescence as a nightmare and yet refuses to take initiatives that would make it less traumatic for all those involved.

Until older women are given the support they deserve, it seems understandable that Lessing, Sarton and Laurence centralize female rage and frustration. Within literature, and literary theory, these emotions are generally seen as the province of the younger characters that populate novels from the nineteenth-century *Jane Eyre* to the quintessential post–World War II novel of female rage, *The Bell Jar*. Authors discussed in this chapter demonstrate that the anger and frustration in their older characters' lives partly arises from the same source, as a protest against the social construction of a role that demands that they are neither seen nor heard. They may technically be victims, but their rage destroys self-pity and prevents them from taking on that mantle.

Maudie, Caro, Laura and Hagar's wrath is also born of the frustration of living with a body they can no longer take for granted. Their subsequent dependency is represented as a bitter pill for them to swallow as the autonomy that they possessed as younger adults, shown in their memories, is slowly eroded. It is no coincidence that Newton and Sarton use the term *prison* for residential nursing homes or that Sarton's "luckier" character, Laura, feels "imprisoned" in her body. The imagery of incarceration that recurs in these novels speaks of the lack of control the protagonists feel at both a physical and social level.

However, the novels are concerned with more than outrage; they also portray a love and affection between female characters that crosses the divides of age and class. *The Diary of a Good Neighbour* paints such a convincing portrait of Janna and Maudie's friendship that the following declaration, made by the older protagonist to the younger, is entirely believable: "I have been thinking, this is the best time of my life.... I know you will always come and we can be together."[108] Despite her physical problems, and perhaps even because of them, Maudie surprisingly finds a stability and a happiness that she was denied throughout her life as a more obviously autonomous individual. The narrative never denies that her disabilities frustrate her or that Janna is disheartened by the effort it takes to care for her without social support, yet the life-enhancing nature of their relationship is unmistakable. Analogies can be drawn between Lessing's representation of this pair, Sarton's depiction of Caro and Anna Close, and Laura and Mary O'Brien, and Forster's portrayal of Mrs. McKay and Bridget.

These authors are aware, however, that not all relationships are so outstanding. Contemporary society still treats nurturing as a solely female task, and this results in the care of dependents (old and young) being constructed as a female responsibility. Forster and Laurence's respective representations of Jenny and Doris (Hagar's daughter-in-law) emphasize that this can be conceived as an onerous charge, and their relationships with the aged protagonists are characterized by moral decency rather than love.[109] Unfortunately, not even this can be said of the interactions between the Hatfields and Caro. They are represented as having absorbed dominant anophobic discourse and cannot see beyond Caro's frailty and age to treat her as an individual. Their bullying response to her is uninterrupted by the world outside Twin Elms and endured by the older protagonist until she reaches her breaking point.

Realistic literary representations that portray characters until the moment of their deaths are a rarity. Those that do not avoid the subject work toward demystifying death, and in the process, insist that old age, the most common signal of its increasing imminence, is a normal part of life. This sentiment is particularly vivid in *The Reckoning*, although Laurence's representation of the event reminds the reader that death is not always greeted with such calm acceptance. Neither writer is trying to suggest that there is a correct way of being old or dying (although some ways may be better than others). However, the texts are not devoid of morality and Sarton, for example, represents Caro's death as wrong. This judgment does not concern the fact that she committed suicide (or even becomes a murderer), but is aimed at the circumstances that drove her to such lengths. Finally, by depicting older characters that possess a fluid identity until the very end, Lessing, Sarton and Laurence reinforce the fact that feminist politics can only successfully theorize about women's lives if it includes the experiences of the older woman.

# 3

# *The Passionate and Desiring Older Woman*

## Introduction

Both the novels in the previous chapter, and this one, foreground the ways in which characters cope with the aging female body. Whereas the narratives I have already discussed focus on the ailing body, the ones I am going to consider contain characters who are actually healthy but deemed decrepit by society within a certain context: that of sexual expression. The texts engage with the effects that the cultural erasure of the older, female, sexual body has upon protagonists. Two of the novels that I consider centralize desire and sexuality in senescence: Doris Lessing's *Love, Again* (1996) and Jenny Diski's *Happily Ever After* (1991). *Wise Children* (1991), by Angela Carter, provides a more retrospective consideration of the narrator's life and carnal encounters, including one that takes place on her seventy-fifth birthday. In addition, I will be mentioning Elizabeth Cairn's "Echoes" (1993); William Wharton's *Last Lovers* (1991); and Colette's *Chéri* and *The Last of Chéri* (published respectively in 1920 and 1926). *Last Lovers*, insofar as it has a male author, strictly falls outside the boundaries of my study, as do Colette's novels because they were written in the early part of the twentieth century. Nonetheless, they provide pertinent illustrations of love affairs that involve the older woman and are too useful to ignore.

It is noteworthy that the majority of these texts were written in the last fifteen years. Generally, fiction produced since the 1960s can make use of feminism's discursive inroads into areas such as female sexuality. It comments on the status of the aged woman that it has taken thirty years of the "sexual revolution" for her desires to finally become more visible.

On the whole, though, younger adults still greet the idea of older ones embarking on intimate relationships, or even possessing sexual feelings, with a mixture of repulsion, incredulity and laughter. Society fosters this attitude by encouraging the equation of beauty with youth, and beauty as a prerequisite for sex (although this is arguably a gendered equation). However, even pausing to think about these axioms is enough to expose their falsity. At the most obvious level, it is not only beautiful and/or young people who are involved in sexual activity, and not only "ugly" and/or old people who are celibate, although dominant representations might suggest otherwise. Notwithstanding, many institutional discourses reproduce the concept of senescence as a period of asexuality, including much gerontological material. For example, Peter Oberg, in "The Absent Body—A Social Gerontological Paradox" (1996), refers to the advice of earlier gerontologists who suggested that during senescence, individuals should concentrate on "socializing instead of sexualizing interpersonal relationships."[1] This recommendation arises from a model of sexuality that makes assumptions about older adults, but also presumes that younger adults are all busy "sexualizing" their relationships.

Lessing, Carter and Diski challenge the construction of old age as a period devoid of sexual feeling and represent older passionate characters who expose the instability of the discursive boundary that divides the young and insatiable from the old and celibate.[2] They mock the idea that sexual fantasy and expression in old age is abnormal, taboo or inappropriate, while managing to avoid the pitfall of suggesting the other extreme: that older women should necessarily be sexually active. In fact, I will argue that the older sexual character reveals the fragmented and partial nature of the paradigm of compulsory heterosexuality, which is convincingly framed as a tool of social control by, among others, Foucault in the first volume of *The History of Sexuality* and Judith Butler in *Gender Trouble* (1990)—works to which I will be referring to support my readings of the novels.

Two dominant stereotypes perpetuate the received wisdom that older people do not possess acceptable desires. One is that of the "dirty old man" (and its less common equivalent, the "dirty old woman"), and the other, that of the aged individual who is beyond carnal desires. On the one hand, there is caricature, and on the other, denial: a treatment that Carole S. Vance in "Pleasure and Danger: Toward a Politics of Sexuality" (1984) sees as the fate of socially marginalized groups generally, whose sexuality is represented "in mainstream culture either rarely (literal invisibility) or inaccurately through caricature or other distortion."[3]

The figure of the "dirty old woman" helps to obscure the realities of older women's sexuality, and while not as ubiquitous as she once was, she remains a stock comedy character. For instance, the late 1990s British television comedy show *Harry Enfield and Chums* depicts two old female characters (played by actress Kathy Burke and Harry Enfield) luring men into situations where they can seduce them. The humor of the sketches revolves around the grotesqueries of the characters, with their lasciviously intoned catch-phrase of "Oh, young man," and the bizarre situations they manipulate to capture their "prey." This representation of the lecherous older woman connects to earlier images such as the eponymous heroine of Chaucer's "The Wife of Bath's Tale" (although middle-aged by contemporary standards) and figures described in the texts that arose around the European witch hunts of the seventeenth century.

By combining two historians' perspectives on this time of mass hysteria, it is possible to glimpse the prevalence of stereotypes that portrayed the older woman as possessing a monstrous sexual appetite. Marianne Hester, in *Lewd Women and Wicked Witches* (1992), stresses the largely gender-specific nature of the witch hunts and writes that the "contemporary witch stereotype included lustful behavior and leading 'a lewd and naughtie kind of life.'" She goes on to assert that it is virtually impossible to "ignore the sizeable number of women who, in the trial pamphlets, were associated with sexual deviance."[4] James Sharpe, in *Instruments of Darkness* (1996), brings a class- and age-conscious viewpoint to his analysis of events, stressing that not all women were equally likely to be accused of witchcraft: "In practice a disproportionate number of accused witches tended to be old, socially isolated ... and poor."[5] When Hester and Sharpe's conclusions are considered side by side, it seems reasonable to suggest that older women were viewed as more than capable of possessing a sexual appetite, even if it was "diabolical." Historian Lois W. Banner, in her study of the older woman/younger man relationship, *In Full Flower—Ageing Women, Power and Sexuality* (1993), suggests that it was not until the eighteenth century that this stereotype was eclipsed by a more saintly one. She believes that a broad cultural shift in the definition of the feminine as concerned with spirituality, as opposed to carnality, sanctioned the role of the caring grandmother for the older woman: marginalizing the image of the voraciously carnal witch, "most probably in an attempt to undercut its disruptive potential."[6] It would seem, from Banner's suggestion, that the sexuality of the older woman, like that of her younger single counterpart, has been for centuries a consistent source of social anxiety.[7] Asserting the polarized roles of grandmother/witch is part of a familiar motion, discussed in the introduction, whereby attempts are made to manipulate female behavior using the basic dualism of virgin/whore. The virginal stereotype of the grandmother continues to be the more influential in the popular imagination, either because she is too "grotesque" for anyone to want as a lover or too wise to be concerned with matters of the flesh. The latter mind/body dichotomy is apparent throughout much Western philosophy and discussions of sexuality.

Lessing, in *Love, Again*, the first text under discussion, challenges the reality of such a severance when her sixty-five-year-old protagonist, Sarah Durham, finds herself unexpectedly emerging from a calm she assumed appropriate to old age and falling passionately in love with two younger men. The novel is explored alongside a discussion of ways in which the body has been socially constructed as separate from, and inferior to, the mind, and how the older character throws light on the artificial nature of this disjunction. Angela Carter, in *Wise Children* (1991), takes a far more irreverent stance on the topic of the sexuality than does Lessing, as might be expected from an author who self-confessedly aims to demythologize dominant discourse. In this novel, Carter, among other things, exposes the unnaturalness of compulsory heterosexuality by showing that this supposedly universal paradigm excludes the older heterosexual body that she brings to the fore. Jenny Diski's *Happily Ever After* (1991) similarly mocks the idea that the old do not indulge in sexual activity. It highlights the fluidity of desire and the importance of considering its place in women's lives. To best explain this aspect of the narrative, I have turned to various feminist ideas about female sexuality and, in the process, considered their lack of commitment to the older woman.

Feminist theory, though, is insistent that sexuality is represented as bounded by social structures and the individual psyche (as suggested by the idea that the most influential sexual organ is the brain), but it is not forgotten that its sensations and patterns are played out on the body. The radical aspect of this interpretation becomes clear in a comparison with those produced from within sociology (one perspective from which sexuality is analyzed). Anthony Synott, in *The Body Social: Symbolism, Self and Society* (1993), is convincing in his suggestion that, until recently, sociology tended to ignore the role of the body in society. He even goes as far as to suggest that Bryan Tuner's *The Body and Society*, published in 1984, "inaugurated the sociology of the body."[8]

In specifying this date, Synott ignores work by Merleau-Ponty and Beauvoir that was produced in the first half of the twentieth century, and feminist texts such as Susie Orbach's *Fat Is a Feminist Issue* (published in 1978).[9] Nevertheless, despite the fact that his suggestion of a date when sociology engaged with embodiment is questionable, his appraisal that the field has long marginalized the physical is not. Peter Oberg, in "The Absent Body," published in 1996, makes a similar assessment of social gerontology. He explains that it designates the older body the responsibility of "geriatrics," while it concerns itself with "other aspects of ageing (psychological and social)." Oberg adds that on the rare occasions social gerontology includes the body, it is solely in the "spirit of welfarism" that deals with the "functional body."[10] The importance of functionality cannot be underestimated, but framing bodies solely in this context ignores the fact that they serve other purposes, such as generating the pleasurable sensations caused by activities as diverse as eating, bathing, and making love.

Sidelining the body also discounts the ways in which it can impinge on the psychological and the means by which society can intimately affect its management. Synott describes the relationship as one whereby the "body is not a 'given' but a social category with different meanings imposed and developed by every age, and by different sectors of the population."[11] The politicizing of the body allows for a reading of it that insists it is "both an individual creation, physically and phenomenologically, and a cultural product; it is personal, and also state property."[12] This dynamic is apparent in texts whose authors appreciate that the sexual body does not simply vanish after a certain socially dictated age, of which Lessing's *Love, Again* is one.

## *The Body and Its Repression in* Love, Again

*Love, Again* is nominally centered on the staging of a play by a small theatre company run by the central protagonist, Sarah Durham, and three colleagues. Lessing concocts a historical character on whom the production is based: the French composer and diarist Julie Vairon, who, at the end of the nineteenth century, committed suicide just before her marriage because she feared becoming a bourgeois wife. The close-knit and flamboyant atmosphere of the company creates opportunities for sexual intrigue, and the subject of the play causes Sarah to face her ideas about love and the nature of her passionate feelings. Her first infatuation is for the flirtatious Bill: a beautiful, bisexual actor in his twenties; and then for the more sincere married producer, Henry (who is in his early thirties). Lessing represents Bill as a "crush," and although Sarah is ambivalent about his personality, she still has difficulty overcoming her desire for him. When she eventually does, her companionable relationship with Henry develops into one of mutual attraction that includes an interest in one another's opinions and aspirations. Although never consummated due to Sarah's insecurity about being an older woman, this is not a platonic affair, and she finds the strength of her physical demands disconcerting.

The "love" of the title is not the peaceful emotion that dominant discourse would suggest appropriate to someone past the stage of menopause, but is overridingly linked with sexuality. Lessing places the body at the forefront of this narrative, as she does in *Diary of a Good Neighbour*, portraying Sarah's gradual realization that the appetites of the older body are not easily repressed. Her stance at the beginning of the text is typified when she receives a telephone call from one colleague about another: "Yesterday Mary had rung from the theatre to say that Patrick was in emotional disarray because he had fallen in love again, and she had responded with a sharp comment. 'Now, come on, Sarah,' Mary had rebuked her."[13] The older protagonist wonders at her intolerance of other people's passions, but thinks that the idea of "growing old gracefully" fits her outlook toward aging:

> She found herself at sixty-five telling younger friends that there was nothing to getting old, quite pleasurable really, for if this or that good took itself off, then all kinds of pleasures unsuspected by the young presented themselves.... She said this sort of thing in good faith, and while observing the emotional tumults of those even a decade younger than herself even indulged private shudders at the thought of going through all that again....[14]

Many articulate novels about aging implicitly include these sentiments, but *Love, Again* exposes that they are not applicable to all older characters. After Sarah is described as feeling that she "could not believe she would be in love again," the narrator adds that this was said with "complacency, forgetting the hard law that says you must suffer what you despise."[15] Such foreshadowing prepares the reader for the narrative destruction of Sarah's placidity, although it does not condemn her for her initial viewpoint and acceptance of material (such as imaginary memoirs) that position senescence as a time of bereft of sexual desire. Such homilies are, after all, part of a larger philosophical tradition that separates the mind and body. Therefore, it is useful to consider some of the discourses about the subject that feed Sarah's not unusual point-of-view at the start of the novel.

The body has been represented in a number of ways over the centuries, a few of which Synott lists in *The Body Social*: "as a tomb (Plato), a temple (Saint Paul), an enemy (Teresa of Avila)," and "a machine (Descartes)." These are distinct ways of thinking, but all support a dualism that posits the opposition of mind/soul and body, and the inferiority of the body within this dichotomy.[16] Plato is commonly cited as the first to write about this polarization and the belief that the coexistence of the elements was characterized by conflict.[17] Synott makes the point that this idea of the mortal body and immortal soul "was absorbed by Christianity" but failed to result in a singular perspective. Christian opinion has ranged from seeing the body as constantly trying to undermine the purity of the soul to respecting it as divinely given.[18] Yet, the hierarchical worth of the mind over the body remains intact, as it does in Descartes's philosophically central statement made in 1637, "*Cogito, ergo sum*" (I think, therefore I am). Oberg, in "The Absent Body" sees this oft-quoted declaration as part of a grand narrative whereby the "distancing of humankind from nature ... during the development of civilisation and modernisation receives its analogical counterpart in a distancing from the body."[19] Both Oberg and Synott see this attempted "distancing" as the main reason for the gerontological (and sociological) reproduction of the disembodied subject.

Sarah, too, at the beginning of *Love, Again*, not only sees physical desire as behind her, but as uncivilized, as illustrated in a conversation she has with a potential financial backer, Stephen Ellington-Smith, when they first meet. He confesses to an obsession with Julie Vairon about whom he has written a book. Sarah tries to hide her horror at this admission, and casually remarks, "Oh well, we are all mad." In response, he fires back, "I do wonder what it is you are mad about," and she replies, "Ah, but I've reached those heights of common sense. You know, the evenly lit unproblematical uplands where there are no surprises."[20] Her connection of passion with madness and common sense with the absence of desire exhibits her belief that the mind should be able to subdue the unruliness of physical longing.

Sarah's conviction about the inappropriateness of an older people, particularly women, being "madly" in love becomes even more understandable when the basic polarization of mind and body is considered alongside discourses of age and gender. Susan Bordo, in *Unbearable Weight: Feminism, Western Culture and the Body* (1993), produces a succinct, gender-conscious reading of the history of the body in Western philosophy. She argues convincingly that when it is represented most negatively, it is associated with women, who "are that negativity, whatever it may be: distraction from knowledge, seduction away from God, capitulation to sexual desire, violence or aggression, failure of will, even death."[21] These associations are internalized, explains Bordo, and account for women's discomfort with their bodies and guilt over their "femaleness" (she studies eating disorders from this perspective).[22]

Unfortunately, Bordo does not consider how discourses of the disembodied older woman complicate the conventional paradigm of woman-as-temptress. Lessing does, however, revealing the female body as making a transition from, supposedly, speaking a language of silent provocation to becoming mute. She explicitly comments upon this process when she represents Sarah's thoughts about the comparative desirability of her older and younger self: a juxtaposition elicited by her increasing obsession with the beautiful Bill and an attempt to assess the likelihood of a relationship. At this point in the text, Sarah's company has taken the play to Julie Vairon's hometown for a run of performances, and the cast has gathered for dinner on a sensual Mediterranean night. Sarah watches the younger characters, thinking to herself, "From being *this*—and she looked around at the young people—one becomes *this*, a husk without colour, above all without the lustre, the shine."[23] She cannot conceive of herself as still attractive and, regarding the flirtatious behavior of the female actors, she is reminded of her younger self, musing: "How could I be so callous? When I was young—and not so young—men were always falling in love with me and I took it for granted."[24] Society produces a myriad of representations of female seductresses but only grant her this role for a short time. Lessing sets up Sarah as highly passionate in her earlier life, adding poignancy to her lament about senescence rendering her invisible, like "a miserable old ghost at a feast."[25]

This analogy repeats one contained in a homily Sarah refers to at the start of *Love, Again*. The tract describes supposedly wise older people watching the "posturings" of the young and sharing with "each other ironies appropriate to ghosts at a feast."[26] Although in both instances the ghosts are metaphoric for the marginalization of the old, the earlier example describes an acceptance of exile, while the later one describes Sarah's social withdrawal caused by feelings of physical inadequacy. Just as illness can force the individual to face the fact of their embodiment, Lessing shows sexual desire as disrupting the body-as-taken-for-granted. The author makes a similar comparison when Sarah, in analyzing her feelings, thinks that "if the condition she was in were not tagged with the innocuous 'in love,' then her symptoms would be one of real illness."[27]

Lessing further gestures to this connection when describing Sarah's reaction to a card Bill slips under her hotel door. The message reads, "I have to tell you how much it means to me, getting to know you," and is described as causing her "agonizing physical symptoms":

> It seemed impossible that he would not come over at once, and into her bed. Such are the side products of the physical swellings, wettings and aches shorthanded in the word *burn*. Her body rioted, but her mind, as much under threat as a candle flame in a strong draught, made derisive comments.[28]

Dominant discourses make her feel foolish about her body's behavior, and as she can no longer dismiss her feelings for Bill as maternal, she judges them unreasonable and inappropriate. Nevertheless, she invites him to her room in response to the missive and he agrees. When he turns up, several younger members of the cast accompany him, and he comes as a friend rather than a lover. Sarah manages to hide her bitter disappointment from them but not herself, and presumes her carnal feelings are not reciprocated because she is no longer attractive.

Lessing does not allow the reader to make such a straightforward assumption: Bill obviously flirts with Sarah, and not long after this scene, she discovers that he already has a partner (who, on this occasion, is male). Further, Lessing represents several peripheral characters who obviously find Sarah sexually attractive, including one younger man who explains how he is specifically drawn to older women. Yet, this does not change Sarah's opinion that she is no longer desirable or sexual. Even her own fantasies no longer feature herself: "Images of her own charms could not fuel eroticism as, she only now understood, they once had, when she had been almost as much intoxicated with herself as with the male body that loved hers."[29] The "narcissism" that was a part of her "sexual landscape" has been destroyed by the relentless cultural attitude that in senescence the body becomes totally subdued by the mind/spirit.

However, despite the continuing influence of this dualism during the twentieth century, there has been a philosophical questioning of its veracity. Synott suggests that the works of Nietzsche and Sartre began the break with Platonic tradition by insisting on the self as body. Commenting on the late-twentieth-century developments of this perspective, Oberg writes that "there is an increasing tendency to become one's body; a person's true identity becomes expressed via the body."[30] This observation points to a postmodern movement whereby the body is framed as "plastic" and thus subject to refiguration. Synott describes recent paradigms as not only discussing the body as plastic (as opposed to being "given"), but also referring to it as "bionic," "communal," "engineered" and "chosen." New technologies of plastic surgery, artificial body parts, *in vitro* fertilization, artificial insemination, and organ transplants are causing a gradual shift in the way the body is characterized. These redefinitions complement postmodern theories of a consumer culture that would enable the individual to purchase the body they want. While this concept is interesting, both theoretically and as a means of allowing individuals to imagine constructing the self through the body, it should be accepted with caution, and returns us to the question: How "plastic" is the body?

One answer to this debate has already been touched upon, when I argued that the old, physically deteriorating body demarcates a point beyond which the idea of physiological fluidity becomes difficult to maintain. In *Unbearable Weight*, Bordo reaches a similar decision, although from a different starting point. She does not deny that the body reflects the fact that we are living in a postmodern, fragmented, contradictory society.[31] Yet, she believes it is problematic for feminists to embrace the suggestion that it is entirely malleable, a text to be constructed.[32] Bordo stresses that images continue to be normalizing and homogenizing and cause women to aim for a specific physique (although this changes to suit the fads of the period and culture).

Bordo briefly touches on the aging body when she considers how female public figures are changing cultural expectations of what middle-aged and old women should look like. She rightly argues that the media frames attractive older celebrities as heralding a liberating development for women in their suggestion that being fifty or sixty can still be "sexy." Yet, Bordo astutely insists that individuals such as Cher and Jane Fonda have not made the aging female body more acceptable, but instead established a new norm, "achievable only through continual plastic surgery, in which the surface of the female body ceases to age physically as the body grows chronologically older."[33]

At the beginning of *Love, Again*, Sarah is proud of her body because she, too, has been able to defer the appearance of old age: "She looked at a handsome apparently middle-aged woman with a trim body.... She did not often look in the mirror: she was not anxious about her looks. Why should she be? She was often thought twenty years younger than her real age."[34] Her self-acceptance hinges on the fact that she looks younger than she is, a precarious position, which becomes increasingly untenable as the novel progresses (as demonstrated by Sarah's aforementioned self-comparison to the younger characters). Lessing, though, like Bordo, does not mock individual women for wanting to appear younger (or have bigger breasts and smaller stomachs). Bordo sums it up when she writes that individuals "know the routes to success in this culture—they are advertised widely enough—and they are not 'dopes' to pursue them."[35] Instead, she is suspicious of a culture that suggests to women that these measures are normal ways to gain success, as, implicitly, is *Love, Again*.

Lois Banner, in *In Full Flower*, adds a useful class perspective to the discussion of women turning to plastic surgery, hormonal treatments, and costly creams in an effort to retain a youthful appearance. She reminds the reader that these treatments are expensive and asks, rhetorically, "Will even further distinctions come into being between the wealthy and poor in the matter of appearance?"[36] While treatments will become cheaper and more easily available, it verges on the ridiculous to suggest that women struggling on a pension are going to be able to afford these luxuries. Furthermore, there comes a point where these measures no longer work and the consumer still looks older than twenty-five (or whatever the desired age is), and the basic paradigm that senescence is synonymous with ugliness is left intact. Surgical procedures do not even make the individual who undergoes them anatomically younger, which would seem a less shallow, or somehow more logical, goal.

Yet, such a judgment underestimates the role that appearance plays in everyday life and its connection to society's treatment of the senescent. Banner writes that "distinctive appearance is the most common characteristic of ageing. Despite individual differences in ageing, all ageing people eventually develop white hair, a wrinkled skin, increased fatty deposits, ageing spots."[37] These characteristics relate to what sociologists term "social identity." Oberg in "The Absent Body" explains that this form of identity is based on "social information ... conveyed by bodily expressions and manifestations" that are read by people when they come into contact with one another. This differs from "personal identity" insofar as this concerns individuals' "own picture of themselves based on biography and selective choice of aspects of their lives."[38] Frequently these two versions of identity do not entirely overlap, and in the case of the old, they are often polarized: the older individual's psyche disassociating itself from a body that causes a negative cultural reaction.

The denial of the body feeds the Featherstone and Hepworth's "mask of ageing." Oberg puts a particularly disturbing spin on this bodily disassociation of older people, paralleling it to that of torture victims whose captors aim to specifically attack social identity.[39] Both groups "estrange" themselves from their bodies, but while torture victims' behavior is rightly regarded a reaction to an extreme situation, "the mask of ageing" is normalized by society. This means that dominant definitions of senescence remain intact and investigations into why millions of people are alienated by them are not forthcoming. Moreover, in everyday life, older women have to find the courage to either avoid attempting to pass as younger or choosing to accept their changing physical appearance with the subsequent social penalties that this incurs. Bordo frames the latter action (in the context of critiquing postmodern ideas of the body) in the following way: "To resist *this* normalising directive [to be youthful and slender] is *truly* to go against the grain of our culture, not merely in textual 'play' but at great personal risk."[40]

Those who manage to integrate their outer appearance with their ideas about themselves will have a better chance at defining the aging body as normal (rather than pathological). Yet, the contemporary cultural climate makes this a difficult and fraught task and one that Lessing represents Sarah as unable to manage. When the protagonist's attention turns from Bill to Henry, she thinks that he symbolizes "the kind of love that, had she been in her thirties and not—well, better not think about that—would have led (to coin a phrase) to an ongoing committed relationship."[41] She tries to repress her feelings because the idea that someone of sixty-five could embark on such a relationship with a younger man seems perverse. Lessing, once again, links this attitude to her poor self-image in a scene that parallels Sarah's earlier contemplation of her reflection:

> The person who is doing the looking feels herself to be exactly the same (when away from the glass) as she was at twenty, thirty, forty.... She has to insist that *this* is so, *this* is the truth: not what I remember—*this* is what I am seeing, this is what I am. This. This.[42]

By this point in the text, she has totally lost her complacency about being able to pass for a younger woman. She believes her older body, and the unflattering connotations that accrue to it, fail to reflect what she perceives as her "ageless" feelings (although they appear to the reader to revolve around her attempts to come to terms with a particular stage of life).[43] In forcing herself to contemplate her image, Sarah attempts to subdue the passions that she believes she no longer has the physique to indulge: "She might allow herself to dream of Henry's embraces, but at once her mind put her situation into words, and it was the stuff of farce and merited only a raucous laugh."[44]

Continuing with the analysis of Lessing's representation of her protagonist's struggles with her appearance, it is worth considering further the part played by the face in society's perception of desirability.[45] Synott writes that it "symbolises the self, and signifies many different facets of the self. More than any other part of the body, we identify the face as *me* or *you*."[46] He suggests that it is the prime indicator of beauty, and that physical "attractiveness touches practically every corner of human existence."[47] Using Gordon Patzer's "definitive" research on the subject, contained in *The Physical Attractiveness Phenomena* (1985), Synott illustrates how being perceived as beautiful affects social evaluations of the individual, listing some of its advantages including higher salaries and marks in school and more lenient prison sentences. He calls the phenomena of attractive individuals being attributed with positive personality traits the "halo effect" (and, conversely, those who are unattractive suffer from the "horns effect"). Synott suggests that this bias has permeated Western culture since Plato's time, when beauty was equated with goodness and ugliness with evil, believing that this paradigm has been widely accepted except by feminist theory. Synott mentions Beauvoir's *The Second Sex* as the first study to explore how narrow ideas of attractiveness affect women. Although this area of feminist inquiry has proliferated ever since, this is not true when considered in the context of the older woman.

When issues surrounding the senescent are brought to bear on a discussion of aesthetics and social identity, there emerges a further explanation of society's ageist attitudes. For although what is considered beautiful varies between eras and cultures, there is no evidence that older women have ever been widely regarded as attractive. Most probably this is linked to the fact that women are prized for fertility, which is signified by a youthful appearance. Some extraordinary older individuals escape condemnation, and personal opinion complicates aesthetic boundaries, but aged women have never personified the ideal of beauty. Subsequently, the "horns effect" comes into play and is discernible in representations of the older woman; from the wicked witch of fairytales to the mother-in-law complained about to advice columnists and satirized in comic stand-up routines. The common theme between these stereotypes is that old is ugly and therefore evil.

Even at a less extreme level, discourses of attractiveness help account for the disbelief with which older women's sexuality is met. As psychoanalyst Roberta Galler writes in "The Myth of the Perfect Body," published in 1984, "lack of 'perfection' is equated with the lack of entitlement to sexual life."[48] Although this equation is relevant to all those who do not fit dominant definitions of beauty, Galler is actually referring to those with disabilities, and she specifically includes the body of the aging woman alongside that of the disabled one. Lessing shows an appreciation of the fact that, however cruel it might be, a "normal" appearance is regarded as crucial to desirability. In one of the many scenes in which Sarah muses on being old and passionately in love, she bitterly concludes that she is:

> in exactly the same situation as the innumerable people of the world who are ugly, deformed or crippled, or who have horrible skin disorders. Or who lack that mysterious thing sex appeal. Millions spend their lives behind ugly masks, longing for the simplicities of love known to attractive people. There is now no difference between me and those people barred from love, but this is the first time it has been brought home to me that all my youth I was in a privileged class sexually but never thought about it or what it must mean not to be.[49]

Sarah's use of the term *mask* and her equation of aging with deformity is telling, as is her realization that the female heterosexual body is not a lifelong attribute. She adds: "Yet no matter how unfeeling or callous one is when young, everyone, but everyone, will learn what it is to be in a desert of deprivation, and it is just as well, travelling so fast towards old age, that we don't know it."[50] The idea that younger women are oblivious to the fate of older ones and that feminist theory is culpable of duplicating this stance is an observation to which I find myself returning repeatedly. Galler writes on the subject: "Feminists have long attacked the media image of 'the Body Beautiful' as oppressive, exploitive, and objectifying. Even in our attempts to create alternatives, however, we develop standards that oppress some of us."[51]

In the final part of *Love, Again*, defeated by her internalization of the image and connotations of the "Body Beautiful," Sarah attempts to return to her initial feelings of calm. She fails to keep an illicit appointment with Henry and does not return his calls or letters. She consciously attempts to regain her equilibrium but is plagued with a barely restrained emotionalism. Lessing represents the character as "bad-tempered ... as if she only just managed to keep an even keel, but the slightest demand, or even a too-loud voice, was enough to tip her over."[52] Also, words that "had the remotest connection with love, romance, passion ... brought tears to her eyes."[53] After some months of this pattern: "Sarah's anguish had lessened to the point that she would say it had gone." However, she is constantly alert as to anything that might rekindle her desire: "She knew that the gates separating her from that place were flimsy, no more than hastily tacked up pieces of thin wood...."[54] The certainty she possessed at the beginning of her journey has disappeared, as has her belief in the inherent placidity of senescence. She restores her mental boundaries along the lines of the Cartesian dualism while realizing the artificiality of her actions.

Ruth Saxton, in "The Female Body Veiled: From Crocus to Clitoris" (1994), discusses Lessing's *The Summer Before the Dark* and its middle-aged protagonist, Kate, making peace with her body (she finishes the narrative in the same state of mind in which Sarah begins hers). Although Saxton's study was written before the publication of *Love, Again*, her assessment that an implication of Lessing's work is that "the thinking female must either avoid or outgrow her sexuality" is relevant to both texts.[55] Saxton sees this, though, as Lessing rejecting the female body, whereas I have argued that she represents characters trying to survive society's rejection of the older female body.[56] Sarah and Kate's maneuvers are sensible when considered, for example, in relation to Germaine Greer's analysis of female sexuality in *The Change* (1991). She writes that suggestions that older women have a right to a sex life might be experienced as "a series of rather mocking demands on them, namely, that there should be someone in their lives who wants to have sex with them, and they should also be wanting sex with that person."[57] Providing a useful note of caution, she asserts that it is a lucky woman who does not experience strong sexual urges in senescence.

## *Drag, Perversions and Challenges to Compulsory Heterosexuality in* Wise Children[58]

Despite the obstacles over which Sarah cannot raise herself, disabled and older women do exercise their sexuality, and I am now going to focus on literature that represents this. Desire is not easily eradicated even by oppressive social structures, as Catherine Belsey, in *Desire: Love Stories in Western Culture* (1994), suggests: "Desire in all its forms ... commonly repudiates legality; at the level of the unconscious its imperatives are absolute; and in consequence it readily overflows, in a whole range of ways, the institutions designed to contain it."[59]

The "overflowing" motion recognized by Belsey, which reveals institutions' parameters, is similar to one discussed by Judith Butler in relation to sexual acts that potentially disrupt static models of sex and gender. The task Butler recommends to feminists in *Gender Trouble* is "not to celebrate each and every new possibility *qua* possibility, but to redescribe those possibilities that *already* exist, but which exist within cultural domains designated as culturally unintelligible and impossible."[60] As I have been insisting, the sexuality of the older individual is "culturally unintelligible," and its appearance in fictional narratives can thus be regarded as part of a larger attempt to "redescribe" current categorizations of sex, gender and desire. This chapter expands upon this idea, as the implications of a scene in which Carter represents sex between the narrator of *Wise Children* and her centurion uncle cannot be fully appreciated unless connections between age and compulsory heterosexuality are taken into account. Although the novel's focus is not as concentrated on the older heterosexual body as is *Love, Again*, it does challenge both dominant models of sexuality and gender through its representation of passion in senescence.

*Wise Children*, Carter's last novel, is structured as the autobiographical story of the narrator, Dora, and her younger twin, Nora. It traces their loves and career in the theatrical world where they made their living as what the narrator describes as "hoofers." This irreverent description captures the tone of a novel that shuttles between past and present tracing the relationships, familial and otherwise, that dominated the sisters' lives as the illegitimate offspring of the Shakespearean actor, Melchior Hazard.

Lucie Armitt, in *Contemporary Women's Fiction and the Fantastic* (2000), states that "the whole novel deals in the paradox of representing the unrepresentable."[61] Armitt correctly locates this theme as common to Carter's work and suggests that death is *Wise Children*'s central "unrepresentable" subject, characterizing Dora as a "genuine latter-day Scheherazade ... effecting one more stay of execution," whose tales are populated by ghosts and characters who refuse to die, or stay dead.[62] Although this interpretation is valid, I find the simple fact that the protagonists are old and sexually aware the most significant "unrepresentable" aspect of the novel.

Carter is well known for her denial of female stereotypes, and *Wise Children* follows this pattern, refusing to marginalize or homogenize its older female characters. Besides Dora and Nora, Carter also creates Lady Atlanta Hazard, Melchior Hazard's first wife, with whom the twins share a house. Carter plays with portraying her as a Miss Havisham figure who dwells on her past, but puts a typical spin on the myth by representing her as co-existing with her grief and continuing to take an interest in the present. At Melchior's one-hundredth birthday party, the culmination of the text, she is allowed to shine, as demonstrated in the following extract when Dora notes the effect "Lady A" has upon a young man who has been co-opted into helping her from a cab: "She looked like a ... very ancient bride until, out from under her veil, she gave him a flash of her Lynde-blue eyes and he blushed, he straightened his back, he bore her off with surprise and pride."[63]

This "unveiling" of a spirited identity reminds the reader, as much as the other characters, not to underestimate the seemingly frail Lady Atlanta. Carter endows a further key figure in the novel with the same individual personality: the twins' surrogate mother, Grandma Chance. Sarah Gamble, in *Angela Carter: Writing from the Front Line* (1997), explains that the forward-thinking grandma—naturist, vegetarian and lover of crème de menthe—is "reminiscent of Carter's description of her own maternal grandmother."[64] This might account for the fondness with which the author treats the character and her eccentricities. She is framed by the text as a role model for the twins' own old age, with their propensity for nurturing and penchant for a song and dance. This quartet of older female characters demonstrate varying degrees of contempt for the boundaries that delineate appropriate behavior in senescence, echoing the dissolution of the hierarchical binary of the legitimate and illegitimate that runs throughout the novel (most obviously in the context of family relationships). This reading is reinforced toward the end of the text when Peregrine suggests to the narrator that Grandma Chance might have actually been her biological mother, the consequence of a "last fling ... pinning old Melchior down on the mattress."[65]

Carter portrays the protagonists in such a way as to question the construction of femininity more generally, revealing the links between gender and compulsory heterosexuality before demolishing discourses that insist on the naturalness of each institution. The suggestion that sexuality is socially constructed is implicit in *Love, Again* but becomes more explicit in texts in which older women do indulge in sexual acts. In order to unravel Carter's narrative perspective on the subject, it is useful first to return to Foucault's work on power and sexuality.

The introductory volume of *The History of Sexuality* considers ways in which individuals are manipulated by a proliferation of discourses on sexuality. Foucault aims to reveal that the "repressive hypothesis," the idea that sexuality is socially repressed, is not the underlying force behind dominant sexual ideologies. Instead, this hypothesis is actually part of a "process" that "spreads" sex, "over the surface of things and bodies, arouses it, draws it out and bids it speak, implants it in reality and enjoins it to tell the truth."[66] Sex is constructed as a dark secret that must be endlessly discussed because it promises to logocentrically tell us the truth about ourselves.[67]

Foucault exposes the insidious power that underlies such rhetoric by discussing how individuals are categorized according to the acts in which they indulge and how certain sexual practices are judged unacceptable. He stresses that this labeling process is random insofar as the natural division that is seen to exist between, for example, heterosexual and homosexual activity was constructed in the nineteenth century: "The sodomite had been a temporary aberration; the homosexual was now a species."[68] This new "specification of individuals" contributed to the creation of a scientific discourse on sexuality (itself part of the movement toward an increasingly panoptical society). The authority that this provided allowed for the policing of sexual activity, and so Foucault asserts that the "growth of perversions is not a moralising theme that obsessed the scrupulous minds of the Victorians. It is the real product of the encroachment of a type of power on bodies and their pleasures."[69]

In terms of the older woman, Carole Vance, in "Pleasure and Danger: Toward a Politics of Sexuality" (1984), discusses the categorization process in the late twentieth century and concurs that a sexual hierarchy still "rewards some acts and stigmatises others."[70] Those concerned with procreation are usually socially rewarded, but as Foucault points out, even these have been, at times, a focus for interrogation and suspicion. Society, though, is even less trusting of acts that are not, and never have been, even tenuously involved with procreation. Included in this category would be "perversions" such as sodomy and intercourse involving post-menopausal women, the latter of which appears to have been treated with suspicion since, at least, the time of the European witch hunts.

Within the context of age-disparate relationships, perhaps older women are regarded as occupying the time of a younger man who could be involved in procreative sex. Even in the cosmopolitan society depicted in Colette's *Chéri* (1920), where the middle-aged Léa and her younger lover's relationship is accepted for six years, all parties involved expect that it will only last for a limited period and will end when Chéri finds a young wife. The tragedy of the tale is that, despite this unwritten pact, both protagonists find their hearts are broken when Chéri does what he perceives as his duty and marries. In *The Last of Chéri* (1926), the sixty-year-old Léa is depicted as having recovered from the affair, but Chéri never does, and he muses, just before taking his own life, "We've been well punished, you and I: you, because you were born so long before me, and I, because I loved you above all other women."[71] The force of socialization is so strong that neither he, nor Léa (nor Colette), seriously consider that the now-thirty-year-old hero could possibly return to his former lover indefinitely.

If both parties in a sexual relationship are old, their non-procreative acts are still distrusted and treated to denial and vilification.[72] This is not to reassert the repressive hypothesis, but as Foucault states, "I do not claim that sex has not been prohibited or barred or masked or misapprehended since the classical age."[73] The sexuality of the older woman is prey to these discursive ruses, as has been noted, particularly the effects of "masking" and misapprehension, in discourses produced by experts as much as those emerging from popular culture. As mentioned earlier, when gerontology discusses the sexuality of older women, it is in terms of physiological statistics or the arrangement of institutions so as to prevent their inhabitants' opportunities for indulging in sexual activity. In this sense at least, the sexuality of older people can be seen as parallel to that of children: officially it does not exist; nonetheless it is anticipated and prevented by those with discursive social influence (rarely the old or young themselves).

Butler agrees with Foucault that debates about sexuality are generative and have to do with the distribution of power but reconceptualizes this relationship in terms of gender. Among other things, Butler suggests that gender is not an effect of sex (of the male/female sort) but that both are culturally mediated: There is not a prediscursive identity, or what Butler calls an "essence," which can be referred to unproblematically. Rather there is: "*a stylized repetition of acts.* The effect of gender is produced through the stylization of the body and, hence, must be understood as the mundane way in which bodily gestures, movements, and styles of various kinds constitute the illusion of an abiding gendered self."[74] Butler points out, as have other feminist theorists, that one of the ways in which gender is stabilized is through the assertion of compulsory heterosexuality with its recommendations of acts and gestures suitable for men and women. Further, she argues that there is no sexual activity that can escape this system, as homosexuality is discursively situated in binary opposition to heterosexuality, therefore supporting the latter category's supposed primacy and naturalness.

Catherine Belsey is equally skeptical about the possibility of a culturally uncontaminated sexuality. She believes that the acceptance of this fantasy results in the belief that "if we get our sexual relations wrong, if they do not work out for us, that is in one way or another the result of a failure of adjustment."[75] Further, that "the cure must be a return to nature, which cannot get it wrong, even though ... nature is what has to be taught—in sex education classes and popular handbooks."[76] Placing blame on the individual for not doing it "right" distracts from the myths of sexuality: that all older women, for instance, return to a kind of virginal state or that men play a more carnally active role than women.[77]

Returning to Butler, she provides a way of recognizing and interpreting gendered and sexual practices that can be strategically labeled subversive (within current practices and matrices of power). One instance of such an act in *Wise Children* is the Chance sisters' use of makeup, which might at first seem to support rather than question gender norms. However, one specific practice of stylization that Butler cites as disruptive of gender boundaries is drag. But as Bordo rightly notes, Butler "does not consult (or at least does not report on) a single human being's actual reaction either to seeing or to enacting drag."[78] While Nora and Dora are fictional characters, they point to the practice of older women consciously reproducing a particular face of femininity (that is supposed to be youthful and sexually alluring), making them everyday drag artists. Carter, from the start of the text, foregrounds gender as performance in her representation of the intricate methods the Chances use to manufacture a feminine appearance. Within the first few pages, Dora narrates: "We'd feel mutilated if you made us wipe off our Joan Crawford mouths and we always do our hair up in great big victory rolls when we go out.... We always make an effort. We paint an inch thick."[79] Their mouths are not their own but styled after a dead film star, pointing to the theatrical ingenuity they use to, literally and metaphorically, "put on their faces." Dora spends a great deal of time detailing the order in which they apply their makeup: foundation, rouge, eyeshadow, mascara, and lipstick. After one of these passages she comments: "It took us an age but we did it; we painted the faces that we always used to have on to the faces we have now."[80] She realizes that she is creating the illusion of the feminine, as does her sister. "'It's every woman's tragedy,' said Nora, as we contemplated our female masterpieces, 'that, after a certain age, she looks like a female impersonator.'"[81] Carter deflates the potentially tragic aspect of this comment by having Dora muse, "'Mind you, we've known some lovely female impersonators, in our time.'"[82]

Carter uses the trope of the female impersonator to challenge the naturalness of gender in an earlier novel, *The Passion of New Eve* (1977). In this text, the character Tristessa is biologically male but lives as an actress and convinces the world of his femaleness to the extent that he is billed "the most beautiful woman in the world."[83] While this a more obvious mockery of essentialist notions, Carter's explicit connection of Dora and Nora to drag artists in *Wise Children* serves the same purpose but also acknowledges that older women are excluded from dominant definitions of femininity.

The narrator of *Wise Children* clearly recognizes this fact, and previous to the Chances' grand entrance at their father's party, Dora spots their reflection and comments: "two funny old girls, paint an inch thick, clothes sixty years too young.... Parodies."[84] Yet, throughout the text there is a pervading sense that there is no stable original to which can be referred in senescence. Even when younger, the Chances' status as twins, with its concomitant idea of doubling, undermines certainty about appearance. On the evening of their seventeenth birthday, the narrator asks the more sexually confident Nora, "Give me your fella for a birthday present ... why should he notice any difference? Same eyes, same mouth, same hair."[85] They carry out the deceit successfully through the simple disguise of swapping dresses and perfume. In the theatrical world of the Chances, the lines of the real and illusion are irrevocably blurred.

Carter thus illustrates, in a fictional form, Butler's theory that there is no fixed original sex to which gender corresponds even when allegedly close to the feminine (or masculine) youthful ideal. She further destabilizes gender boundaries by representing Dora's continued interest in sex. If it is accepted that compulsory heterosexuality helps police gender divisions, as I do, it may seem paradoxical to suggest that a sexually active seventy-five-year-old can challenge this model. Yet, the role designated to the older woman, like that of the child, is to be sexually unaware, and this is as much part of the paradigm as the expectation that younger women should be involved in a heterosexual relationship. Therefore, when Dora sleeps with her substitute father at her biological father's hundredth birthday, there is an acute sense that the protagonist's actions undermine the status quo. As Sarah Gamble comments, it "is an event which consciously breaks a number of taboos," including "old people doing it" and "uncles doing it with nieces."[86] This scene demonstrates that some heterosexual acts question the accepted connotations of heterosexuality: the narrator, who is described as a "female impersonator" shamelessly asking for a "fuck" with her hundred-year-old uncle and further, getting one. Carter foregrounds the revolutionary aspect of this sex scene when she describes "one ecstatic moment" that the narrator later thought:

> would bring down the chandelier and all its candles, smash, bang, clatter, and the swagged ceiling, too; bring the house down, fuck the house down, come ("cum"?) all over the posh frocks and the monkey jackets and the poisoned cake and the lovers, mothers, sisters....[87]

Within the context of the novel, Dora sees her actions as flouting the pretensions of a family that constantly made her feel an outsider because of her profession and status as a bastard. Within a wider context, this scene mocks discourses of sexuality that insist older women are passionless, and/or asexual, as this is not just an act of revenge but the fulfillment of an oedipal desire for a man who has always treated her like a daughter.[88] Further, Dora writes afterward: "Now I remember how everything seemed possible when I was doing it, but as soon as I stopped, not, as if fucking itself were the origin of illusion."[89] Like Foucault and Butler, Carter suggests that sex may be constructed as connecting people with their inner selves, but that it is far more outward looking, contributing to all kinds of effects, including that of a gendered and ageist society.

This is a useful point at which to emphasize that Butler's ideas support the argument that sexuality is not "the *sunnum bonnum* of life" (as Lois W. Banner phrases it in *In Full Flower*).[90] If gender is performative and not tied to some core identity, then sexual activity can be framed as something that we do: a set of actions, as opposed to what we are (the stable self that sexual activity allegedly expresses). This does not mean that it is unimportant. Feminism should continue to work toward less repressive models of sexuality, as Linda Singer highlights in an essay entitled "True Confessions: Cixous and Foucault on Sexuality and Power."[91] She usefully engages with the fact that within a Foucauldian economy, even the production of potentially liberatory discourses could be seen as "contributory to the proliferation of operative hegemonies," and the product of a mistaken belief in the freedoms gained from confession.[92] However, she gestures to Foucault's lack of engagement with issues of gender and says that his work "can be read less as a contestation than as a prolongation of a patriarchal logic which constructs sexual difference and then selectively ignores it."[93] Singer uses Cixous and her call for women to "engage with the representational apparatus" as a theoretical counter for Foucault's mistrust of such a strategy.[94]

> Because sexual difference is a product of a political deployment, woman's silence must be regarded as a tactical construction, and not as some case of collective congenital aphasia. Because women's silence has been produced politically, it can also be contested, most forcefully by women's refusal of that position in writing.[95]

## *Romance and the Fulfillment of Desire in* Happily Ever After

Diski clearly aims to contest the construction of the older woman as disembodied in *Happily Ever After*. Like *Love, Again* and *Wise Children*, the narrative exposes the protagonist's sexually passionate nature, contests the notion that the heterosexual body disappears in senescence and insists on the fluidity of desire. What sets Diski's text apart is that it explores these elements in relation to a fulfilling and sustained adult relationship between the older female protagonist, Daphne, and her middle-aged love, Liam. Feminist debates about sexuality, some of which I have already referred to, provide a useful way of interpreting Daphne's actions. Additionally, *Happily Ever After* contains some interesting observations on the explicit roles of writing and fantasy in matters of desire, which leads to a further consideration of the possibilities fiction offers for the "re-presentation" of sexuality in senescence.

At the beginning of the text, Daphne decides that she is going to be happy. The reader learns over the course of the novel that she was psychologically abused by an unstable mother and led an even more traumatic adult life, experiencing bouts of depression and alcoholism, punctuated by a brief career as a successful author. Diski taps into the idea of age bringing wisdom and represents Daphne realizing, in her sixty-eighth year, that "in the ordinary way, life had a value, and in their ordinary way, people generally tried to hold on to it in themselves and others."[96] This new perspective inspires her to attempt, after a silence of forty years, a fourth novel, the subject of which will be her prospective love affair (her first in twenty or so years) with her alcoholic landlord. Despite his initial resistance, and even repulsion, they begin a relationship, and he falls in love with his tenant, leaving a difficult marriage with his young promiscuous wife, Grace.

Diski depicts the entire course of the affair and its various patterns of desire. Daphne's passion for Liam is only matched by her need to leave her childhood home, to which she had returned as a lodger. Diski is interested in the idea of people being haunted by their pasts, and her characters are literally able to hear the ghostly cries of a young Daphne, locked in a cupboard by her mother. Thus, Daphne and Liam's flight from the house to Europe in a motorhome is framed as the triumph of the individual over an unhappy past, demonstrating the redemptive nature of their relationship. Their journey takes them to a remote part of Spain, where Liam suggests they renovate a dilapidated cottage to create a home together. The ending of the novel promises the closure of contented domesticity, but Diski moves beyond the conventional ending of the romance (of which this text contains many elements) and represents Daphne leaving Liam to continue her travels: "She was at the end of Europe, and at the age of sixty-nine, later this evening, she would drive her home off the boat and on to the dry, hot land of Africa; a new continent after all her years on a small island at the edge of Europe."[97] The "happily ever after" of the title is recast by allowing the protagonist to continue developing and adventuring rather than being bound by the domestic narrative.

Catherine Belsey makes a interesting suggestion about the connection between desire and its textual representation that elucidates Diski's decision to use conventions from the romance genre and make Daphne a novelist. Belsey argues that fiction, particularly popular fiction and the "love story," is the privileged site for explorations of desire because it "is entitled to be figurative, paradoxical and elusive": an ideal medium in which to represent an emotion that can be characterized in the same way.[98] She suggests that writing itself is a form of romance and vice versa, as the "human being in love necessarily writes, inscribes desire in the hollows of enunciation, means passion in the physiology of sex."[99] Diski makes this symbiotic relationship explicit through Daphne's choice of topic for her novel, and she is described as taking "a good two hours to complete her fifty words, because she liked to spend a lot of time reliving the moments she was writing about."[100] Here Diski hints at the element of desire that revolves around absence (Liam is not present when Daphne writes) and the human need to try to define an emotion that is, in many ways, indefinable. This basic paradox obviously does not prevent authors from trying to capture the essence of passion. Belsey writes that although it has "been done before ... something seems to remain unsaid. And it is primarily this that motivates still more writing."[101]

Even so, as might be expected in an ageist culture, there are relatively few love stories that represent desire between two old protagonists, although, perhaps surprisingly, there are more that revolve around older characters involved with younger ones. The "May to September" narrative is more often thought of as being played out by an older man and younger woman than vice versa, but as Lois Banner argues in *In Full Flower*, this is not necessarily the case in reality. Banner is interested in the hidden history of relationships between older women and younger men, explaining that the starting point for her study was an awareness of the growing number of age-disparate relationships in which women were the older partners. She searches for examples of real-life couples who fit this description but have been historically marginalized because of the social invisibility that accrues to old age, particularly female old age.

Banner considers opinions on the appeal of this relationship, citing, for instance, Benjamin Franklin's belief that older women are better conversationalists, and because they no longer consider themselves beautiful, are more sexually willing. She also mentions the Freudian interpretation that suggests an Oedipal fixation "draws certain young men to act out fantasies of incest with their mothers by union with older women."[102] Yet, Banner correctly believes that this reading foregrounds the psychological at the expense of the social. For instance, male partners might find that the political and economic power wielded by certain older women adds to their attractiveness. Colette emphasizes this aspect of such a relationship in *Chéri*. The fifty-year-old female protagonist, Léa, provides for her twenty-five-year-old lover's sensual needs, but also teaches him about material things and supports him financially (duplicating a status quo that she herself had experienced with older male partners in her youth). *Chéri* also reminds the reader that many interpretations of the age-disparate relationship underestimate the active role women take in choosing to start a relationship with a younger man. Léa, with a preference for the younger body, understands what she is doing when she returns Chéri's first tentative advances.[103] Diski represents a similar confidence in Daphne. Nonetheless, in literary terms, there seem to be fewer well-known novels about this sort of relationship by female authors than male ones, represented by texts such as William Wharton's *Last Lovers* (1991), Brian Moore's *The Lonely Passion of Miss Judith Hearne* (1956) and Tennessee William's *The Roman Spring of Mrs. Stone* (1950). (Only Wharton's protagonist is old though; the other two female characters are middle-aged.)

Both male and female writers generally appear uninterested in relationships between senescent peers: Even Carter's *Wise Children*, which at first glance seems to discuss this pairing, depicts intergenerational sex between the narrator and her uncle. Fay Weldon and her novel *Rhode Island Blues* is exceptional in this sense. She handles the relationship between the same-generation protagonists, Felicity and Charlie, with her usual insight, directly addressing the discourses that represent older women as asexual in asides such as: "As for lust, it was not the prerogative of the young."[104] The relationship is both sexually and emotionally satisfying and represented as offering the eighty-two-year-old true love and a companionship she had not found until that point (despite being married three times). Weldon's departure from her more usual, skeptical portrayal of romantic relationships might have something to do with the fact that Felicity is a worldly character and goes into the partnership under no false illusions. The message that Felicity's granddaughter learns from her grandmother's example is that, "Really there was no hurry to get everything right."[105] The possible advantage of age finally allowing the individual to "get things right," in terms of intimate relationships, is mirrored in Diski's novel (and discussed later in the chapter).

Novels that choose to represent sexuality in senescence say more about the subject than is specific to one particular sort of relationship or age-group (as shown in the discussion of compulsory heterosexuality and *Wise Children*). Belsey mentions the correlation between the specific and the general in the introduction to her text: "Desire, I am convinced, can go anywhere, and I would support all efforts to legitimate sexual dissidence. But I am also interested in the common ground."[106] Taking a similar stance, I want to consider the common ground that feminists have found in discussions of female sexuality, and then use the theories to further analyze Daphne's role in *Happily Ever After*.[107]

The first point to make about feminist scholars' views on female sexuality, and its representation, is that there is little agreement. Ann Snitow, Christine Stansell and Sharon Thompson explain in the introduction to *Desire: The Politics of Sexuality* (1984), that feminist theorizing about sexuality oscillates between two perspectives: on the one hand, a "self-righteous feminine censoriousness" and on the other, a somewhat "cavalier libertarianism, which deals but minimally with vulnerability."[108] A brief consideration of the history behind these two perspectives will help explain their entrenched, and often adversarial, nature.

Beginning with nineteenth-century attitudes, the priority for feminists at this time was to try to protect women from unwanted pregnancies, which resulted in the portrayal of heterosexual sex as about female victims and male aggressors. This image of sexual exploitation resonates throughout the following century of feminist inquiry, as can be sensed in debates about rape, pornography, and sexual harassment. While earlier feminist discussions portrayed male desire as virtually uncontrollable, later critiques saw that this paradigm naturalized male sexual aggression and made it difficult to challenge. Maneuvering discussions of rape and pornography away from issues of desire and onto power relations has allowed for a more incisive exploration of the dangers that greet women who express their sexuality in a patriarchal society.

Yet these discussions, while necessary, focus debate around male sexuality and marginalize female desire (in much the same way as the Victorian "angel in the house" image designated the perpetuation of morals and sexual restraint as a specifically feminine task). This attitude makes even consensual heterosexual sex a battleground, and has led to the suggestion that all heterosexual sex is rape because of the current social powerlessness of women. However, the Foucauldian idea that an individual can be weak in relation to one institution but strong in relation to another complicates this idea. In a specific scenario, it is possible that a woman could possess more power than her partner, as happens and will be discussed in relation to *Happily Ever After*. Furthermore, desire is too mutable to be inexorably linked to one person as representative of dominance (apart from perhaps in sadomasochistic relationships, but even this is questionable).

In a climate where the focus is only on sexual danger, it becomes difficult for women to admit that they enjoy "sleeping with the enemy." Snitow, Stansell and Thompson state that this was especially true for a period in the late 1970s when lesbian sexuality came to the forefront of feminist discussion. From being marginalized, lesbianism and the "woman identified woman" were touted as the politically correct choices for feminists. The influential nature of this perspective was relatively short-lived, because it made heterosexual feminists feel guilty and alienated by the stigmatization of their sexuality. Lesbians also protested at the misrepresentation and "sanitization" of their desire insofar as it downplayed the physical aspect of their relationships.

Alongside these tensions, social changes, most obviously the availability of the female-controlled contraceptive pill, claimed to herald an age in which women could begin to experiment with their sexuality without the fear of pregnancy checking their desires. While the gains in female freedom that resulted from these drugs cannot be downplayed, retrospectively it seems as if women were given the go-ahead to express what can be characterized as a traditionally masculine sexuality. Further, while the fear of unwanted pregnancy diminished (although it is still unclear as to whether taking oral contraception brings with it an increased risk of a variety of medical problems), now women had to deal with the, admittedly lesser, hazard of being seen as frigid if they were not involved in intimate relationships. This may seem a minor consideration, but it has real effects, not the least on younger women who may sense an obligation to become involved in sexual activity before they feel ready.[109]

As this brief history demonstrates, stark divisions have arisen in feminism over issues of sexuality. Theoretical disagreements are partly the result of the fact that sex contains contradictory elements both within a single encounter and more generally. "Intercourse can be rape; it can also be profoundly pleasurable. Sexual experience with men or women can be abusive, objectifying and degrading, but it can also be ecstatic, inspiring, illuminating."[110] Contemporary feminist theory, represented in texts such as *Pleasure and Danger* and *Desire: The Politics of Sexuality*, addresses both aspects of sexual activity in an effort to produce a climate in which women feel able to express both their worries and desires. Some of the questions that Snitow, Stansell and Thompson believe could organize discussions about sexuality provide further insight into, among other areas, age-disparate relationships.

> What is the psychological relationship between sexual taboo and arousal? Does sexual excitement depend on creating and recreating taboo? Is there such a thing as a progressive taboo? In what ways is sex managed differently in relationships with a relatively equal balance of power than in relationships between people who—for any number of reasons including race, class or gender—are vastly unequal?[111]

Although age does not appear in this list of factors, it has the potential to make a relationship "unequal." *Happily Ever After* provides one fictional answer to the ways in which sex is managed in such a situation. Moreover, it also provides insights into how the taboo of the sexually active older woman feeds into Daphne and Liam's relationship.

Diski begins the novel by focusing on the conventional female body and the socially sanctioned relationship between Liam and his ex-student Grace. Liam is portrayed as having given up a comfortable home life at the sight of Grace's breasts (which he spends the first couple of chapters, one of which is actually called "Grace's Breasts," contemplating in a drunken stupor). She no longer willingly has sex with him, so he is reduced to coercion and begging for the "privilege" (as well as for intimate details about her extra-marital affairs). Liam is described as characterizing this relationship in metaphysical terms, ones that resonate with the mind/body platonic–Christian hierarchy:

> He had given up everything for sex: wife [his first one], children, home ... he thought of this place of his as a metaphysical gutter; a combination of Harry Lime's rat-infested sewers and Dante's flaming inferno; but, in fact, he hadn't got there yet. Not to the final depth and degradation of the physical world, not to the exquisite agonies of eternal spiritual punishment.[112]

Liam frames the sexual degradation he experiences with Grace as an essential part of his motion toward spiritual "redemption." Diski sets up this idea of woman as catalyst for damnation and then undermines the paradigm by introducing Daphne. Her body is not seen as a "silent provocation" to Liam (at least not until he falls in love with her), and within a literary context, she is neither the usual heroine of a romance nor an obvious femme fatale.

In fact, the first time that Liam, unwillingly, sees Daphne naked, she repulses him, and he finds her lecherous comments disturbing. Diski represents his attitude toward the aging heterosexual body as normal: playing on those dominant paradigms of beauty discussed earlier and the ideology that an older woman expressing desire is perverse. She also satirizes the romance genre's convention that the romantic couple initially experiences antipathy toward one another by representing Daphne as actually having to tie Liam to the bed, where he has passed out in an alcoholic haze, in order to overcome the force of his preconceptions. When he finally comes round and finds Daphne "exploring" his body, his protests are vehement: "'Don't do that! Stop it! Don't touch me! Leave me alone! Will you leave me alone!' ... He felt, at first, hideously vulnerable, used, at risk from whatever terrible whim might come to the black-hearted crone grazing over his unprotected, naked body."[113] Diski, inverting Grace and Liam's relationship, brings the comic, dirty-old-woman stereotype to the fore before banishing it with a description of Daphne's sensual reawakening:

> She began to get a feel of his landscape, different from her own, though the components were often similar.... She felt a precise con-

nection between her fingertips on his flesh, her brain, and the tightening in her throat, chest and lower abdomen. An old channel was reactivated, and desire ran its familiar route from out-there to in-here.[114]

As this extract demonstrates, Daphne's passion may have been latent but had certainly not disappeared with the onset of senescence.

Liam, like Daphne, slowly becomes aroused. "He suddenly found himself caught up in the pornography of bondage and reification that was being acted out on him.... Disgust did a *pas de deux* with desire, until they were twisted together as indistinguishable sensations."[115] Although Liam is a white, middle-class, middle-aged male, it is the older woman who, both literally and metaphorically, possesses authority at this point. Diski not only demonstrates the flexibility of power in sexual relationships, but she also demonstrates the way in which discourses of sadomasochism and pornography grapple with, and finally override, those that suggest older women are not sexually desirable.

William Wharton's *Last Lovers* is a useful text to read alongside Diski's because it is also concerned with how differing constructs of sexuality become confused, merge and fight for supremacy in a particular situation. Set in Paris, the narrative begins with a description of the meeting between Jack, a fifty-year-old American artist, and the seventy-one-year-old blind Parisian, Mirabelle. Their platonic friendship gradually develops into a sexual relationship, and Wharton interweaves several discourses of sexuality in its depiction. Again, the older female character takes the initiative and seduces the male protagonist. Wharton frames this in a more romantic way than does Diski: Jacques never finds Mirabelle repulsive or frightening but initially fails to think of her sexually.

Wharton manipulates the idea that blind people have a better sense of touch in the seduction scene. At first Mirabelle explains that she just wants to "see" him through her fingers: "Please Jacques, may I touch your face? May I let my fingers tell me what my eyes cannot, how your nose fits between your eyes, your mouth, your lips, how they are formed so I can have a picture in my mind."[116] This carries on night after night, with Mirabelle exploring more of Jack's body until they eventually have intercourse. As she is a virgin until this point, Wharton uses her innocence as a device to allow Jack to explain sex to her. For the most part, these explanations seem inane, functioning as gratuitous titillation in an otherwise intelligent and touching text. However, they bring into focus the discourse of the virgin, or more precisely, the recently deflowered virgin being taught about sex by a more experienced mentor. These images work against those that define the older woman as asexual. Further, this fantasy combination of the "voracious virgin" not only complicates the notion of the older woman's sexuality but also the possibility of generalizing about the management of sex in partnerships that are socially unequal. It is worth repeating Belsey's assertion that desire seems to constantly overflow the boundaries that attempt to confine it.

Returning to Daphne's seduction of Liam in *Happily Ever After*, when he becomes aroused, he strains against his ties, "wanting to explore the loose flesh around the neck, to weigh the drooping breasts in the prickling, sweaty palms of his hands, to caress the fallen buttocks and the hanging folds of her belly with his mouth."[117] As is evident from the language used to describe Daphne's body, Diski does not deny the effects of age upon it. She makes a powerful statement by refusing to romanticize the portrait and insisting that a body described in these terms can still arouse passion and be considered desirable. The narrative later plays on a child's relative innocence to make an explicit point about the institutionalized nature of beauty and its connection to sexual attractiveness. Divya, a young girl, lives with her depressed mother in the basement of Liam's house. Her unhappy childhood echoes Daphne's own, but she finds solace in talking to the older protagonist (who justly worries about her welfare). One day Divya catches a glimpse of Daphne's breasts and asks whether Liam likes them "saggy." Daphne replies:

> "I'm happy to say he does.... You see, dear, what a person likes has a lot to do with what they think they should like. And sometimes people just find themselves liking things they didn't know they liked at all...."
> "But they must feel nice with all that soft squidgy skin, and the little nibbles at the end."
> "Exactly dear."[118]

Divya's acceptance of the older body echoes Daphne's own and can be contrasted with Grace's reaction to finding Liam and Daphne naked in bed together. Grace is shocked rather than angry, not because of her partner's infidelity but because of his choice of partner: "She had not thought very much about beauty as an abstraction, so she hadn't dwelt on the slightly curious fact that old *objects* were considered beautiful, often because of the signs of time rather than in spite of them."[119] Diski foregrounds what could be considered a paradox in philosophies of beauty, but her italicization of the word *objects* (as opposed to *subjects*) demonstrates that it is not normally related to individuals.

Before Liam embarks on a relationship with Daphne, he is described as sharing Grace's narrow view of sexual attractiveness as linked solely to youth. The narrative explains that his preference stems from a dread of "the effects of time. Specifically, he dreaded decay and death."[120] Liam considers Grace's youth an "amulet" so that "when the fear grasped at him he could bury his face in Grace's breasts and hide from the old ogre, who would not see him in the magical place that defeated death."[121] This strategy obviously cannot work as it is impossible to prevent the aging process, and so it continues to haunt him. It is only after his first sexual encounter with Daphne that he is represented as facing his fears and gaining comfort from his refusal to turn away: "He would discover something within decay that defeated the vandalism of time and the obscene graffiti it scored into human flesh. Death may not yet be defeated, but the power of ineluctable time might be weakened by a close and loving scrutiny."[122] In this way, Diski challenges the conventional, sinister connotations of older women's association with death.

Elizabeth Cairns in "Echoes," published in 1993, uses a different technique than Diski in emphasizing the continued sensuality of the older body. In this short story, the two protagonists, Melinda and David, who are in their early sixties, are reunited at the funeral of an old college acquaintance forty years after their last meeting. The narrative depicts their next rendezvous, at which they become lovers again, and the emphasis of the story is on the enduring nature of their feelings for one another. Besides its depiction of a relationship between peers, what is interesting about "Echoes" is that it emphasizes the role that personality plays in creating sexual desire. So far I have downplayed this aspect of attractiveness because I assume, to a great extent, that it is obvious, but also because I did not want to focus on appearance as the key factor in carnality. Cairns's representation of the lovers does not ignore the body but demonstrates how the psychological affects perceptions of the physical:

> He had grey hair on his chest and she became suddenly aware of all the years she hadn't known him, of all the things that had happened in those years…. But when their bodies joined the forty years ago was now. They were the same people, lovers…. They had left their age, like coats, hanging on the door. Bodies were the feelings that surged and spiraled in your core, not their case.[123]

Neither character denies the effect of age upon their bodies, but they redefine the physical as something more than appearance: Their lovemaking is of the surface but also the interior. Carter makes a similar point about the workings of what might be labeled memory, desire, energy or personality and its connection to sex in *Wise Children*. Dora writes about her encounter with Peregrine:

> He was himself when he was young; and also, when we were making love, he turned into, of all people, that blue-eyed boy who'd never known my proper name…. Don't think I'd gone wandering down off Memory Lane in the midst of it all; but Peregrine wasn't only the one dear man, tonight, but a kaleidoscope of faces, gestures, caresses.[124]

Dora's thoughts serve to further stress the idea that sex is not just about the surface of two bodies, be they young or old, but involves feelings that are in many ways "ageless." (I am not suggesting that an individual possesses an ageless identity, rather that some feelings, such as the experience of sexual pleasure, may be consistent over the years).

Returning to *Happily Ever After* and its denouement, Diski makes a final interesting point about desire and the older woman. She throws into relief the static nature of narratives that end with the couple poised to enter a life of domestic bliss by choosing not to represent a conventional romantic ending. Belsey persuasively argues that the more usual "happily ever after" arises from the authorial recognition that desire is often a fleeting emotion. Other feelings may precede desire: contentment, apathy, hatred, perhaps love, but that which endures is not desire. This is because it is linked to lack: "At the level of the unconscious, its objects are no more than a succession of substitutes for an imagined originary presence." It is the search for "a completeness which is desire's final unattainable object" (an idea originally discussed by Freud).[125] It is this restlessness that means that for desire, "domesticity is not an option."[126] Belsey writes that authors of the most conventional romances recognize this fact and choose not to represent extended domestic scenarios, as she explains: "the fulfilment of desire in a happy ending is also the unhappy end of the story, since the characters now move on to the transcendent domestic plane where they live happily ever after, immobilised by their own reciprocal happiness."[127]

Diski does not use this template, but neither does she revert to that of the tragic love story whereby the desire of protagonists and readers are simultaneously "sustained" through the dissolution of the relationship and a narrative maintenance of the state of "lack."[128] In *Happily Ever After* there is no tragedy. Daphne does not want a domestic life, and while Liam does, he is content to finally have found a peaceful place in which to continue his philosophizing. The note Daphne leaves him acknowledges their mutual passion, but also her need to search for new experiences:

> I've left, dearest. I'm off on my way south.... Isn't it wonderful that the world is round? If I keep going, I'll be passing your way on my second go. So perhaps I'll see you then. If not, I love you madly, my darling, and I'm taking all our memories, and all your fingerprints from last night with me. I think I may give up washing. Have a lovely life. Yours ever, your darling Daphne.[129]

Diski represents Daphne as understanding the nature of passion and its restlessness. Her actions can be explained by considering the notion that desire is fueled by a sense of lack alongside the idea that the older woman is more whole than her younger counterpart (in terms of self-knowledge, at least). Daphne's ability to leave a relationship without trauma or desperation result from lessons she has learned throughout her life that have taught her that sexual passion is just one facet of existence. She prioritizes her desire in a different way than her younger self and so avoids the intense but damaging affairs that had previously characterized her love life. Appreciating that her relationship is valuable, she still realizes that she can only rely on herself to sustain the feeling of completeness that is the source of her newfound *joie de vivre*. In some ways this is a cliché, and the sort of goal recommended by agony aunts to lovelorn letter writers, and yet, as with stereotypes, platitudes do sometimes contain elements of truth. Unfortunately, because of the silence that surrounds the aged, the connection between a potential spiritual/psychological confidence in senescence and the importance of sexual intimacy is more of a speculation for future discussion than an informed reading. Louise Banner, though, in *In Full Flower*, notes a similar pattern in real-life age-disparate partnerships, prompting her to write: "At the end of the long journey I have taken in writing this book, I find myself more interested in personhood than in relationships."[130] She states that if an affair crumbles, the older partner often sees this as a "way station on the road to maturity.... The relationships had represented an acting out of needs for dependence and power, a way of healing old wounds before moving on to a greater independence."[131] Banner believes the feminist interest in aging is beginning to counteract the secrecy that has previously surrounded age-disparate relationships. She urges discussion about the subject, as well as about aging more generally, for reasons similar to mine: "Just as gender justice means more than material gratification, so the wisdom of ageing means more than simply extending the definition of youth into age, of allowing older people to think of themselves as young."[132] Colette represents the radical nature of those who refuse to judge themselves in terms of youth in *The Last of Chéri*. In this text, Léa is depicted as having come to terms with her age, although she had thought this an unlikely prospect when younger. Chéri, on the other hand, projects his fears of aging onto her, and although he loves her, he cannot come to terms with the fact that she is both content and old. Perhaps if he had accepted her age, the ending of the novel might have been less tragic.

*Happily Ever After* clearly represents both Daphne's literal and metaphorical shedding of her past and continuing journey as a processual subject. However, like Sarton's *As We Are Now*, the text does not does suggest that all individuals will have this opportunity. At the end of the novel, the young girl, Divya, is murdered at the hands of a deranged social worker who believes her future to be hopeless, reminding the reader that not everyone can heal the scars of their youth. Less drastic barriers to development continually arise, not least those discourses that characterize older individuals as static and resistant to change or unable to express their desire. Yet as Snitow, Stansell, and Thompson write, "Sexual pleasure, at its best, allows us to lift our eyes to the horizon to see what might be coming in our direction," and this experience is far from the sole province of the young and beautiful.[133] Again, an appreciation of this fact is not just pertinent to the old, but to women of all ages.

## *Conclusion*

Having suggested that sexual intimacy may have a different relevance for an older woman than a younger one is not to reassert the marginal nature of such feelings in senescence. It is more than necessary to support feminism's exploration of the pleasures involved in sexuality for women from all generations, including the oldest. As I have pointed out though, the seemingly taboo nature of sexual activity in senescence often prevents even the most progressive of theories from considering its existence. Lessing represents the damage that is inflicted on the protagonist of *Love, Again* who only has the polarized images of grotesque lecher or passionless grandmother with which to make sense of her feelings. Sarah muses on the fact that she has several books that position old age as a period of emotional calm:

> Once, she would never have opened a book by an old person: nothing to do with her, she would have felt. But what could be odder than the way that books which chime with one's condition or stage in life insinuate themselves into one's hand?[134]

By the end of the novel, the irony of this reflection becomes apparent. While the sentiment is sound—that literature can open up ways of considering a subject is an axiom of this study—there are few texts to which Sarah could refer that reflect her feelings of being old and sexually passionate. Lessing recognizes the gap in discussions of sexuality that correspond to the older women and participates in filling it (as do all the other authors discussed in this chapter). In Sarah's fictional world, she does not have recourse to such literature, and so feels that her only way to survive is by subduing her body to her mind.

This sort of challenge to the Cartesian dualism is not specific to texts that represent the senescent. As Belsey asserts, desire is "a state of mind which is also a state of body, or which perhaps deconstructs the opposition between the two, throwing into relief in the process the inadequacy of a Western tradition that divides human beings along an axis crossed daily by the most familiar of emotions."[135] Yet, desire's potential to undercut the mind/body hierarchy is particularly potent when possessed by older women who are assumed to have "naturally" tamed the body. Society conveniently overlooks that this is partly due to the internalization of norms that suggest the old are unattractive and not entitled to express their sexuality.

The older character who acts upon her desire, as occurs in *Wise Children* and *Happily Ever After*, is a particularly transgressive figure. The cultural unintelligibility of her actions exposes the shortcomings of the supposedly universal model of compulsory heterosexuality. In excluding the older woman, this paradigm reveals itself as invested in controlling the procreative functions of women. Maya Angelou makes this connection explicit in an essay entitled "Age and Sexuality" (1998), when she discusses an occasion when her then-seventy-four-year-old mother threatened to leave her adored husband because he was afraid to have sex with her after his stroke. She mocks those who believe that old age excludes sexuality, but ends more seriously by writing: "Parents who tell their offspring that sex is an act performed only for procreation do everyone a serious disservice."[136]

In the same way that older female characters who perform supposedly natural heterosexual acts and are damned for it reveal the true face of compulsory heterosexuality, their very attempts to appear as normal women critiques the symbiotic model of stable gender identities. Carter's depiction of the Chance twins' creation of an acceptable image of femininity dramatizes Butler's assertion that gender is only performance. Butler's use of drag artists to make this point demonstrates that feminist theory often does not extend its thinking to include the older woman and loses a valuable figure with which to question contemporary paradigms of femininity.

Carter and Diski do not make the same mistake and grasp the opportunity to centralize the anti-authoritarian tendencies of the sexually passionate older woman. Yet, their celebrations are not at the expense of real women, or characters such as Lessing's Sarah, who does not possess the *élan* of Dora and Daphne. By seizing the older heterosexual body from the experts who attempt to hide it away, and by showing it giving and receiving pleasure, they expose the fallibility of the discourses that suggest otherwise, whether based on the aesthetic, spiritual or social.

# 4

# The Contented and Developing Older Woman

## Introduction

The female characters that I will be discussing here occupy a relatively respectable literary and social position because they are not, for example, involved in romantic relationships or interested in exploring their sexuality. Instead, the protagonists indulge in more prosaic activities: preparing meals for friends; caring for pets; seeing to housework; and immersing themselves in the local community. Texts that focus on such activities insist that everyday life is filled with comparable pursuits, and although not earth-shattering, are of note because they are what individuals spend a great deal of their time doing. This is a useful perspective for those interested in representations of older women because they are popularly portrayed as leading restricted lives (which many do because of the limited social opportunities they are afforded). In the late twentieth century, at least, this "narrowness" is framed as leading to passivity and mental stagnation. Molly Keane's *Time After Time* (1983), Barbara Pym's *Some Tame Gazelle* (1950), and May Sarton's *The Education of Harriet Hatfield* (1990), counter such pejorative judgments by emphasizing that the prosaic offers its own satisfactions, concentrating on the routines and rituals that sustain characters on a daily basis.

This narrative strategy has been criticized by some: Nicholas Shakespeare, in a review of *Time After Time* and borrowing an image from the text, suggests of Keane that, "In a sense she writes in such a monotonously beautiful way that much more needs to happen. By the end I felt I had watched a swan crane its neck to leave the water; but never quite taking off."[1] A similar charge has been leveled at Pym's work. In this chapter I reinterpret the fact that relatively little happens in terms of dramatic events as allowing readers to note the processual nature of subjectivity and the ways in which subjects create their own narratives from their experiences. Unlike Lady Slane in *All Passion Spent* (1931), Vita Sackville-West's classic tale of an older woman retrospectively assessing her personal history, the protagonists who appear in this chapter are rarely introspective, and thanks to their relatively good health, are portrayed as in the prime of life.

Keane, Pym and Sarton engage with the fact that the dominant conception of senescence is as a time of decline and show their protagonists refusing to be reduced to passivity and despair and taking active steps to retain, and create, a sense of personal meaning in the face of the limited subject positions available to them.[2] This is not characterized as taking a conscious effort, but simply as a continuation of the techniques used by people of all ages, in a variety of situations, to deal with life. Led by this approach, I do not emphasize the difficulties experienced by the characters, but rather the techniques they use to integrate them into a fulfilling existence.

Margaret M. Baltes and Laura L. Carstensen offer a gerontological perspective on the ways in which older people cope with changing circumstances in "The Process of Successful Ageing" (1996). Their research into "selective optimisation with compensation" adds a helpful gloss to novels that primarily represent the day-to-day experiences of older women. Baltes and Carstensen see the older individual as choosing "high priority domains" in their lives (selection) and using alternate means to accomplish "the same outcome [as expected when younger] in a specific domain" (compensation).[3] The final process of optimization is characterized as "the enrichment and augmentation" of whatever resources are needed to continue the tasks that have been prioritized.[4] The most telling part of Baltes and Carstensen's study is when they state that "the process of optimisation will be contingent largely on stimulating and enhancing environmental conditions. Thus, society plays a central role in providing environments that facilitate optimisation." They add that, unfortunately, the environment in which older people find themselves frequently thwarts this process, as does a society that will "under-demand rather than over-demand" of an older person.[5]

Simone de Beauvoir draws a similar conclusion in *Old Age*. She despairs of the limited opportunities older people have for pursuing the projects that are central to a thriving life. However, as pointed out in an unpublished paper by Jean Grimshaw, "Aging, Embodiment and Identity" (2001), Beauvoir's definition of *projects* is tied to those found meaningful by dominant discourse and largely excludes more pedestrian activities. Baltes and Carstensen's emphasis on the individual value of domains/projects, on the other hand, allows productive readings to be made of the activities I discuss in this chapter. They write, "We cannot predict what any individual's successful ageing will look like until we know the ... goals that the individual considers important, personally meaningful and in which he or she feels competent."[6] This more personalized approach allows that, for instance, the setting up of a feminist bookshop (*The Education of Harriet Hatfield*); offering guests a good meal (*Some Tame Gazelle*); or restoring broken china (*Time After Time*), can be as individually fulfilling as the creation of a work of art.

Like Beauvoir, and Baltes and Carstensen, the historian and anthropologist Michel de Certeau, in *The Practice of Everyday Life* (first published in France in 1980), and its companion volume, *Living and Cooking* (1994), discusses how Western society under-demands of its members, but he sees this as a problem for the majority of the population. Using Foucault's ideas about the distribution of power as a starting point, he investigates the ways in which people can resist restrictive discourses and create a modern "network of anti-discipline."[7] Analyzing practices such as reading, walking, and cooking, he considers "the ways in which users—commonly assumed to be passive and guided by established rules—operate."[8] Certeau focuses on active interventions into social spaces or, as Jeremy Aherne describes it in *Michel de Certeau: Interpretation and Its Other* (1995), the "irreducible mark of human subject within social order."[9]

Certeau believes that theorists should prioritize the subject's response to his/her positioning in the grids of power, an attitude captured in the following passage:

> It is true that the grid of "discipline" is everywhere becoming clearer and more extensive, it is all the more urgent to discover how an entire society resists being reduced to it, what popular procedures, ... what "ways of operating" form the counterpart on the consumers' (or "dominee"s') side, of the mute processes that organize the establishment of the socioeconomic order.[10]

This allowance of, and focus on, tactics of resistance supports a more subversive reading of representations of the everyday than is normally conceded. As Certeau explicitly states, the "tactics of consumption" are, in fact, part of "the ingenious ways in which the weak make use of the strong."[11]

Not only can the practices used by older individuals to pursue their goals be politicized but they can also be viewed as courageous. This is not the sort of bravery referred to in the statement, "It's amazing what she can do at her age." For, as Barbara Macdonald points out in *Look Me in the Eye* (1983), this statement implies "that you admire the way she does not show her age, and it follows that you do not admire the ways in which she does, or soon will, show her age."[12] Instead, the courage discussed in this chapter comes from the strength it takes to honor one's values and ideals, which requires fortitude at any stage of life.

While this is a serious point, the texts that I read do not all use a serious tone to make it. In fact, *Time After Time* and *Some Tame Gazelle* are amusing novels and use humor to undercut the dominant construction of senescence as void of interest. This is no coincidence: Kate Fullbrook, in "Jane Austen and the Comic Negative" (1987), characterizes comic fiction generally as refusing "death" and as "the literary mode of endless struggle."[13] The characters in Keane and Pym's texts are certainly not simply waiting to die, but put their heart and soul into their various passions. The authors literally refuse to take seriously the notion that the lives of older people are bereft of meaning, and in doing so question the divisions between, and subsequent connotations of, youth and age. Regina Barreca, in the introduction to *Last Laughs: Perspectives on Women and Comedy* (1988), points out that this failure to "reproduce the expected hierarchies" is a further recurring feature of female comedy.[14]

With this as an overriding axiom of their narratives, Keane and Pym are happy to laugh at the eccentricities of their older characters. In representing quirky older protagonists, who in *Time After Time* also possess a variety of disabilities, the authors do not patronize the senescent, nor marginalize them in a doubtful act of political correctness. Mary Klages, in "What to Do with Helen Keller Jokes: A Feminist Act" (1992), speaks of a similar dynamic at work in the telling of Helen Keller jokes. Klages pertinently points out that women who repeat them refuse to buy into the admonition not to make fun of people "less fortunate": which relies on the idea that the lives of disabled people are bound with "misery and suffering."[15] The jokes also bring the disabled body, with its differences left intact, to the fore of a culture that routinely denies anything but normal physicality. Both points translate to readings of the older body, and in Keane's text, as I will discuss, the disabled and senescent body in fact merge.

My redemptive interpretations of representations of the ordinary, then, use theories about the potentially radical nature of both humor and images of the everyday. I will begin with a discussion of Kingsley Amis's black comedy, *Ending Up* (1974), as it is demonstrative of the literary and wider social discourses with which Keane, Pym and Sarton's texts engage. Amis produces a more usual portrayal of the quotidian routines of senescence, representing them as stultifying and mundane and using his humor to reaffirm the dominant conception of the old, and their pastimes, as intrinsically abnormal.

## Black Humor and Bitterness in *Ending Up*

*Ending Up* focuses on the daily life of five aged, and very different, characters who share Tupenny-hapenny Cottage. Amis depicts Adela as the downtrodden housekeeper who is constantly baited by her ex-officer brother, Bernard, whose only pleasure derives from devising malicious tricks to play upon his cohorts. Shorty, Bernard's ex-batman (and one-time lover), is characterized as a pleasant alcoholic, and Marigold, Adela's old school friend, as clinging to her youthful mannerisms while becoming increasingly forgetful. The final member of this "family" is George, Adela and Bernard's brother-in-law, an ex-professor of European history, bed-bound after a stroke five months earlier. The novel traces their strained relationships and daily routines, climaxing in a farcical ending.

Bernard and his schemings are the focus of the novel, and Amis takes delight in creating scenarios in which the protagonist plays upon his peers' concerns about aging. He torments Marigold by hiding her post and encouraging her to think she has become senile, and attempts to make Shorty believe he is incontinent by pouring a container of his own urine on the trousers of his sleeping "friend." The denouement of the novel provides a succinct summation of the overall tone of the text. First, Shorty mistakenly drinks one of Bernard's powerful laxatives and dies on the toilet. Meanwhile, Bernard, in order to make the others worry about the vandals he has invented to scare them, falls off the ladder he is using to cut the phone lines and dies. Marigold, in the middle of this event, fatally trips over a tennis ball she had left on the stairs earlier in order to catch out one of the others, and George, hearing the noise, pulls himself out of bed but loses consciousness from the effort. When Adela returns and sees the bodies, she suffers a heart attack, and the reader presumes that George eventually dies because there is no one left to help him and the phone lines have been sabotaged.

Although Amis's focus is clearly on Bernard's disgust at being old (intensified by the knowledge that he only has a few months to live), *Ending Up* does contain a less bitter view of aging. George is represented as the most content of the inhabitants at the cottage. Despite his physical disabilities and reliance on others, he continues to invest energy in his plans. On a relatively immediate basis, he successfully manages to overcome the nominal aphasia caused by his stroke. He then decides that despite being bed-bound, he can continue his academic work, provided Shorty brings him the texts he needs. This project, which in Beauvoir's terms is worthy of the label, uses the processes of "selective optimisation with compensation" lauded by Baltes and Carstensen. Amis describes the change that this activity brings about in George: When he first arrived at the cottage, he was "listless, overborne by his handicaps, concerned only with getting through the day. Now, his mind was full of schemes and prospects."[16] Although the character experiences difficulties finding an editor who will publish his research, it is the work itself, rather than the acclaim of being publicly recognized, that drives him onwards.

This aspect of *Ending Up* is not developed in relation to the other characters and is overlooked by the book's reviewers who prefer to concentrate on the more familiar paradigm of senescence that equates it with loss and despair. The black humor of the piece derives from Amis's obvious exaggeration of society's vision of aging, and yet reviewers generally did not receive it as such. They accepted it instead as a comedic but essentially realistic take on old age. Michael Ratcliffe, in *The Times* (1974), states that Amis is writing from a "cool disgust that man's life—every man and woman's life should come to this," and continues, "the novelist himself refrains from diagnosis and prescription throughout."[17] In response, it is highly questionable as to whether "every man and woman's life" degenerates into either maliciousness through boredom (Bernard, Marigold and Shorty), or exploitation through kindheartedness (Adela, George). Ratcliffe's evaluation of Amis as refraining from "diagnosis" is also debatable. Undeniably, the characters could be described, as does one critic, as "grotesques," but the suggestion that Amis somehow reflects the basic experiences of senescence (even if it is through the medium of black humor) speaks of the limited expectations of old age and, moreover, the ageism, both internalized and externalized, of the reviewers, and perhaps, readers more generally.[18] Barreca writes that the male "comedy-of-despair," of which *Ending Up* is an example, works on "a number of 'universals' or 'givens' ultimately reaffirming rather than undercutting existing cultural systems."[19] Undoubtedly, Amis uses caricature, but there is no suggestion that old age can be anything but stultifying. Supporting dominant ideas of aging, his representation of senescence is bitter, and yet he does not rage at society's treatment of the old but at death itself, which even his text shows is unavoidable.

## *Female Humor and Flourishing Characters in* Time After Time

Molly Keane's *Time After Time* challenges this familiar but one-sided representation of aging; although the events it portrays are not what would usually be considered dramatic, they are depicted as important to the characters. Fullbrook discusses a similar attitude in Jane Austen's work, an attitude which insists "that life is always extreme, that everyone lives on the razor's edge whether they want to or not," mocking "gothic extremity" in the process.[20] Keane nods to the gothic in *Time*

*After Time* by setting it in the decaying Irish mansion of Durraghglass, but she, too, focuses on the seemingly workaday tensions and passions of the Swifts who live there.

Keane's critically acclaimed "comeback" novel, *Good Behaviour*, was published after a silence of twenty years in 1981, and *Time After Time* followed two years later. Her depiction of senescence is very different to Amis's, primarily because, as critic Joy Grant comments, "unlike some younger authors, she pays scant attention to the process of ageing; to Molly Keane, ageing is clearly a mere incidental to living."[21] Grant's observation is relevant to the remainder of texts in this chapter, although it is more accurate to suggest that every stage of life creates particular challenges and problems. For example, the young adult is expected to successfully attend school, find a job, manage a house, and perhaps start a family. The female authors of the novels under discussion approach the trials of old age similarly: as hurdles to be conquered rather than insurmountable brick walls.

Amis, on the other hand, displays an attitude similar to those who portray the declining body as always overwhelming the individual. *Ending Up* relies heavily on the physical difficulties experienced by the quintet for its comedic moments (also allowing the denouement to appear vaguely feasible). Scatological humor is central to the narrative, with its descriptions of Bernard's daily struggles with hemorrhoids and his planting of stink bombs outside the toilet to "frame" the snobbish Marigold. Keane, conversely, works with the paradigm that the body can be managed, and the divergent humor of the texts is linked to this difference in authorial perspective. She avoids portraying disabilities as the sole province of the aging by depicting the Swifts as having lived with them from a young age. Jasper, the only male sibling, lost his sight in one eye as a child, and the widowed April, the oldest at seventy-four, started to lose her hearing in her twenties. May was born with only two fingers on one hand and constantly tries to prove her adroitness with the other to avoid pity: "Nothing was beyond her will to prove super-normal dexterity."[22] The youngest sister, sixty-four-year-old Baby June, has learning difficulties, and Keane writes that "being a little slow was a more subtle deformity than May's hand, April's growing deafness, or Jasper's one-eyed state."[23] Yet, to compensate for her lack of academic skill, she developed her expertise in horsemanship, husbandry, and gardening (producing much of the food consumed at Durraghglass).

Keane, like Amis, uses these characteristics to create humorous situations, for example by allowing April to hear selectively and ignore unpleasant conversations while catching asides that were not meant for her. However, *Time After Time*, unlike the majority of *Ending Up*, emphasizes the Swifts' resourcefulness and ingenuity in dealing with their problems. Keane also exaggerates not just situations caused by their disabilities, but their other characteristics. She depicts with relish their competitiveness, the affection that they lavish on their respective pets, and the baby-talk they use to communicate with them. The following extract combines these elements and characterizes their meals together. After eating, Jasper (a cat lover) pseudo-innocently asks, "Isn't it time for doggie-dins?" and April goes to the sideboard to put down the three dogs' plates:

> She picked up the smallest dish and looked searchingly at its contents. "My woofie-woof's dreadfully hungry and there doesn't seem to be any meat in his dins," she said.
> June didn't criticize [her dog] Tiny's dinner, or even look at it closely, there was too much on her mind. But May moved in to the matter at once: "Where's the beef I scraped all the blue mould off and left chopped up in their soup and brown bread?"
> Jasper gave her a nearly rat-like grin: "You've just eaten it," he said. "I put it in the pie."
> "Ah, don't mind him," June felt as usual that she must keep on Jasper's right side. "He's only joking."
> "I believe him," May said stonily.
> "And you'd be right." Jasper rose to his elegant height....[24]

The humor in this extract is not reliant on caricaturing the senescent, but rather on the peculiarities of the individuals and their relationships.

The event around which the plot is structured is the unexpected arrival of the Swifts' blind Jewish cousin, Leda (in Greek mythology her namesake was ravished by Zeus disguised as a swan), whom the siblings have not seen since childhood and believed to have died in a German concentration camp. Leda's favorite pastime is manipulating people: "She could find a use for any person or circumstance even before she knew how such a one or such an event could forward her aims."[25] Relishing the opportunity to play one sibling against the other (similar in this respect to Amis's Bernard), her presence arouses many old jealousies as the Swifts' jostle for her attention. This allows her to note their weaknesses and gradually learn their secrets: April's partiality to alcohol and marijuana; May's occasional shoplifting; June's fondness for her farmhand, Christy; and Jasper's plans to endow the neighboring monastery with land in exchange for help in the cultivation of his dream garden. Keane mocks the Swifts' snobbery, which hides such un-genteel plans and habits, and plays with the reader's expectations that older characters would not indulge in such clandestine, and "youthful," pursuits.

Leda's visit ends when, in a rage at being sexually "brushed-off" by Jasper (who reminds her of his dead father with whom she had a fleeting affair), she reveals the siblings' various secrets at the breakfast table.

In turn, her daughter arrives and informs them that her mother was never in a concentration camp and, in fact, is wanted as a Nazi collaborator. Leda's fate is to be hidden away in an exclusive nunnery with April, whom she detests:

> "Isn't this nice?" April said.... "I'll have the room with the view," she went on, "because that doesn't affect you darling." She crossed to the window. "What a nice tidy garden—perfect for pi-pi. I do think Tiger is going to be happy. Are you happy, Baby-doll? Please say you're happy, little man."
> "I'd like to kill you both," Leda wrote in a furious indecipherable scrawl and handed the message back to April.
> "You know I can't read your writing." April handed back the envelope....
> Imprisoned, Leda put her hands up to her blind eyes. There was to be no escape.[26]

The Swifts' experiences in dealing with adverse circumstances, and their self-absorption, mean that they cope with the revelations by continuing with their plans. The narrative rewards them for their perseverance, unlike Amis's text that punishes its protagonists with its comi-tragic ending.

Part of Leda's downfall is that, unlike the other characters, she has not acknowledged the changes that aging had wrought on her and so moved on. When she arrives at Durraghglass, she is described as possessing "the terrible freedom of the blind exuberantly unaware of lost beauty, confident, as always, in her ways to women's acceptance and to man's desiring."[27] This attitude is initially advantageous because it makes her bold, but in senescence, she can no longer trade on her looks as she did in her youth. Jasper, whom she desires, enjoys her ability to recall images from childhood but does not find her physically attractive (Keane depicts him as asexual). Leda's utter disbelief at Jasper's rejection leads to anger, but not to any sort of personal insight or development. Barbara Macdonald's admonishments about the dangers of attempting to "pass" as a younger person can be applied to Leda, although her attitude is largely unconscious. Nevertheless, Macdonald's warning that "passing" is fraught with complications—because to show signs of aging and then to be treated as an older person fractures a brittle sense of self— is very pertinent to a reading of Keane's manipulative character.[28]

The Swifts' pastimes are of the sort gestured to by Betty Friedan in *The Fountain of Age*, which she suggests contribute to a feeling of satisfaction in senescence.[29] Keane is certainly explicit in delineating the sense of purpose and fulfillment that the characters gain from their assorted passions. April, for example, pays strict attention to her health and grooming. Her absorption with her body is strangely reminiscent of that which Foucault notes in ancient Greek and Roman citizens (studied in the later volumes of *The History of Sexuality*). Her rituals of exercise, monitoring her diet, and planning her wardrobe consume April's thoughts: "It was her pleasure to rule her body so that she might dress it for her private eye's delight."[30] This boon is explicitly connected to her old age: April found her late husband sexually demanding, and it was only with his death that she could think of her body as her own. This is surprising when considered alongside the current paradigms that equate bodily satisfaction with sexuality and youthfulness. Keane is equally clear about Baby June's source of satisfaction with life, which comes from her love of the land. Although the character worries about her livestock, vocalizing her concerns to the others in order that they appreciate her labors, the author writes that "secretly, she was happy."[31] Her work constantly provides her with challenges and rewards that she takes equally in her stride.

May's happiness, on the other hand, is represented as more of a conscious achievement than that of her sisters. Her interest in flower arranging and antique restoration stems from her efforts to overcome her disability, and Leda's revelations are more damaging to May, with her carefully constructed sense of worth, than they are to the others. The interloper not only advertises her penchant for shoplifting but also informs the siblings that the members of the flower-arranging club, of which May is president, watch her breathlessly because they are fascinated by her crippled hand rather than by the arrangements she creates. After this revelation, Keane writes that "habit and courage can go together," as May continues with her plan to show the club a lovingly restored candlestick.[32] "Small, beautiful objects were, to May, far more important than the breakage of her own self-respect and confidence—established with so much discipline and difficulty."[33] The pride she takes in her work helps to heal her shattered self-esteem. Keane shows her dogged spirit as rewarded when a local antique dealer who catches sight of the candlestick offers the character a part-time job as a restorer.[34] May accepts and leaves the flower-arranging club with her dignity restored and the opportunity to handle a limitless supply of "beautiful objects" in the future.

As May's story shows, Keane's humorous take on the snobbish family and their eccentricities does not preclude an optimistic ending. The cartoonist Betty Swords suggests, in "Why Women Cartoonists Are Rare, and Why That's Important" (1992), that female humor is concerned with "hope and *change*."[35] This narrative perspective is apparent in *Time After Time* and becomes even more noticeable when compared to Amis's nihilistic take on senescence. Keane's hopefulness is reflected in her representation of older characters that flourish, and while the Swifts individually do not fit the conventional picture of a hero, in an ageist society, their will to continue can be interpreted as courageous.

Certeau expresses a similar respect for the ordinary person and their everyday actions in both the first volume of *The Practice of Everyday Life* and the second, subtitled *Living and Cooking* (1994) and co-produced with fellow researchers Luce Giard and Pierre Mayol. In a chapter entitled "Envoi" and written with Giard, Certeau talks with regret about their epistemology being too unsophisticated to allow for an elaboration of "the inventive proliferation of everyday practices." He adds that "there remains so much to understand about the innumerable ruses of the 'obscure heroes,' who live their lives in anonymity."[36] Certeau and his colleagues constantly express their admiration for the fortitude needed to undertake certain activities from within interlinking, and often repressive, networks of power.

## *Single Women and Contentment in* Some Tame Gazelle

Barbara Pym could be described as a specialist on the subject of "obscure heroes" and the prosaic. The fact that very little of dramatic intensity appears in her work is noted by both her admirers and detractors. In *Some Tame Gazelle*, she laughs at the idiosyncrasies of her characters, while commending their courage and tenacity. Martin Cooley comments on this technique in *The Comic Art of Barbara Pym* (1990): "Potential tragedy as well as potential farce are averted when Pym takes the reader into the enclosing medium of the characters' ingenious but somewhat off-center interpretations and surmises."[37] *Some Tame Gazelle*, like *Quartet in Autumn* (1977), focuses on day-to-day occurrences and the personal narratives that characters create to interpret their lives. Michael Cottsell, in *Barbara Pym* (1989), helpfully discusses critiques of her style by asking if the author's fictional world really is "quaintly 'irrelevant' to the world that normally offers itself as relevant?"[38] He rightly decides that Pym's works actively query the worth of what society usually deems pertinent by valorizing the small events and decisions of which life, for the most part, consists.

Pym's embrace of the irrelevant over the relevant is reflected in a typical response to one reviewer's charge that her work (in particular, *The Sweet Dove Died*) is obsessed with trivia: "What are the minds of my critics filled with? What nobler and more worthwhile things?"[39] This waspish reply hints at the anger that many critics see as driving female humor, with its anti-authoritarian and disruptive tendencies.[40] Cottsell frames Pym's reclamation of the "daily round" as an assertion of its literary interest and part of her refusal "to identify with meaninglessness."[41] He captures the tone of her writing when he states that her work suggests that:

> meaning must be sustained amongst us by good humour, a delight in the absurd, recurrent small gestures, taking an interest, loving anyway. Life delivers disappointments but if those disappointments are accepted ... small joys and satisfaction await us.[42]

*Some Tame Gazelle*, Pym's first novel, focuses on the "disappointments" and "satisfactions" of two unmarried, middle-class sisters, Harriet and Belinda Bede, and their life in a small rural village. The Bedes are interested in the parish church mainly because of the opportunities it offers for socializing and the romance it brings into their lives rather than from a fervent religious feeling. (They do have faith, but it is of an unquestioning and comforting variety). The narrative revolves around their involvement in local fêtes, concerts, and slide shows, and their organization of the domestic arrangements of their home. Harriet is described as "especially given to cherishing young clergymen," whom she frequently invites to supper, and Belinda nurses a longstanding "crush" on the married Archdeacon Hoccleve, with whom she had gone to Oxford University.[43]

Before going further, I want to acknowledge that this novel was published a good ten years before any of the other books I discuss (and therefore, strictly, falls outside the parameters of this study). As well as being one of the first novels to rouse my interest in narratives of aging, *Some Tame Gazelle* is one of the few texts I have come across to valorize the mundane and allow its protagonists to lead such obviously fulfilling lives.[44] As such, it is too valuable a text to ignore. It was published in the 1950s, at a time when dominant ideology represented women as happy to be back in the home after their excursion into the public sphere during World War II. On the surface, *Some Tame Gazelle* might not seem to counter this perspective. But as Niamh Baker insists in *Happily Ever After: Women's Fiction in Postwar Britain, 1945–60* (1989), Pym's work represents women in a way that challenges the prevailing post-war image of contented wife and mother.

I agree with Barker and feel that Belinda and Harriet's sedate avoidance of all attempts to make them give up their chosen way of life illustrates her point. They both receive offers of marriage from men with whom they are casually acquainted. Count Bianco, an Italian neighbor, regularly proposes to Harriet, and Mr. Mold, a deputy librarian and friend of the archdeacon, asks her to be his wife after only a few meetings, an offer that the female protagonist declines graciously. Yet afterward, Harriet is represented as providing her sister with "many ludicrous and exaggerated imitations" of his proposal. Belinda responds by chiding Harriet for being unkind, but the author adds that this was "in the intervals of laughing, for her sister was really much funnier than Mr. Mold could possibly have been."[45] The sisters' laughter at supposedly solemn matters punctuates the novel and deflates the seriousness with which, for instance, romantic matters are often treated in society and literature.

Pym represents Mr. Mold as being equally unperturbed by the refusal, and on the train journey home, he considers that "he had probably had a lucky escape."[46] The male characters approach the business of suggesting marriage as something that they should do—an attitude Pym refuses to reward by allowing them to capture either of the sisters, for whom she obviously has great affection. Bishop Grote, who proposes to Belinda (mistaking her for Harriet whom he knew in his youth in a comedy of errors), regards it as his duty to return to his mission in Mbawawa with a wife in tow. The second Belinda receives the proposal from the bishop, who reminds her "of a sheep more than anything,"[47] she flatly refuses, adding that she "wished Harriet would come, so that she could tell her all about it. After all, she supposed, it was something to have been considered worthy to be the wife of a bishop, even if only a colonial one."[48] Pym cannot resist the opportunity to invite the reader to laugh at the snobbery of the character, and undercut the niceties of the situation by describing Belinda as supposing that she should be flattered, rather than actually being so.

Therefore, while both sisters pay lip service to romance, neither really wants to find it at the expense of the contented lives they have built together. Ellen M. Tsagaris, in *The Subversion of Romance in the Novels of Barbara Pym* (1998), makes the point that "Pym was dismayed by a society that advocated women's systematic search for a husband."[49] She was not anti-marriage; for example, *Some Tame Gazelle*'s last scene centers, without cynicism, on the wedding of the curate and the archdeacon's niece. Nonetheless, Pym was against discourses that suggested women could not lead full lives unless romantically attached. Belinda's thoughts at the end of the novel demonstrate this perspective: "Harriet would accept the attentions of Count Bianco and listen patiently and kindly to his regular proposals of marriage. Belinda did not go any further than this in her plans for the future: she could only be grateful that their lives were so little changed."[50]

This modest thankfulness is characteristically Pymesque and part of her technique for puncturing literary pretensions. Barbara Brothers speaks about this aspect of Pym's work in "Women Victimised by Fiction: Living and Loving in the Novels of Barbara Pym," published in 1982. She writes that "Pym mocks the pretentiousness of tragedy but proclaims the dignity of the quotidian" and creates characters who would usually be considered too uninteresting for fictional treatment (a "trait" shared by the majority of protagonists mentioned in this study).[51] Brothers talks about the author's treatment of supposedly tragic events, such as refused proposals and spinsterhood, as being low-key, or at least not dramatized in the ways that might be expected. Barreca, in the introduction to *Last Laughs*, points out that, generally, the female humorist's take on subjects is often erased by readings that project "pain on her pleasure, unhappiness onto her joy."[52] So Belinda's feelings of unrequited love, for instance, might be interpreted as tragic but only if being single is viewed as such. Pym does not, and therefore she represents the protagonist as immensely gratified to feel a connection to the archdeacon without having to care for him. She enjoys the drama he unconsciously brings to her life, and secretly relishes her uncharitable thoughts about his wife, Agatha. Pym, with a characteristically impish touch, describes how Belinda's eyes, after being told that Agatha is stingy with her mealtime portions, "filled with tears and she experienced one of those sudden moments of joy that sometimes come to us in the middle of an ordinary day. Her heart was like a singing bird and all because Agatha didn't keep as good a table as she did."[53] Pym is adept at capturing such nuances of emotion and daily experience, although not all critics regard her depiction of this one-sided passion as part of her narrative commitment to the single woman and the importance of the quotidian. This is perhaps a reflection of the fact that her work seems to divide people into those who love it and those who loathe it (perhaps connected to how interested readers are in the everyday lives of older women).

Daphne Watson, in *Their Own Worst Enemies: Women Writers of Women's Fiction* (1995), would seem to fall in the latter group, and she regards Pym's representation of unrequited love as characteristic of a theme that runs throughout her novels, one that shows women being "manipulated, exploited" and "condescended to" by male characters.[54] Watson interprets the female protagonists as "tremulously self-conscious, never self-aware. This is what makes them victims, they need approval, male approval."[55] While the suggestion that male characters tend to take female ones for granted is valid, as demonstrated, for example, by the archdeacon's expectation that Agatha will manage parish affairs, it is more controversial to characterize the female characters as needing male endorsement.

Watson's interpretation of Pym's work misses the subversive potential of its humor and relies on the polarity of self-consciousness and self-awareness. In *Some Tame Gazelle*, Belinda is shown to be self-conscious, worrying that her shoes are too dowdy for the village fête and that people will gossip about her sharing a meal with the archdeacon and their mutual friend, Dr. Parcell. In the last pages of the novel, though, Pym represents her as thinking about the poem by Thomas Haynes Bayley from which the title of the novel is taken: "some tame gazelle, or some gentle dove / something to love, oh, something to love."[56] Musing over the verse, she rephrases it: "some tame gazelle or some gentle dove or even a poodle dog—something to love, that was the point."[57] Belinda is obviously under no illusion as to her feelings for the archdeacon and demonstrates self-awareness alongside an appreciation of the romantic tendencies of others. That it is the process of loving that she cherishes, rather than the object of affection, is made clear to the reader with the mention of a poodle: an oblique comparison to the archdeacon of the sort that Watson overlooks. Niamh Baker writes about Pym (as well as Molly Keane) that the "unsatisfactory nature of so many of the suitors in their fiction seems to reflect a disillusionment with the nature of men, but not necessarily with the nature of love."[58] The presence of this attitude in *Some Tame Gazelle* shifts the focus from Belinda's needing the archdeacon's approval and onto her generating self-aproval for the choices she makes.

Even more textually explicit is the condescending attitude that Pym's women display toward male characters, supporting Baker's viewpoint and challenging Watson's definition of them as self-effacing. For example, when Belinda spots the archdeacon affecting an "eighteenth-century melancholy" in the churchyard, she

> felt a faint irritation to see him sitting there in the middle of the morning when so many people, women mostly, were going about their household duties and shopping. She supposed that men would be working too, but somehow their work seemed less important and exhausting.[59]

In light of this extract, the female characters' continual comments about men not being expected to grasp household matters is indicative of the importance domestic duties are given by the novel. The female characters in *Same Tame Gazelle* may only insist on their knowledge of the domestic, but village life, as portrayed by Pym, constantly merges public and private spheres. Village fêtes and slide shows, for example, are organized using the same methods as the afternoon tea and evening meal, and the female characters take responsibility for both. Therefore, female protagonists are actually asserting their social competence when expressing their doubts about the male inability to "darn a sock."

Watson also interestingly comments that Belinda's love for the archdeacon "is portrayed as a comfortable kind of emotion rather than unhappy or disturbing" and is a result of Belinda's inherent placidity.[60] This appraisal is actually relevant to both of the sisters' experience of love (and that of many of Pym's female characters). Their desire is of a different quality than that expected of fictional heroines, and is not of the same caliber as that exhibited by the characters in the previous chapter. They do not demonstrate the turbulence of Sarah Durham, the cheek of Dora Chance or the determination of Daphne Drummond, but then, why should love be any more homogenous a feeling for the old than for their younger counterparts? Watson regards the Bedes' composure in a scathing light, hence the title of her study (*Their Own Worst Enemies*). Indeed, Belinda's ideas about love may disconcert readers used to the high dramas generally associated with romantic relationships (and in much fiction there is no other sort). However, many people, regardless of age, experience comfortable feelings for someone else, and Pym's narrative interests allow for an articulation of aspects of a relationship that fiction often ignores, such as treasured conversations, reminiscence, and the ordinary pleasure found in another's company. These are signs of love and cause Barbara Frey Waxman to comment, in *From the Hearth to the Open Road*, that it "need not be banished from ... ageing lives, and Pym has reminded us of its persistent and affirming presence in these lives."[61]

As an aside to this reading, it is interesting to consider a comment Pym made about the novel to her friend and biographer, Hazel Holt, in 1976 (some twenty-six years after the novel was published). Part of the Pym "mythology" is that *Some Tame Gazelle* is an imaginary extrapolation of her undergraduate affair with fellow student Henry Harvey.[62] Holt characterizes Pym's youthful relationship as more of an infatuation than a full-blown affair, although a lifetime friendship emerged from the episode.[63] In the text, Belinda is based on Pym and the archdeacon on Harvey. The young author seemed relatively accurate in her predictions for her future life, as she did share a house with her sister, on whom the character of Harriet is loosely based, and Harvey lived in a village about thirty miles away. Yet, everyday life proved to be more optimistic than she imagined. In talking to Holt about the "occasional weekend holidays" she took with Harvey, she is said to have exclaimed, "Fancy ... Belinda and the Archdeacon going on a Winter Break together!"[64]

Pym's concentration on the experience of the aging unmarried character, which, as Waxman phrases it, helps "to persuade readers that such a woman has intrinsic interest as a human being," even if without any "particular distinction," is distinctly polemical.[65] *The Practice of Everyday Life*, particularly volume two, further supports a radical reading of Pym's work. A large proportion of this volume is dedicated to unraveling the "profound meaning of differences and preferences" that women demonstrate in the planning and preparation of the "*plat du jour*."[66] Luce Giard, who writes this section, frames this everyday task as:

a domain where tradition and innovation matter equally, where past and present are mixed to serve the needs of the hour, to furnish the joy of the moment, and to suit the circumstance ... such life activities demand as much intelligence, imagination and memory as those traditionally held superior, such as music and weaving.[67]

This analysis of the numerous skills subsumed under the heading of cookery throws an interesting light on Pym's representation of the Bede sisters' attitude to food and life more generally. Throughout *Some Tame Gazelle*, the sisters continually discuss meals: what to serve to whom and when; what mixture of dishes are suitable; and so forth. When the sisters entertain the new curate, Belinda thinks,

Were all new curates everywhere always given boiled chicken when they came to supper for the first time? ... It was certainly an established ritual in their house.... The coldness, the whiteness, the muffling with sauce, perhaps even the sharpness added by the slices of lemon, there was something appropriate here, even if Belinda could not see exactly what it was.[68]

At several points in the novel, the character is represented as indulging in similar reveries, including the earlier example when she becomes joyful at being complimented on "the table" she keeps. Attributing this attitude to fussiness on the part of the protagonist is only one, narrow, reading. A more productive one would suggest that Pym is representing the daily creativity of characters in their production of meals in response to the time, ingredients, and money available. In this context, Belinda's pride in the compliments she receives seems justifiable.

The effort Belinda puts into planning her meals also reflects her feelings for her guests and her desire to make them as comfortable as possible. Undoubtedly her worries about what to feed the visiting seamstress, Miss Prior, are comic but her desire not to patronize the poorer character are just (particularly as Miss Prior does judge the meal she is served).[69] Food also allows the sisters to express their affections. Harriet is constantly trying to tempt the curate, Mr. Donne, with delicacies such as duck and blackberry jelly to supplement his otherwise paltry diet, and Belinda gets positively dreamy about the prospect of baking a cake for the archdeacon: "Perhaps when Agatha went away ... a cake ... perhaps with coffee icing and filling and chopped nuts on the top, or a really rich fruit cake."[70] The potentially sensual nature of food is accepted and developed in a narrative space that allows for the exploration of the everyday and is part of continual authorial refusal to denigrate the practices of the older women.

## *Self-Knowledge and Marginalized Identities in* The Education of Harriet Hatfield

This impulse is also found in *The Education of Harriet Hatfield*, Sarton's nineteenth and last novel, in which she represents the healthy and financially solvent Harriet Hatfield of the title. Sarton deals far more explicitly with discourses of aging than do Keane and Pym, foregoing humor as a strategy to undermine the status quo and preferring to more directly challenge pejorative representations of the old as immanent by basing the narrative around the recently widowed Harriet's decision to launch herself into the wider world. Virginia Rounding, in an article entitled "A Charmed Circle" (1990), describes one of Sarton's overall goals as the depiction of "exemplary lives" (a phrase Sarton uses in *The Magnificent Spinster*, published in 1986). Rounding explains that this phrase refers to the "lives of people who seem to have attained an inner wholeness, and who are able to give themselves freely to those they come into contact with."[71] This is a fair description of the heroine at the end of the novel, and as the title suggests, it actually traces Harriet's journey to the point, focusing on her education (in its broadest sense) and growing self-knowledge.

Primarily, the sixty-year-old protagonist learns about herself by becoming more involved with the community and opening a feminist bookshop. She makes this decision after the death of her partner of thirty years, when she realizes that she wants to become more mindful of herself and the world. In the relationship, she had happily played the domestic role, supporting Vicky's career as a successful publisher. When Vicky dies, Harriet is provided with the impetus, and financial means, to leave behind her sheltered life. The novel represents her grief alongside the first months of the shop's opening: the daily routines of managing the bookstore; the harassment she receives when a local reporter publishes the fact that she is a lesbian; the friends she makes; and most importantly her growing political awareness and sense of autonomy. As in *Some Tame Gazelle*, there is no dramatic denouement, but a similar summing-up by the heroine of her state of mind: "One ... problem appears to be settled ... and then another breaks over my head like a huge wave. But it's all right, I say to myself. It's the way things are. It's the real world and I am fully alive in it."[72]

Central to this attitude, and the text itself, is the idea that personal development does not stop at a certain age. The narrative is written from Harriet's perspective, and so the reader is privy to her feelings about the events that overtake her. She learns different things from the women of various ages and social backgrounds who come into the shop: from Nan, the black wife of a professor, she learns the venom of racism; from the dour Mrs. Stoneworth, the sheer hard work involved in caring for a partner who has become an invalid; and so forth. The character's learning process is very much tied to the widening, rather than narrowing, of her world, and as such, contains dynamics that are in direct opposition to those that drive, for instance, *The Reckoning* and *The Stone Angel*. Again, the variety of approaches with which authors treated in this piece of work represent personal growth in senescence demonstrates their non-homogenizing principles and commitment to heterogeneity.

It is not just Harriet who gains from her plunge into the public sphere, for the bookshop and her sympathetic ear provide, respectively, a refuge and sense of acceptance to those characters who cross her path. Because of this growing appreciation and tolerance for the diversity of people's lives, her brother finally confides to her that he, too, is a homosexual. After the revelation, she muses:

> I see that I have a lot to learn about Andrew. At sixty I seem to be learning a lot, chiefly learning, in fact. Growing up! It may appear humorous to some people, people who tease me about my innocence, but it makes my life extremely interesting. What more can one ask at sixty?[73]

Sarton deals with discourses of homosexuality, as the passage demonstrates, in terms of aging and development rather than in a romantic context (for instance, representing Harriet finding a new lover). The protagonist finds herself facing the problem of defining her relationship with Vicky when telling her new confidants about her past. Initially she is disconcerted about being described as a lesbian because she finds the term too confrontational and restrictive. Talking to old friends, she says, "I don't think of myself as labelled and stuck in a closet as someone outside the pale, you see."[74] Yet, she grows to realize that this is because Vicky, who was economically successful, protected her from homophobia and the strategic necessity of labeling herself.

The pitfalls and bonuses of proclaiming oneself a lesbian resemble those inherent in describing oneself as old. It is worth bearing this in mind when reading the following passage from Judith Butler's essay "Imitation and Gender Insubordination" (1991), in which she discusses her unease about using the term *lesbian*:

> The prospect of *being* anything ... has always produced in me a certain anxiety, for "to be" gay, or "to be" lesbian seems to be more than a simple injunction to be who or what I already am.... To write or speak *as a lesbian* appears a paradoxical appearance of this "I," one which feels neither true or false.[75]

Butler continues by asking the Foucauldian question: "There is political necessity to use some sign now, and we do, but how to use it in such a way that its future significations are not *foreclosed*? How to use the sign and avow its temporal contingency at once?"[76] Harriet's reluctance to describe herself as a lesbian fictionally reenacts the dangers of labeling with which Butler is concerned. Yet, after the newspaper article in which the character is "outed" and homophobic slogans are daubed on the shop front, she claims the label, realizing that, precarious though it may be, sometimes the individual needs to speak as part of a group that shares common concerns (as Butler acknowledges in her essay).

The author uses the device of Harriet's explaining her public articulation of her sexuality to an old friend to make explicit the processes involved in this decision. Initially, Harriet talks about it terms of her growing sense of community: "Every homosexual these days feels in some way at risk. Maybe when an old lady comes out it makes them feel less isolated."[77] In addition, Sarton points out that the protagonist's economic security allows her to be open about the subject: "No one can fire me; I'm not young. I am—don't laugh—a 'lady.' So can't you see that I must stand up for the hundreds of women who can't, who don't dare because for them the risk is too great?"[78] Clearly being old is not always a social disadvantage as the character's age raises questions about the validity of the youthful "militant" lesbian stereotype. Harriet's sedate and upper-middle-class manners are at odds with the imagined figure of the homophobe's narrow vision, much as her developing character and decisions about her sexuality contradict ageist visions of stasis in senescence.

Sarton's representation of Harriet's changing attitudes also dramatizes Foucault's argument that in claiming a marginalized identity, the individual may be negatively prejudged, but can also formulate a clearer reverse discursive position, challenging social prescriptions attached to a particular label.[79] Harriet copes with the stigma of aging by revisualizing it as a time for absorbing new experiences and lessons, and she says defiantly to her brother: "For me it is good to be as old as I am, and alone."[80] The character's positive affirmations about age, and sexuality, may appear unusual in light of the issues Charity V. Schoonmaker, a retired psychiatrist, discusses in an essay entitled "Aging Lesbians: Bearing the Triple Burden of Shame," (1993). The "triple burden" to which the title refers is a result of a society "which devalues women, punishes lesbians and debases the aged."[81] Her essay urges psychotherapists, at whom it is aimed, to take into account these social prejudices when treating older lesbians: advice that adds a necessary coda to Sarton's more optimistic representation. However, this argument does not make Harriet an unfeasible character, as one of the thought-provoking axioms of

Schoonmaker's paradigm is that as "we grow older, we become more different than alike inasmuch as our life experiences differ so widely."[82] This comment, which is eminently sensible, counters the overridingly homogenous views of the aged that abound in our society. Considering this idea, one might expect a multiplication of discourses about the subject. Yet, as I have been arguing and as Friedan notes in *The Fountain of Age*, this is not the case, and it "is only in the individual experiences of people and groups finding new uses for their own unexpected added years that we get hints of what might be possible for us all."[83] Harriet may be a protagonist in a novel, but her "life" creates a dialogue about the possibilities of aging, encouraging an affirmative response to the process.

Sarton's novel is not as didactic as I have made it sound: The more stressful aspects of Harriet's new life are countered by representations of its quieter moments—the pleasure she gains at the beginning of the text from walking her dog; visits from old and new friends; the success of the bookshop; and a glass of good wine. Harriet's friendships are central to her, and thus the text, and because she has moved to a new area, the reader is presented both with her sustenance of long-term relationships and the gradual development of new ones. Sarton is excellent at providing an insight into the give-and-take of such an endeavor. For example, Harriet becomes involved with a homosexual couple who provide both emotional and practical support when she is harassed (they listen to her worries and wash the slogans off the wall of the bookstore). But they "complicate" her life insofar as when one of them is diagnosed with AIDS, she responds by offering them her time and support.

Although this is a normal part of friendship, it is unusual to find a contemporary text that portrays the dynamic as existing in platonic relationships between men and women, an observation Sarton makes in *The Magnificent Spinster*. Sarton uses a metafictive device in this novel by depicting the seventy-year-old narrator, Cam, writing a biography about her friend. Due to this technique, readers often feel that when Cam comments about the process of writing, they are gaining an insight into Sarton's perspective. The following extract, then, can be read as explaining the significance that friendship holds in both *The Magnificent Spinster* and *The Education of Harriet Hatfield*: "It is odd that, on the whole, novelists speak little of friendship between opposite sexes, and especially these days, when sexual encounters dominate everything else in most fictional characters. I am writing about a woman who had a genius for friendship with both sexes."[84] Like Pym, Sarton demonstrates her awareness that some areas of life are seldom represented in fiction, and the absence of singularly dramatic events would seem to permit the fictionalization of these, more workaday, relationships.

Virginia Rounding levels one criticism at the text that concerns the coziness of some of Sarton's scenarios, including her depiction of friendship: "It may make the reader want to join the charmed circle around the fire, drinking tea and discussing Margaret Atwood's latest novel, but at times it sounds a little too good to be true."[85] One of the reasons for this critique is that Harriet (and Cam in *The Magnificent Spinster*) are wealthy and can afford lifestyles that are infinitely appealing. However, Sarton is not oblivious to the difference that financial stability can make to the individual, as illustrated in the contrast between Caro in *As We Are Now* and Laura in *The Reckoning*. Furthermore, the "twist" in *The Education of Harriet Hatfield* is that a proportion of the harassment Harriet receives is not because she is a lesbian, as she had thought, but because she is financially comfortable. Her dog is shot by an older woman who is jealous that Harriet has enough money to deal with her homophobic harassment (hiring a lawyer, replacing damaged property and so forth). By representing a variety of characters, some of whom are well-off, Sarton challenges the ubiquity of images of aging that suggest it can only be a period of economic hardship.

## *Conclusion*

All of the novels treated in this chapter challenge representations of the old that characterize their lives as full of deprivations of various sorts. Although the activities they represent are not radically different from what might be expected of the aged, the perspective from which they are approached insists on the value of these pastimes. As discussed, Baltes and Carstensen, and Friedan also argue convincingly that successful aging is linked to the continuation of tasks prioritized by the individual. In *Time After Time*, the only character who suffers disappointment is Leda because she has no such interests and so is portrayed as prey to dominant discourses of aging. The Swifts, on the other hand, cherish their plans, eccentric as they may seem (and Keane uses them to create much of the humor in the novel), and negotiate their limited social positions with flair.

While their activities fall outside of Beauvoir's conception of what constitutes a worthwhile "project," if they were to be viewed as such, her insistence on the key part they play in a fulfilling life is illuminating for the novels. As it stands, perhaps her desire not to see mundane activities as life-enhancing contributed to her representation of the senescent as unable to find room for maneuver within what are, undoubtedly, limiting paradigms of aging. Certeau and his colleagues are more optimistic about the possibilities for "anti-discipline" and argue that, in Foucauldian terms, we are not such "docile bodies." Giard talks of the necessity of accepting "as worthy of interest" the various "ordinary practices so often regarded as insignificant," and encourages "a will to learn to consider the fleeting and unpretentious ways of operating that are often the only place of inventiveness to the subject."[86]

This comment is particularly relevant to the older woman, with her marginalized social position and amount of time she is represented as spending in the domestic sphere. Pym revels in the conventionally unimportant, such as the organization of the Bedes' home, questioning dominant views of what constitutes worthwhile labor, a trait shared by Keane and Sarton. The authors' interest in "unpretentious ways of operating" sets them apart from their academic counterparts and society at large. Certeau, and his co-researcher Giard, hint at this conclusion by stating that for "the last fifty years, the ordinary has been the terrain for literary reflection."[87] This statement needs to be qualified when applied to representations of older women because they are rarely the subjects of literary observation.

Sarton's novel may seem to dwell less on the prosaic because it balances depictions of the domestic with Harriet's new career in the public sphere. However, within a wider literary framework, the running of a shop would usually only serve as a backdrop for the protagonist's involvement in, for example, a romantic narrative. Sarton's text, in appropriating for an older woman what would be an everyday activity for a younger one, simultaneously damns a society that would make Harriet exceptional for attempting the job and reveals something about the usual concerns of fictional worlds.

Pym and Keane, as discussed, use humor to deflate social and literary pretensions. They work with the premise that life is seldom as dramatic as it is in books, and ask the reader to acknowledge this fact. Barbara Brothers makes this point in relation to Pym: "In life the day-to-day activities of others seem like so much trivia. But then people, as opposed to characters [in fiction] dwell on trivialities."[88] This recasts people's relationship with the prosaic as one of importance, asserting that in seemingly quiet lives there exists the same feelings of drama as represented in exaggerated forms throughout literature.

Contrasting Amis's portrait of old age with Pym's and Keane's highlights the difference in narrative tone. The readers of *Ending Up* are expected to laugh at the characters and see their obsessions as childish, and they are urged to think themselves lucky that they have more important concerns. Amis kills off his characters in disgust, while the female writers allow the protagonists to continue contentedly beyond the end of the text. Barecca writes in *Last Laughs* that a lack of closure is common to women's comedy and symptomatic of a perspective where:

recognition replaces resolution. Resolution of tensions, like unity or integration, should not be considered viable ... because they are too reductive to deal with the non-closed nature of women's writing ... the realization that rules can be suspended, and absolutes are only powerful when allotted power, when a unified, linear progression is given over to the recognition of multiplicity and diversion, all "else" becomes possible.[89]

The non-endings which characterize *Time After Time* and *Some Tame Gazelle* (and *The Education of Harriet Hatfield*, although not a comedy) point to the future. In doing so, they represent figures that dominant discourse would find unfeasible; "making possible" single older female characters who will continue to be interested in their lives and projects long after the narrative has finished. All of the authors directly challenge the paucity of "quiet" lives, which is useful and noteworthy, if only because this is the sort of existence that society, and literature, generally allots the older woman.

# 5
# *The Wise and Archetypal Older Woman*

## Introduction

The texts in this chapter set aside the prosaic to represent literal life-and-death situations. The narratives work toward a suitably dramatic climax that is often precipitated, and always explained, by the older-female protagonist. Despite having argued that there is a scarcity of fiction featuring such characters, the novels to which I am referring belong to a genre that is densely populated by them: classical detective fiction. Initially it might seem as if senescent female detectives are portrayed stereotypically, a practice I have protested against, yet I want to suggest that bringing an age-conscious perspective to the genre exposes a more radical side to their representation. The authors tend to manipulate pejorative stereotypes of aging and refer to more archetypal images to produce heroines who are wise, independent and irreverent. As this technique is common in the genre, this chapter is not structured around a series of individual novels, but instead offers a broader explanation of these approaches.

The older-woman detective has featured prominently in this form of popular literature for over a hundred years. Her first appearance is attributed by Patricia Craig and Mary Cadogan, in their 1981 study *The Lady Investigates*, to the American author Anne Katherine Green and her sleuth, Amelia Butterworth, who appeared in *The Affair Next Door*, published in 1897.[1] It was not until the years between the two world wars, though, that the old-lady sleuth became engraved on the popular imagination through the work of female British writers who began their careers in this period.

The most famous author to emerge from this era, retrospectively dubbed the "Golden Age" of detective fiction, is Agatha Christie, with her amateur detective, Miss Marple, who made her debut in *Murder in the Vicarage* (1932), and her last appearance in the 1970s. Two other writers whose creations had equally lengthy careers are Patricia Wentworth, with her professional investigator Miss Silver (first appearing in 1928 in the *Grey Mask*), and Gladys Mitchell's home office psychologist, Mrs. Bradley, latterly Dame Bradley (who first starred in *Speedy Death*, published in 1929).[2] These characters—and more minor ones such as Miss Climpson, who was employed by Dorothy L. Sayers' creation, Lord Peter Wimsey; and Josephine Tey's Miss Pym—emerged from this period and led to the older woman becoming one of the stock figures of classical detective fiction.

From a historical point of view, it is likely that older protagonists were chosen by authors of the period because women who had passed "beyond" marriageable and child-rearing age seemed to possess more freedom than their younger counterparts. As Barbara Macdonald and Cynthia Rich point out in *Look Me in the Eye*, this comparative independence accounts for the fact that middle-aged and older women drove the first wave of feminism at the turn of the twentieth century. Authors who wanted to depict a female character undertaking a path that often involved, among other things, travel and mixing with unsavory characters, probably felt that these activities were more "appropriate" for the older woman.

The precedent set by Christie, Wentworth and Mitchell mean that critics who analyze this branch of crime literature do not find it unusual that the older-woman protagonist has such a high profile. Equally, feminist theory makes relatively little of the fact that a thriving sub-genre in which the older woman is a central character constitutes a literary anomaly. The reason for both camps' lack of commentary lies in a shared disregard for discourses of aging and the effects that they have upon the individual and representations of the senescent.[3] Traditional critiques of classical detective fiction tend to marginalize the figure of the old sleuth, and feminist theory about the genre duplicates this sidelining. There emerges a pattern in criticism about crime fiction whereby the older character is briefly mentioned and then the focus of the study switches to the younger female detective (obviously some theorists do consider the older sleuth in depth, and they will be cited). I want to begin my analysis where the majority of critiques end: focusing on issues of both gender and age, and in doing so, offering an alternative way of approaching novels featuring the older female sleuth.

Theorists such as Julian Symons, in *Bloody Murder: From the Detective Story to the Crime Novel* (first published in 1972 and updated in 1985), suggest that the classical detective story is currently out of fashion. Although the popularity of this type of crime fiction has undoubtedly declined since its zenith in the "Golden Age," at least in terms of authorial interest, it is still produced by numerous writers and enjoyed by vast numbers of readers.[4] Works from between the wars remain in print, and contemporary authors, from Ellis Peters with her "Brother Cadfael" series to Umberto Eco and *The Name of the Rose* (1983), continue to base their works on the narrative structures of classical detective fiction. Writers such as Corinne Holt Sawyer are still penning texts that specifically represent the older woman, with her detectives Caledonia Wingate and Angela Benbow, and Hamilton Crane (the pseudonym of Sarah Jill Mason) with her investigator/artist, Miss Seeton. These texts are published in America but are easily accessible internationally through Internet bookshops. In British literature, Ruth Dudley Edwards's ribald protagonist, Jack Troutback, who appears in novels such as *Matricide at Saint Martha's* (1994), continues the tradition of the older sleuth popularized by authors emerging from the interwar years.

For the most part, this chapter concentrates on novels by "Golden Age" authors—in particular, works by Gladys Mitchell and Patricia Wentworth, who continued to produce books into the 1970s. I range between their earlier and more contemporary novels, as the generic conventions of ratiocinative fiction lends the work of the individual, and different authors, an air of continuity and "timelessness." Christie's Miss Marple is mentioned, but as she already receives a lot of critical attention, I wanted to bring to the reader's attention a pair of slightly lesser-known detectives.

Two questions loosely structure the chapter, and they arise from the already outlined approach to the novels. First, what characteristics are attributed to the older woman that make her attractive to authors and readers of these texts? And second, what features does classical detective fiction possess that make it a genre suitable for interesting representations of aging? As these questions indicate, my concerns are quite broad and therefore will be answered in reference to a number of texts, with a more detailed analysis of a recent novel by Holt Sawyer to bring the reader up-to-date with a 1990s representation of an older female sleuth.

## *Crime Fiction as Popular Fiction*

Classical detective novels constitute just one sub-genre of the wider field of crime fiction, which includes such categories as the police procedural (a definition of the work of, for example, Patricia Cornwell), hardboiled (Raymond Chandler), spy/thriller (Ian Fleming) and adventure novels (Dick Francis).[5] Before considering some of the more obvious differences within the genre, it is useful to place crime fiction within the wider context of popular fiction, an area that I have not yet mentioned.

In the last half of the twentieth century, literary critics suggested that the established literary canon supported particular ideologies that reserved the ideal of literary greatness for white, middle and upper-class Anglo-American males. This "elitism," Glenwood Irons writes, in his introduction to *Gender, Language and Myth* (1992), "has no rationale in post-modern society."[6] Divisions, therefore, that were once seen as irreversibly separating "high" and "popular" art became more nebulous, with academia, for example, taking popular fiction more seriously and regarding it as worthy of analytical scrutiny. Various theorists have suggested that the two types of art should no longer be viewed in binary opposition, but rather as parts of a literary continuum. Nonetheless, it would be naïve not to acknowledge that there are differences in the aesthetic quality of texts (however this is decided). John Cawelti, in *Adventure, Mystery and Romance*, published in 1976 and one of the early academic studies of popular fiction, helpfully suggests that "there are different kinds of artistry rather than a single standard in terms of which all fictional creations should be judged."[7] He further points to the fact that this is also true within popular fiction and that each "conventional formula has a wide range of artistic potential."[8]

On an obvious level, for example, the latest novel by Corinne Holt Sawyer will be distributed, marketed and received in a different way than the latest book by A.S. Byatt, or in terms of popular fiction's own internal hierarchy, a more gritty Patricia Cornwell mystery. At a different level, the concept that popular fiction has its own conventions is also demonstrated by the evaluation that it contains its own "narrative visions" and myths, distinguishable from those found in more canonical texts.[9]

Joanna Russ, a critic and writer of science fiction, picks up on this paradigm in "What Can a Heroine Do?" first published in 1972, suggesting that certain genres possess the potential to represent women following more courses of action than are allowed in traditional texts. She, too, regards this textual potentiality in terms of literary plot patterns and myths, and states that readers:

> do not only choose or reject works of art on the basis of these myths; we interpret our own experience in terms of them. Worse still, we actually perceive what happens to us in the mythical terms our culture provides. Make something unspeakable and you make it unthinkable.[10]

The converse of this sentiment is also true: Make something "speakable" and you make it thinkable (one of the axioms of this study). Russ sees three genres as revolving around relatively ungendered myths and so allowing authors the opportunity to move beyond representing female characters as romantic heroines: science fiction, supernatural fiction, and classical detective stories, in which the myth is centered on "Finding Out Who Did It (whatever 'It' is)" [*sic*].[11]

Russ does not expand on the reason behind this generic potential, but Sally Munt, in *Murder by the Book? Feminism and the Crime Novel* (1994), proposes an idea that helps explain it, although she shifts the emphasis from characters to authors. Munt believes that crime fiction as a whole is "fundamentally friendly" to female authors wishing to portray autonomous female characters of all ages (and fully able to express explicitly feminist concerns). She convincingly argues that this is because women "infiltrated" the genre from the very beginning, using, for example, parody as a strategy to disrupt the seemingly masculine framework of the narratives.[12] The concept of female humor as a technique for subversion was discussed extensively in the last chapter and recurs throughout this one. Munt goes as far as to suggest that there has been a feminization of the genre, a point that she believes has been conveniently overlooked or ignored by more traditional critics.

## *Archetypes in Classical Detective Fiction*

The type of approach to crime fiction against which Munt argues is characterized by the observation Marty Roth makes about female detectives, whom he describes as "feminine notations that perform a masculine function."[13] The function that he believes they execute is the fulfillment of an adolescent fantasy, in which the detective is an all-knowing and all-seeing kind of superman. Munt uses this concept of detective as hyper-talented outsider, but she places the character in a different paradigm that is more conducive to feminist appropriation and readings. She astutely suggests that in crime fiction, "the Othering of the detective is always already in the text; feminist writers can exploit this."[14] Her useful description of the detective's position makes explicit the connection between the sleuth and the older-female protagonist who is Other on two counts—because of her gender and because of her age.

Munt challenges earlier interpretations of the genre in this way to support her suggestion that the genre has been feminized. Not only does she dispute that the iconography of crime fiction is tied to dominantly masculine concerns and figures, but she also believes that interest in the "psychological effects of a crime" is a "legacy wrought by women writers of the genre."[15] Although this latter point is not particularly pertinent to a discussion of ratiocinative novels, which are not overly concerned with the psychological, it works to counteract the concept of crime fiction as a masculine medium.

Munt, in specific reference to the classical detective model, writes that female authors disrupted "male authority myths and deployed stereotyped female characters satirically against themselves."[16] Before discussing the manipulation of stereotypes, it is interesting to focus on another strategy used by authors to challenge male-authority myths: the invocation of an alternative myth of female authority, that of the "old crone," the mythical wise woman who, although on the margins of the community, is valued for her experience and knowledge. Some examples of the type of mythical figures that can be related to the older sleuth are Hecate, the Greek goddess of witchcraft and the moon, also the oldest member of the mythological tripartite of the Maiden, Nymph, and Crone (also known as Demeter, one of the triple goddess's titles);[17] Athene, goddess of female skills and warfare; and the Gorgon's sisters, the Graeae (three crones who share an eye and tooth and guard their sister, the Medusa).[18] These mythological figures have been virtually ignored in conventional literary criticism of the genre. The classically styled detective is usually compared to a knight, or a knight-errant, who undertakes a quest for truth, and yet the image of the wise crone would seem an obvious cipher for the older sleuth.

Annis Pratt, in *Archetypal Patterns in Women's Fiction* (1982), points out that there is both a general, and a more specific, literary critical blindness to female archetypes: "Male archetypalists, alternately attracted and repelled by 'the feminine', had difficulty in getting enough perspective upon it to admit it into their thinking."[19] This observation is more than fair when considered in relation to the numerous textual references to the sleuth-as-witch that are infrequently noted by male critics. In Wentworth's *The Watersplash* (1954), Miss Silver is described as conveying "an impression of belonging to the same period as her [Victorian] pictures and walnut chair." Misleadingly sedate and softly spoken, she is proud of the talents that have made "her independent and in a modest way prosperous."[20] She is also incredibly determined, and when she eventually solves the crime, her policeman friend, Frank, exclaims, "The chief really does suspect you of at least white witchcraft. I don't think it would surprise him if you were to fly out the window on a broomstick."[21] Gladys Mitchell also makes the connection between sleuth and crone relatively explicit, using images evocative of witchcraft and witches to depict Dame Bradley. In the following passage, Bradley is described by Simon Innes, the thirteen-year-old narrator of *The Rising of the Moon* (1945), who, with the assistance of his younger brother, helps Dame Bradley to solve a series of murders that occur in his hometown. Early in the novel, the brothers visit a local junk shop, a favorite haunt, to talk to the proprietor, and while there they catch their first sight of Dame Bradley: "Mrs. Cocketon had a customer, and we were obliged to wait. The customer was an unusual-looking old lady with sharp black eyes, a yellow face, hands like claws and a general expression of knowing all about you and making allowances."[22] Throughout Mitchell's novels, Dame Bradley's hands are described as claw-like, her eyes beady, and her laugh a "cackle": a portrayal more than coincidentally close to the fairy-tale representation of a witch.

Even when the connection between older-female archetypes and detectives is made obvious, it is downplayed in much theory. Julian Symons is not expressly concerned with studying archetypes in his consideration of psychological reasons for detective fiction's continuing popularity. However, he does discuss the figure of the witch doctor in terms of the role he plays in both the ancient and contemporary imagination. Symons believes that the genre is compelling because it reenacts the scenario whereby "the primitive tribe is purified through the transference of its troubles to another person or animal;" the "murderer is an appropriate villain" who is then punished and banished from the community. The detective is analogous with the witch doctor "who is able to smell out the evil that is corrupting society, and pursue it."[23] While this is an interesting hypothesis, what is most revealing is that Symons does not even consider that the witch or wise woman is equally feasible in this role.

Such reference to archetypal female figures would help to explain the popularity of the older woman as ratiocinative investigator, and why she is more prominent than her male counterpart (although many male sleuths could be classed as middle-aged, such as G.K. Chesterton's Father Brown and Christie's Poirot). Male archetypal figures are often connected to large-scale heroics, and as crime fiction tends to be conservative, and produced in an ageist society, it is unlikely that an older man would be represented as involved in the "quests" that provide the younger male detective with his mythological resonance. Female archetypes, on the other hand, are linked to the more intimate cycles of life, including death and perhaps murder. (Although Hades is one of the gods of the underworld, he "never knows what is happening in the world above.")[24]

The power accorded female archetypes has varied in the past, and although in classical European mythology they were still accorded positions of authority, it is from this period that the image of the triple goddess emerged. The splitting of the more archaic figure of Mother Earth into three components weakens the imaginative strength of the female deity and demonstrates the patriarchal tactic of polarizing female roles, as found in the enduring virgin/whore dichotomy. (Men do not generally have to face such labeling, although, of course, they cannot escape some sort of social classification.) Contemporary society's disjunctive attitude toward the different stages of life has allowed the "maiden" and "nymph" phases of a woman's existence to take center stage while the "crone" is banished. Nonetheless, although marginalized, she refuses to disappear, and classical detective fiction constitutes one strand of her cultural survival. As Pratt writes, "Archetypal patterns ... in women's fiction constitute signals from a buried feminine tradition that conflict with cultural norms and influence narrative structures," including those of the genre under discussion.[25]

The female mythological figure's connection with the darker side of life, or, rather, elements of it that humankind cannot control and thus find frightening, makes the older protagonist's connection to crime and murder less strange. This is particularly true when the role of the mythical three Furies (or Erinyes) is taken into consideration. These crones were said to live in the underworld and, among other things, "hear complaints brought by mortals against the insolence of the young to the aged ... of hosts to guests ... and punish such crimes by hounding the culprits relentlessly, without rest or pause."[26] The link between the Furies who punished unavenged criminality and the older detective is so relevant as to be startling—particularly with regard to the Furies' special interest in prejudice against the old, an aspect of the myth that is normally ignored. Christie gestures to this association by titling one of the later Miss Marple mysteries after a sister of the Furies, *Nemesis* (1971). This figure originally was seen as punishing only the self-satisfied but later became linked to vengeance more generally. Miss Marple was given the nickname by a fellow older character in an earlier novel (*The Caribbean Mystery*, 1964) who witnessed her investigate and solve a murder and posthumously called upon her expertise in *Nemesis*.

Dame Bradley, who is consistently represented as witch-like and gleeful in her demeanor, seems even more analogous with the Furies than the more sedate Miss Marple or Miss Silver. Briefly turning to a more recent use of archetypal imagery, "The Laugh of the Medusa" by Hélène Cixous (1975) provides a further insight into Mitchell's writing. Patricia Craig notes that Mitchell's work "took the detective story as close as it comes to the shaggy dog story."[27] The impudence of the central protagonist is definitely part of her novels' appeal and an example of the "fizzing irreverence" that Munt argues produces a genre conducive to interesting representations of women.[28] This irreverence shows itself primarily in Dame Bradley's humor, an example of which can be found in the following exchange from *Mingled with Venom* (1978). The conversation takes place between the detective and a dramatic young character who, after the death of his grandmother in a small Cornish village, demands of the sleuth: "There is a smell of death around these parts, don't you think?" Dame Beatrice replies "cackling, ... 'No, only of decaying shellfish.'"[29]

Mitchell represents Dame Bradley as refusing to dramatize the situation and puncturing the young man's pomposity with a typically witty answer. This could be termed a "laugh-of-the-Medusa" strategy, as it seems to arise from a source of female power that Cixous talks about in the essay of the same name. In it she urges women to represent vivid images of wild women who are "bowed but not broken." She links the strategies that women use to allow them to express their bodies and spirit to the idea of defiant laughter. The medusa, whom Graves describes in *The Greek Myths* (1955) as possessing "so ugly a face that all who gazed at it were petrified with fright," laughs at her vilification, refusing to be ashamed of what she is.[30] (This portrait seems particularly apt in discussions of the senescent, whose physical signs of aging—wrinkles and so forth—are framed as ugly.) Cixous does not explicitly discuss this image, but her essay is very much concerned with this type of feminine *jouissance* in the face of repression:

> We the repressed of culture ... our wind knocked out of us, we the labyrinths, the ladders, the trampled spaces, the bevies—we are black and we are beautiful. We're stormy, and that which breaks loose from us without our fearing any debilitation. Our glances, our smiles, are spent; laughs exude from all our mouths....[31]

Mitchell's representation of Dame Bradley taps into the everywoman that emerges from Cixous's description, particularly because of Bradley's capacity for amusement and acknowledgment of the darker sides of the feminine. At the end of *Mingled with Venom*, she discusses with her secretary, Laura, an innocent but callous character who had been involved in the case she had solved. Her aide asks:

> "...that young thug will go on and prosper?"
> "Why not? He has proved that he possesses the ruthlessness which, in this life, is said to be the hallmark of success."
> "I'd rather be a failure!"
> "Oh, I don't know," said Dame Bradley mildly. "I can be ruthless myself on occasions."[32]

This sentiment, which the narrative has proven true, adds a more openly defiant quality to the sleuth's humor than can be traced, for example, in Pym's depiction of the Bedes' giggles in *Some Tame Gazelle*. They, like the secretary, are held back by an awareness of what is socially polite, whereas when Bradley cackles, it is with a disregard for social mores that is worthy of Hecate herself.

## Structures of Ratiocinative Fiction

Having offered an archetypal explanation of why the older woman is a popular choice of protagonist in ratiocinative fiction, it is revealing to consider how the basic narrative structure of this "analytic or puzzle solving" branch of the crime genre serves to accommodate her continual presence.[33]

Julian Symons, in *Bloody Murder*, makes a useful, if broad, distinction between more contemporary crime models and those employed by classical detective fiction. In earlier texts the emphasis of the narrative is on the "how?" of a crime rather than the "why?" that drives later novels.[34] The former school of crime writing is generally traced back to two short stories published in the 1840s: "The Murders in the Rue Morgue" and "The Purloined Letter," featuring the character Auguste Dupin and written by the American, Edgar Allan Poe. It was not until the end of the nineteenth century that the narrative structure of the ratiocinative detective story became widely used, popularized most notably by Sir Arthur Conan Doyle and his detective, Sherlock Holmes, and it dominated the genre until the mid–1940s.[35]

There are numerous studies of the formulae that are manipulated to produce a classical detective story: the "rules" that, for example, were listed, only half-jokingly, in 1928 by the author S. S. Van Dine (who wrote criticism under the name of Willard Huntingdon Wright).[36] Both contemporary and earlier critics agree on many points: for example, that murder is the crime most suited to fictionalization, Van Dine stating that "three hundred pages is far too much bother for any other crime but murder."[37] He believed that romance had no place in the detective story and that neither the criminal nor the detective should be a professional. Fantastic solutions were to be avoided in terms of paranormal occurrences and in the sense that the reader should be provided with enough clues so that s/he could reach the same conclusion as the detective.

Marty Roth, in *Foul and Fair Play* (1995), comments that this latter "rule," "is a bluff by admission: what the detective novelist really must do is play fair *and* mislead."[38] He explains that authors accomplish this by providing an important clue and then instantly sidetracking the reader by depicting an event that eclipses the clue. This technique illustrates how narrative rules can be manipulated or occasionally discarded in order to bring variety and innovation into the genre. In the Miss Silver novels, for example, there is often a love story between two characters, one of whom is in danger from the criminal, as in *The Allington Inheritance* (1960), or unjustly accused of a crime, as in *The Watersplash* (1954). While this does not entirely break Van Dine's rule that there should be no "love interest" within the novel as the detective is not directly involved in the relationship, it bends the interdiction and heightens the stakes involved in the detective's search for truth.

A further ingredient of the ratiocinative narrative, and one that is usually honored in those that feature the older detective, is that the crime takes place in a small community: a village (often the setting for Miss Marple's investigations); a school (as in Gladys Mitchell's *Spotted Hemlock* [1958]); or a country house (as in Patricia Wentworth's *The Clock Strikes Twelve* [1945]).[39] The detective is often an outsider from the community, or if not, marginalized in some way (such as being an older woman). They are represented as remedying the disruption caused by the crime and returning things to the status quo. This tidying-up process is generally viewed as comforting to the reader insofar as the narrative depicts criminality as something that can be contained and banished, as discussed earlier in relation to the witch-doctor/witch analogy.[40]

Yet, there are other readings of this scenario that reveal a connection between the classically styled and "hard-boiled" crime novel in terms of the anxiety that they express. Cawelti writes in *Adventure, Mystery and Romance* that the isolated nature of the communities in which the detective finds her/himself constitutes a "symbolic representation of the relation between order and chaos, between surface rationality and hidden depth of guilt."[41] As Cawelti suggests, the classical detective novel is concerned with revealing the peacefulness of the ordinary as a façade, or as Roth phrases it in a description of the tonal qualities of the bucolic settings: "The atmosphere ... is far from pastoral, it is ghost-ridden."[42] The "ghosts" that fade in and out of the background are the repressed passions of the seemingly calm community. Sally Munt supports this interpretation in *Murder by the Book?* in which she writes that the classical detective novel is far from reassuring for the reader: "Since communities always thrive on suspicion their insecurities can never be resolved."[43] She suggests that social instability, in terms of class and personal economics, leads to tensions that are manipulated by novelists in texts whose offer of closure is only a feint.

Despite these readings, after the ideological upheavals caused by World War II, classical detective fiction was popularly judged as offering an unrealistic portrayal of the world.[44] The hard-boiled paradigm, which had gradually emerged from America in the 1930s, and is exemplified in the works of Dashiell Hammett and Raymond Chandler in the 1940s, began to dominate the genre on both sides of the Atlantic. The following comment by Chandler about Hammett's work colorfully summarizes the differences between the two types of crime fiction and the contempt with which the earlier model was viewed:

> Hammett gave murder back to the kind of people that commit it for reasons, not just to provide a corpse; and with the means at hand,

not with handwrought dueling pistols and tropical fish. He took murder out of the Venetian vase and dropped it into the alley. He was spare, frugal, hard-boiled....[45]

The shift in generic tone caused by the popularity of the hard-boiled stories affected the concerns of crime literature as a whole. Authors began to depict the psychological makeup of criminal and detective (and to a lesser extent the personalities of the other characters), as indicted earlier, the "why?" of the textual case became increasingly important. Such is the continuing influence of this subgenre that some of the most challenging representations of younger women detectives in the 1990s, by authors such as Sue Grafton and Sara Paretsky, continue to use its narrative structures.

Hard-boiled narratives (and those novels influenced by them) are less accommodating to representations of the older woman than those of classical detective fiction. In an order to explain why, it is necessary to compare the formulaic elements of each subgenre. Beginning with the realism attributed to hard-boiled novels, one of the factors contributing to its aura of authenticity is the position of the detective as embroiled in, rather than apart from, the criminal underworld.[46] S/he is not safe from verbal or physical abuse, and solving the crime does not promise any hope of a return to moral equilibrium for sleuth, for reader, or, more generally society. Although crime literature is generally regarded as supporting dominant ideologies, the hard-boiled narrative, and those that followed in its wake, rarely restore the status quo of their fictional worlds. The criminals are often professionals (as opposed to the amateurs of classical detective stories), implying that crime is not a random event but a phenomenon that permeates all levels of society. The setting of the hard-boiled narrative emphasizes this perspective. Investigations are carried out in an urban environment, which, as Ralph Willett, in *The Naked City* (1996), explains, "functions as text, one characterised by intertextuality, intangible relationships and instability."[47] This is one description of the "mean streets" so often associated with the hard-boiled text, where society's darker side is centralized and shown to permeate the allegedly secure infrastructure.

While the younger female sleuth is able to navigate the fragmented spaces of the urban world and successfully enact feminist revisionings of the mythical "tough-guy" detective, the older woman is not considered capable of negotiating these urban dystopias.[48] Crime fiction's ingrained conservatism means that it has not yet challenged the pejorative characterization of older generations as old-fashioned and unsuited to the pace of city life (although obviously many older people do negotiate this space successfully). As Simone de Beauvoir writes in *Old Age*: "Modern technocratic society thinks that knowledge does not accumulate with the years but grows out of date. Age brings disqualification with it: age is not an advantage."[49] Nor is it credible for a text to represent a gun-toting, physically aggressive, older P.I.

One crime series that gestures to the potential of such a character is Janet Evanovich's novels, the first of which is *One for the Money* (1994). She includes an older female character, Grandma Mazur, who accidentally becomes involved in detecting. The older woman is the grandmother of the main protagonist, the lingerie-buyer-turned-bounty-hunter, Stephanie Plum. As this career change indicates, Evanovich successfully injects humor into the hard-boiled narrative, and Grandma Mazur's spasmodic appearances are largely for comic effect. Although she is represented as feisty when she inadvertently gets drawn into a gunfight, at the end of *Two for the Dough* (1996), the reader is expected to find it funny that she manages to rescue her granddaughter. Yet, Stephanie is not the most efficient of sleuths; in fact she often has to rely on her colleague, Ranger, and Joe Morelli, a policeman and her sometime lover, for help. But Grandma Mazur is represented as spectacularly inept, and despite her streetwise comments that surprise Stephanie, she would have difficulty negotiating the crime-filled urban spaces without a younger guide.

Glenwood Irons would probably approve of the character of Stephanie, as, in his essay "G Is for Gender-Bending" (1992), he expresses his excitement about representations of the "new breed" of younger female detectives. Interestingly, while praising them as autonomous females, he theoretically disqualifies their older predecessors:

> Female detectives like Kate Fansler, Cordelia Gray ... are rewriting the original detective narratives to create a discursive space that is essentially female, young and definitely not "spinsterish". In contrast to the narrow view of the curious grey-haired spinster taken by Christie and other creators of "lady detectives"; the New Woman Detective is not approached from a single perspective.[50]

Irons's disparaging assessment of older sleuths can be noted in his use of the term *spinsterish* and the unexpanded description of older detectives as *curious*. He marginalizes the older character, and this allows him to make generalizations about their representation. Not only do the older female detectives have their own distinct identity from other types of investigators they also differ from one another. For example, Dame Bradley is far more sarcastic and openly opinionated than is Miss Marple or Miss Silver. The latter detectives usually work alone, while Dame Bradley has the assistance of her secretary, Laura, and chauffeur. Miss Silver and Dame Bradley are professional investigators, whereas Miss

Marple is an amateur. Although I sometimes do not stress the individuality of the detective as much as I might in an effort to focus on a more general age-conscious reading of the subgenre, this cataloguing of differences could continue for pages.

Despite views held by critics such as Irons, the older-woman sleuth continues to appear in her classical disguise, working in smaller communities where her knowledge does not have to unravel the constantly changing environment of the city. As mentioned earlier, the shifting emphasis of crime fiction has resulted in an expansion of the genre rather than a replacement of one type of narrative by another, and the feeling that classical detective fiction will be totally supplanted by more psychologically driven texts seems premature. It is more accurate to suggest, as does Patricia Craig in the introduction to the *Oxford Book of English Detective Stories* (1990), that new ratiocinative texts will continue to appear, "decked out in trappings best suited to the period."[51] This comment seems astute, particularly if considered in relation to some of the scenarios utilized by contemporary authors. Nancy Bell, for example, depicts a Texan matriarch, Biggie, as a sleuth. In *Biggie and the Mangled Mortician* (1997), the character is drawn into investigating a murder because the temporary sheriff, who is a homosexual florist, very stereotypically, but also with an irony typical of the genre, is too worried about the cleanliness of his uniform to dirty it by chasing killers. Ruth Dudley Edward's Jack Troutbeck may be the bursar of a female college at Cambridge in *Matricide at Saint Martha's*, but this novel could not be mistaken for anything but a late-twentieth-century text. Edwards updates the "sleuth's" connection to the witch by touching on the bursar's sexuality; she is an active, non-monogamous bisexual, who demonstrates an uncanny insight into college politics alongside a penchant for gin and roast beef. Further, Jack does not directly solve the crime, although she has her suspicions, but she effectively organizes those who can (a contemporary generic development that will be mentioned in relation to Holt Sawyer's novel).

## *The Subversive Deployment of Stereotypes*

One trait that later writers share with the likes of Christie, Wentworth and Mitchell is the subversive deployment of stereotypes. As Munt suggested earlier, the authors of ratiocinative fiction make use of stereotypes, but not in the way that might be expected. Catherine Kenney recognizes this tendency in Dorothy L. Sayers's portrayal of the aged detective, Miss Climpson, and writes that her "use of the spinster may appear more stereotyped than it actually is": a pronouncement that could be applied to any number of authors who represent the older female sleuth.[52] A discussion of the authorial treatment of characteristics commonly attributed to older women will emphasize the point.

Idiosyncrasies associated with the aging process are taken from their usual context and placed in a more productive one. Gossip, a female habit in the popular imagination, is particularly linked to the older woman who supposedly has time to indulge in this activity. Patricia Craig and Mary Cadogan, in *The Lady Investigates*, have noted how, within the covers of classical detective fiction, this form of communication is constructed as a "socially useful activity."[53] All detectives, to a certain extent, make use of hearsay as a way of finding out about victims and suspects alike, and the older woman is particularly adept at gleaning information from other characters in this way. Yet, not all sleuths rely on "gossip" to the same extent. For instance, Dame Bradley, in her role as home office psychologist, is far more direct in her questioning than is Miss Silver, but she still uses information gleaned from casual conversation to supplement the gaps in her knowledge.

Another characteristic popularly attributed to older women is a general narrowness of experience, put down to the fact that their days are filled with inconsequential events and meetings. Like Pym, Keane and Sarton, though, the authors featured in this chapter discredit the tragic overtones of this myth by throwing a positive light on it. Craig and Cadogan hint at this process when they describe Miss Marple as having a life "neither wide nor deep," but a "very productive familiarity with other people's."[54] They go on to say that the surface peacefulness of her routines allow her to develop skills whereby she can recognize familiar patterns and make connections between events and people. This ability is not exclusive to Miss Marple. Miss Silver, in *The Allington Inheritance* (1960), is also represented as possessing an instinctive knowledge of people: "Miss Danesworth met Miss Silver's eyes and experienced what so many people had experienced in similar circumstances. She felt a great many things that she could not put into words.... The conventions did not matter. The only thing that mattered was the truth."[55] Wentworth depicts Miss Silver as so compelling a presence that people want to tell her their stories, obviously a useful skill for a detective, thus manipulating the ideas of women being both intuitive and good listeners. This insightful knowledge of people is, once again, something that supposedly develops with age, and the older female sleuth's ability to see past surface appearances is often commented upon by the narrator and by other characters. Miss Silver's policeman friend, Frank Abbott, describes her to some of her new acquaintances in *Spotlight* (1949): "You can take it from me that as far as she is concerned the human race is glass-fronted. She looks right through the shop-window into the back premises and detects the skeleton in the cupboard."[56]

The detective's comprehension of the worth of seemingly inconsequential objects, the discovery of clues, could be regarded as an activity more suited to the female sleuth than to her male counterpart. Kenney interestingly writes that an appreciation of the importance of minutiae in classical detective stories is "a task of no great difficulty for the intelligent female of the species, whose small domestic frame has often limited her to the scrutiny of such minute detail and whose survival has often depended on it."[57] This subject was also discussed in the last chapter, although again, crime writers use the female connection to the mundane in a specific way. Ellen M. Tsagaris, who writes about Pym, captures the difference in authorial approach in the following quote: "Detectives and mystery writers have always understood that studying life's trivia is an important means of solving a crime.... Pym, however, is unique because she values trivia for its intrinsic worth."[58] This is not to denigrate writers of crime fiction but to gesture to how stereotypes of senescence can be reclaimed in a multitude of ways.

An example of how knowledge from the domestic sphere is transplanted into the public one and used to trap criminals can be found in *Mingled with Venom*. Dame Bradley's interest in plants and herbs allows her to conclude that the victim, Romula, died after eating poisoned horseradish. The sleuth deduces that monkshood, a similar-looking but highly toxic plant, was deliberately substituted for the edible root. Her having previously noticed it growing in the garden of one of her suspects leads directly to her solving the case. This pattern of events combines many of the elements of which Kenney speaks, as Bradley is alerted to clues because of her expertise in cookery and gardening (her knowledge of plant lore also recalling the archetypal wise woman).[59]

Not only do authors reclaim certain denigrated characteristics of aging, but they also show the older detectives consciously disguising themselves by adopting stereotypically aged behavior. Miss Marple and Miss Silver, for example, often take up their knitting in the course of an investigation, conscious that this activity fulfills suspects' expectations about the elderly and results in their relaxing their guard. Kathleen Gregory Klein, in *The Woman Detective: Gender and Genre* (1988), notes in a discussion of Miss Silver that this action is indeed "part of her professional disguise."[60] Mitchell makes this strategy even more explicit than Wentworth, by representing Dame Bradley knitting unwearable garments while waiting to spring a trap on a criminal:

> Mrs. Bradley sat downstairs in the dining-room placidly knitting a shapeless length of mauve wool, adding (apparently as the fancy took her, for she seemed to be following no particular pattern) touches of grey and shrimp-pink, and blandly receiving reports as they came in.[61]

Mitchell's description foregrounds the activity's strategic deployment and demonstrates the parodic nature of her stories: satirical of both attitudes toward the elderly and the "rules" of classical detective fiction (Dame Bradley's "shapeless length" of knitting contrasts greatly with the innumerable pink vests produced by Miss Silver and Miss Marple).[62]

Although critics such as Craig, Cadogan and Klein note the misleadingly innocuous façade of the older detective, they do not go farther and suggest that the authors are also making a statement against ageist attitudes. Pervading ageism in the fictional society (mirroring real life in this instance) is the reason for the detective's success. The characters surrounding the detective, including the criminal, underestimate her because they judge her using popular and, therefore, generally negative views of the senescent. This eventually leads to the criminal's arrest, but often, even the "innocent" members of the community are surprised by the older sleuth's achievement.

In contrast, there are usually one or two characters familiar with the detective who treat her as a competent adult, such as the aforementioned Frank Abbott in the Miss Silver stories. The friend of the sleuth acts as a foil to the doubting characters, allowing negative views of the detective to be made explicit before the narrative shows them to be misplaced. The following exchange between Frank and his superior, Chief Detective Inspector Lamb, provides an example of the type of aspersions directed toward the older detective: "'I had tea with Maudie yesterday.' ... 'Miss Silver? You're not going to tell me she's mixed up with this... What did she say?'" After Frank tells Lamb about Miss Silver's theory on the crime, his chief responds, "'If that Miss Silver of yours was to tell you black was white, you'd believe it! ... All this second and third-hand stuff—well, I ask you, what's the good of it? It's not evidence.'"[63]

Lamb doubts the usefulness of gossip and is scathing about Miss Silver, who then goes on to solve two murders before he does (using her own methods of investigation). This textual dynamic feeds into the parodistic nature of ratiocinative fiction and is essential to the enjoyment readers gain from seeing the underdog (the older detective) triumph over those who denigrate her capabilities. Roth, in *Fair Play and Foul*, talks about pleasure in relation to the genre's use of serialization to satisfy the readers' desire to revisit their favorite detectives.[64] I would add that, in the case of the older woman, the gratification generated by the marginalized figure's validation is central to the character's appeal and a further reason for her continued popularity.

Sally Munt suggests that the lack of theoretical comment about such strategies is due to the masculine critical tradition's concentration on the structural parameters of classical detective fiction. A fascination with its "rules," has diverted attention from the political messages contained within certain novels, including challenges to sexist and ageist ideology. Roth illustrates this viewpoint in his belief that at "the threshold of analytic detective fiction, social and political history was put under a ban by a generic boundary line."[65]

Feminist theorists obviously disagree with these sentiments, although generally they concentrate on classical detective fiction's treatment of gender rather than age. For example, Katherine Gregory Klein, in *The Woman Detective*, has written a relatively comprehensive analysis of the female private investigator. She argues that because of crime fiction's ideological conservatism authors rarely portray female sleuths as both "good" women and "good" detectives. One of these roles must suffer in order that dominant discourses of femininity remain intact, as a woman cannot have a successful career and remain a "proper" woman. Klein cites a few exceptions to this rule, and in the 1994 update of the text, gestures to Grafton and Paretsky's characters as avoiding this trap. However, in the first edition, Wentworth's Miss Silver is described as the protagonist most challenging to this narrative structure because of her ability to combine being a woman and a detective.[66] Unfortunately Klein does not expand on this, but a clue to her reasoning lies in a footnote to an earlier passage. Discussing another older sleuth, she states that the character is successful as a detective because she is represented as an "honorary man," similar in social position to "postmenopausal women in pacific cultures" that were "accorded male privileges."[67]

However, this reading does not cause Klein to question her definition of women as specifically referring to younger women.[68] Her hypothesis about female characters only works if she excludes the senescent: as does her assessment of crime fiction laying a subversive narrative (about female crime-fighters) over a dominant, conservative base. The primary radical narrative in novels that depict the older woman concerns the fact that aging does not have to be about retreat or decline and is embedded at a much deeper level than discourses that insist a woman can fulfill the role of P.I. The dissident narrative voice that centralizes the older character runs alongside the more conservative one so successfully that the majority of critics do not even notice it.

Too much stress on the conservative nature of the genre downplays the feminist discourses that can be extracted from crime writing and seems to be a case of "throwing out the baby with the bath water" (a position that often has to be negotiated in the development of feminist theories). For example, one can both note the rigid class stratification in the earlier works of Wentworth and Mitchell and realize that the representation of aging challenges cultural norms (although within a restrictive framework). Munt is thinking about this kind of approach when she writes about the urges of the resistant reader who looks to texts partially "for an affirmation of sub-cultural beliefs and exploration and dissemination of ideals."[69] This technique is one way of extracting a reverse discourse that seemingly has been absorbed by a more dominant one. It is used throughout feminist analysis and practiced, both consciously and unconsciously, by feminist (and perhaps other) fans of the woman detective in crime literature.

## Murder by Owl Light

I want to conclude this chapter by offering a reading of Corinne Holt Sawyer's *Murder by Owl Light* (1992). The author demonstrates many of the narrative strategies employed by Wentworth and Mitchell, engaging, even more explicitly, with discourses of senescence. Her overt challenges to ageist attitudes are facilitated by her choice of genre and the fact that popular fiction is relatively elastic in its absorption of ideological trends. Cawelti, in *Adventure, Mystery and Romance*, persuasively argues this dynamic, and the example he uses to support this premise concerns the changing role of the American Indian in Westerns: from evil savage to alienated indigenous race.[70] Undeniably the phenomenon of the aging population has resulted in more discussions of senescence, even if they are often one-sided and focus only on the problems of aging. Therefore, it is not surprising that classical detective fiction, which has always been conducive to representations of older women, should seize the opportunity to include some contemporary perspectives of aging.

Holt Sawyer certainly makes use of this potential in her series of novels, five to date, that focus on the widowed friends, and detectives, Angela Benbow and Caledonia Wingate.[71] In *Murder by Owl Light*, the couple assists the police in solving a series of killings that take place at their Los Angeles retirement complex, Camden-sur-Mer, using their inside knowledge and powers of observation to name the criminal. In this respect, they are closer to the preclassical archetype of wise crone as part of the community than the permanent outsiders Miss Silver and Dame Bradley. Angela and Caledonia also work far more closely with the police then do sleuths from the Golden Age," a development that is part of the increased realism of the genre as a whole. The reader realizes that the resources of the modern police force undercut the omnipotence of the amateur, or as Munt puts it: "Forensic science has put paid to intuitive leaps of deduction—genetic finger-printing is far more reliable."[72] This allows for the depiction of more human detectives than are found in earlier texts with authors providing insights into their cares and concerns.

Due to the backdrop of *Murder by Owl Light*, older characters form the majority of those that populate the novel. Holt Sawyer portrays them as a varied group of individuals, refusing the homogenizing tendency that lies behind many representations of older protagonists. Angela and Caledonia encounter this latter attitude throughout the text, and discuss the issue, for example, after meeting Sergeant Benson, one of the less "enlightened" police officers in the novel. "'This man acts...' 'Like most people act toward anyone with white hair.' Caledonia nodded. 'As though we hadn't the brains left to be of use anymore. I know—it drives me crazy too.'"[73]

In accordance with the classical detective model, however, Holt Sawyer provides the reader with a character who values the sleuths, Lieutenant Martinez. The novelist makes this character's challenge to ageist attitudes far more explicit than earlier protagonists. In the following passage, Martinez is advising Benson of the protocol of working with people at the retirement home. Benson begins:

> "I don't mind old people—one at a time. It's just in herds like that ... I can't tell one from the other!"
> Martinez snorted. "I shouldn't laugh ... that's exactly how I felt at first. All that gray hair, all those glasses, all those bent shoulders and wrinkles ... it took days before I could sort them out.... Listen, you'll sort them out believe me. And you'll find them a co-operative group too."[74]

This type of dialogue supplements the more traditional support of the older detectives, of which the following is an example:

> Those two old girls not only still have their wits about them, they're keen observers. And whether because they're bored and gossip comes naturally, or because they mix in everything that is going on, or because people tell them things, they know absolutely everything.[75]

While the text is keen to stress the more positive aspects of senescence, it does not ignore its problems. It frames them, though, as part of the aging process rather than its defining aspect. For instance, one of the residents of Camden-sur-Mer is slowly going deaf, and her peers admit that she is becoming tiresome to talk to because of the repetition this involves. Holt Sawyer represents this as something that, when faced, can be remedied: The character eventually makes an appointment to adjust her hearing aid, and this allows her to participate once more in the social life of the complex.

Returning to the plot, the murderer, Robbie Hammond, is the nephew of one of the community's most recent members, Mrs. Gardiner. Before his aunt moves to Camden-sur-Mer, he randomly murders people connected with the complex, so that he will not be suspected when he attempts to kill her for his inheritance (which he needs to pay off pressing debts). Robbie convinces his aunt that she would be safer in Camden-sur-Mer because she is becoming a danger to herself due to her forgetfulness. Actually, he hides things that she then believes are lost and engineers riskier situations, such as switching the iron back on after she had disconnected it. As paradigms of aging suggest that senility is inevitable, the older woman becomes worried that she is losing her mind and so reluctantly leaves her home. (Holt Sawyer does not suggest that a retirement complex will be everyone's dream.)

Robbie's downfall is his belief that all older people will be as easily duped as Mrs. Gardiner. Just before the denouement, he gets stuck in an elevator with Angela, whom the reader knows has pieced together clues that reveal him to be the murderer. When he realizes that she has discovered the truth, he plans to kill her, but first indulges in a moment of criminal self-congratulation: "You know … it really took me quite a while to learn how to get along. Not just with her—with all of you. But I learned. Talk nicely; be a 'good little boy' and say what the old people want to hear"[76]—except that he misjudges what it is that old people want to hear and their ability to spot his fake sincerity. Typically, this piece of rhetoric allows Caledonia enough time to come to Angela's aid, but more generally, it is his ageist attitude that ultimately allows Angela and Caledonia to divine his guilt and inform the police about his murderous actions. Holt Sawyer finishes the novel with Martinez telling the sleuths about Robbie's confession and takes a final opportunity to comment upon attitudes towards the old. Angela asks her friend:

> "Did you know that originally, the plan called for him to kill one of the residents of Camden because, as he put it, they wouldn't matter as much?"
> "What!" Caledonia's explosion shook the windowpanes.
> "Well, that's what he said. He said you'd lived your lives, and it was time for the older generation to step aside anyway and let the young ones have a chance."[77]

## *Conclusion*

While Robbie's sentiment might pervade society, it has no place in the world of detective fiction, where the sentiment is exposed as corrupt, undercut by the competence of the older female characters and severely punished. Even the classical detective novels that I have mentioned, and that are not as explicit as Holt Sawyer's, contain radical discourses of senescence. It is not unreasonable to think of Miss Silver and Dame Bradley in terms of stereotyping, but with an age- and gender-conscious perspective, it becomes clear that the authors are deploying stereotypes in unusual ways. Miss Silver may look like a Victorian governess, but this is part of her disguise, one that encourages other characters to judge her from an ageist viewpoint and thus reveal information that she uses to name the criminal.

Even with this dynamic in mind, the novels are not entirely radical; the detective's role is essentially to support the social status quo, and it is rarely suggested that older women are, for example, sexually attractive or physically imposing (as are contemporary younger sleuths). Dudley Edward's Jack Troutbeck is an exception to this rule. I have already mentioned her active sex life, and she explains to her younger sidekick, Robert Amiss, that she manages to manipulate the other characters' sympathies by "making the most of being fat and old."[78] However, even without Jack's commanding physical presence, older characters who are represented as independent, quick-witted, and awe-inspiring, in today's ageist culture, must be considered challenging in many respects.

The connection between representations of older sleuths and mythological figures helps to explain this literary oddity, although references to witches are scattered throughout novels that portray aged female protagonists. Sylvia Townsend Warner frames the appeal of this figure in a particularly insightful way in *Lolly Willowes* (1926). The eponymous heroine leaves her position in her brother's house as a middle-aged spinster aunt and, after making a pact with the devil, roams the countryside as a hedge witch. She explains her decision to him by pointing out that there few other roles that a woman can take on in a patriarchal society that allow her to feel of value: "Even if other people still find them quite safe and usual ... they know in their hearts how dangerous, how incalculable, how extraordinary they are."[79] Townsend Warner shows her character actually practicing witchcraft, but at a less literal level, imaginative access to an unrepentant outsider figure would seem increasingly useful as one ages and is pushed farther to society's margins. This idea helps explain the eldritch shadow that lurks in many narratives about female aging.

The importance of texts that feature female senescence can also be stressed in reference to archetypal imagery and the paradigm of the triple goddess. Without a mythology that includes the crone, representations of female experience are bound to remain incomplete. Authors who use this archetype are appropriating ancient images often overlooked in societies that venerate youth at the expense of age. In doing so, they provide a sense of literary continuity to the production of distinct representations of the senescent, offering images of womanhood that have little to do with notions of stagnation and decline. It is for this reason that I placed this chapter where it is. I wanted to finish by engaging with a collection of texts that clearly represent old age in a way that is radically different from dominant portraits.

# *Conclusion*

In the preceding chapters, I have analyzed texts that represent a variety of older protagonists and fictional worlds: from May Sarton's traumatic vision of an elderly character abandoned to her destructive fate in *As We Are Now*; through the gentle comedy of Barbara Pym's *Some Tame Gazelle*; to the ratiocinative works of Gladys Mitchell with their witch-like sleuth, Dame Bradley. While these novels express different hopes and anxieties about senescence, a number of thematic connections and obsessions have emerged. The most obvious link between the works, and perhaps the most important, is the situating of the older female protagonist at the heart of the narrative. Authors who use this maneuver work toward rending the silence, in both society and literature, which surrounds certain aspects of the older woman's life. Further, they provide her with a voice with which to challenge those that insist decline and stagnation are all there is to senescence.

I have interpreted the texts' refusal to replicate the dominant marginalization of the aged or reproduce conventional stereotypes as a political act, as does Barbara Frey Waxman in *From the Hearth to the Open Road*. Speaking of her chosen texts (that she labels *reifungsroman*), she states:

> We cannot underestimate the political power of *reifungsroman* to affect change in younger people's attitudes towards the elderly, in individuals' attitudes towards their own aging and in notions of appropriate social roles for elders.[1]

The sharing of knowledge to which she refers is reminiscent of the consciousness-raising associated with the second wave of feminism. While some may regard this as an outdated tactic, it is appropriate to think about the twenty-first-century reader's reaction to narratives about senescence in these terms. Producing this piece of work has certainly made me more aware of the limitations, and opportunities, that accrue to different stages of life and how this applies to the older woman mainly as a series of interdictions on her behavior and potential.

As I have demonstrated, authors do not rely on a singular strategy to challenge the current social construction of senescence and devise new representations of aging. For instance, May Sarton in *As We Are Now* and Doris Lessing in *The Diary of a Good Neighbour* engage with the stereotype that older people constantly moan about "nothing." Their protagonists do complain, and are angry, but this is because they have to deal with an uncontrollable body on a day-to-day basis, a task complicated by the lack of social support they receive. Here, the authors use a technique also discussed in relation to the older sleuth whereby they reclaim stereotypically aged traits. Sarton and Lessing may be more subtle in their approach than the detective fiction writers of the "Golden Age," but the dynamic is the same. Conversely, Angela Carter, in *Wise Children*, and Jenny Diski, in *Happily Ever After*, represent their protagonists in such a way as to shatter stereotypes. Both Dora Chance and Daphne Drummond flagrantly disregard norms and indulge their carnal fantasies, revealing the ludicrousness of presuming that all older women are bereft of sexual feelings. Lessing, this time in *Love, Again*, dismantles the same misconceived notion, but by representing the damage its internalization does to the older character who cannot express what she thinks of as inappropriate desires, leading to a nervous breakdown of sorts.

The previous chapters have intensively examined some of the ways in which writers react against stereotypes of aging. The examples I have just mentioned were provided to demonstrate my point that writers have been ingenious in creating diverse representations of older women, and they have approached established literary topics from unusual starting points. A subject such as female sexuality, for instance, is a standard of contemporary fiction, but not from the point of view of someone over sixty (or even a middle-aged woman). Further, certain experiences, such as those connected to a failing body, become more probable in old age and this is reflected in representations of the period (correspondingly, they are less likely to appear in narratives that hinge on younger characters).

Connected to this idea that certain topics are mainly portrayed in relation to a particular age group, is the fact that all the novels I have analyzed represent single women (on a pragmatic level, women statistically live longer than men and so outnumber them in senescence). Some characters live with their sisters or families and some live alone; they may have been widowed or have always been spinsters; but only Weldon's Felicity, in *Rhode Island Blues*, is part of a traditional couple. Barbara Pym's insistence that single female protagonists are worthy of literary interest is a response to their marginalization due to fiction's focus on romantic relationships. The novels featured in the preceding chapters do not exclude passionate love: At the very least, protagonists' reminiscences often include memories of earlier romantic liaisons, yet, in wider fictional terms, this remains the realm of the young. On a positive note, older characters could thus be regarded as freed from this "responsibility" and able to form different sorts of relationships and concentrate on cultivating their own selves.

Besides illustrating the fluidity of their subjectivity (their status as processual subjects), the characters' continual involvement with self-discovery is interpretable in a number of ways. Waxman and Nett see it as part of a spiritual female exploration that recurs in female fictions of senescence. Germaine Greer talks about the process in *The Change* when she describes older women, no longer constricted by social roles, as able to ponder who they are and simply enjoy being alive in a way that was lost to them at the onset of adolescence. Vita Sackville-West's character, Lady Slane, in *All Passion Spent* (1931), embarks on this path when she makes a marked break with the routines and concerns of her adult life. Recently widowed, she moves to a small house after a lifetime of duties as a wife and mother. She makes new friends and assesses her past, glad of the opportunity "simply to be herself."[2] Greer and Sackville-West's perspectives on both psychological and more prosaic journeying are remarkably similar (Greer uses *All Passion Spent* to illustrate her arguments about serenity in old age) and a valid way of interpreting the actions of a number of aged protagonists.

However, not all characters are able to emulate Lady Slane's worldly detachment. For instance, in *Love, Again,* Sarah's introspection is clearly an unwelcome effect of outside circumstance, while others, such as Caro in *As We Are Now* and Hagar in Margaret Laurence's *The Stone Angel*, never "spend" their passions. Ironically, neither did Sackville-West in her old age, as both Greer and Victoria Glendinning, in the introduction to the Virago edition of *All Passion Spent*, suggest.[3] So, while it would be pleasant to think that senescence is characterized by spiritual and sexual tranquility, the texts I have interpreted, which are committed to portraying older characters in diverse ways, suggest that this is not always the case.

While the novels I explored cover a variety of experiences, there are "gaps" in their approaches (although, obviously, authors are under no obligation to write about particular aspects of old age). Aged working-class characters and those fulfilling the role of grandmother seem fated to be described in stereotypical terms. Lessing's *The Diary of a Good Neighbour* may represent the effects of poverty, and Anita Desai's *Fire on the Mountain* (1977) the viewpoint of an Indian grandmother, but these texts are exceptions to the rule, as are, to a lesser extent, many of the novels I have analyzed. En masse, they point to the fact that society is still a long way from producing a realistic range of depictions of older women.

Literary criticism can help to challenge reductive images of aging, as Waxman eloquently explains: "Literary critics who enter the discourse of aging come under its spell, educe and analyze its powerful influence for change, and become partners with this radical discourse in its attempts to change attitudes toward older women and old age."[4] Yet, despite the fact that there is a gradually increasing amount of literary critical attention paid to the subject, the field can still best be defined as anophobic: concentrating on representations of younger characters at the expense of older ones.[5] Further texts that foreground older characters are often read without an awareness of ageist discourses, and so their more challenging elements are overlooked. Undeniably, there are many ways of interpreting a single novel, but in the same way that particular ones seem to cry out for a feminist reading, it is surprising how often critics, studying the same texts as I have, downplay age. This is a particularly noticeable discrepancy in criticism about classical detective fiction, although it happens to a lesser degree in a variety of instances.

While this remains the case, older women will continue to be misrepresented or ignored—a tragedy not only for the old, but for women of all ages, as the category of "woman" remains incomplete. Foucault's model of power, used to underpin my understanding of how society works to manipulate aged women, stresses that reverse discourse can only be effective if it recognizes the various guises of dominant discourse. If the specific networks of power that enmesh the older woman remain unrecognizable, they cannot be disrupted, and this results in feminism actually only fighting for the liberation of younger women. In order not to make a similar mistake, I have taken pains to stress, at various points, that the terms *women*, and consequently, *older women*, are used with the understanding that these categories are provisional and tactical. It allows for the assumption of a political stance without insisting that there is a finite number of "real needs" common to a large group of individuals that are simply waiting to be discovered. To this end, I have striven to avoid generalized assertions while recognizing recurrent experiences and attitudes (among the old themselves and society generally) that stem from contemporary paradigms of senescence.

Moving into the twenty-first century, it is more necessary than ever for female writers and theorists to think about the older protagonist, because, as Maroula Johannou states in *Contemporary Women's Writing* (2000), "the chasm in society between the prosperous and poor, the socially powerful and the excluded ... is deepening."[6] Interestingly, several recently published popular novels have represented older and younger characters as close friends: *Chocolat* by Joanna Harris (1999), *Miranda's Big Mistake* by Jill Mansell (1999), and *Thyme Out* by Katie Fforde (2000). In these three British bestsellers, the female protagonists are unrelated and choose to care for each other out of love rather than duty. Although the younger heroines' primary relationship is with a male character, the female friendship is only marginally less important, with the oldest of the pair portrayed as feisty, humorous and wise without being condescending. Perhaps these novels herald the beginning of a widespread refusal to Other the older woman or, at least, the authors' hopes that this is what the future holds.

Having broadly discussed my conclusions, I would finally like to acknowledge the fact that many of the novels I interpret are essentially optimistic in their outlook. But this is because in most other kinds of writing about the aged, pessimistic imaginings outweigh any other sort. The authors I discuss are certainly not naïve, and their narratives incorporate the harsher sides of aging, such as illness and social mistreatment. They simply refuse to cooperate with discourses that suggest that senescence is only to be defined by its more disagreeable aspects and that its trials could not be alleviated by a more humane society. Further, tragedies may strike the older characters, but they are often represented alongside life's more celebratory moments. It must not be forgotten that authors aim to fulfill their reader's desires, one of which is to see the older woman successfully negotiating social hostility. To achieve this sort of sympathetic reaction from the reader, the texts I have examined are adamant that older characters are valuable individuals who experience disappointment, contentment, anger and desire, as do we all. In fact, returning to a point I made in the introduction, they insist that older women are fully human, and the novels in this study have shown why this is a necessary assertion and one that has driven my engagement with them.

# Notes

## Introduction

1. Simone de Beauvoir, *Old Age*, trans. Patrick O' Brian (1970; London: André Deutsch, 1972) 1.
2. Virginia Woolf, *A Room of One's Own* (1929; London: Grafton Books, 1990) 41.
3. Bridget Hutter and Gillian Williams, "Controlling Women: The Normal and the Deviant," *Controlling Women: The Normal and the Deviant*, eds. Bridget Hutter and Gillian Williams (London: Croom Helm, 1981) 20.
4. However, retirement as a marker of adult aging is being rapidly destabilized, due to the increasingly common occurrence of early retirement, as discussed more fully in chapter 3.
5. This process is made more complex as the representations in which I am interested are not stereotypical, and so conventional notions of age-appropriate behavior are not always useful in deciding upon the age of a character.
6. Bill Bytheway, *Ageism* (Buckingham: Open University Press, 1995) 127.
7. Some may argue for the existence of male menopause, but there is no scientific evidence to support these claims.
8. Lilian S. Robinson, "Consciousness Lowering," rev. of *The Change*, by Germaine Greer, *Women's Review of Books*, January 10.4 (1993): 12.
9. Dorothy Perry Thompson, "African Womanist Revision in Gloria Naylor's *Mama Day* and *Baileys Café*," *Gloria Naylor's Early Novels*, ed. Margot Anne Kelley (Gainesville: University of Florida Press, 1999) 89–111. Although Naylor, as an African American, will refer to some of the same discourses as the writers in this study.
10. Paulina Palmer, *Narrative Practice and Feminist Theory* (Hemel Hempstead: Harvester Wheatsheaf, 1989) 3.
11. Shirley Neuman, introduction, *Re-Imagining Women: Representations of Women in Culture*, ed. Shirley Neuman (Toronto: University of Toronto Press, 1993) 4.
12. Nancy Fraser and Linda Nicholson, "Social Criticism Without Philosophy: An Encounter between Feminism and Postmodernism," Thomas Docherty, ed., *Postmodernism: A Reader* (London, Harvester Wheatsheaf, 1993) 423. Fraser and Nicholson are quoting Gayle Rubin, "The Traffic in Women" (1975).
13. Sally Robinson, *Engendering the Subject: Gender and Self-Representation in Contemporary Women's Fiction* (New York: University of New York Press, 1991) 189.
14. M. E. Bailey, "Foucauldian Feminism: Contesting Bodies, Sexuality and Identity," *Up Against Foucault*, ed. Caroline Ramazanoglu (London: Routledge, 1994) 119.
15. Foucault's later work was not translated into English until the 1980s.
16. Michel Foucault, *An Introduction*, trans. Robert Hurley (1976; London: Allen Lane, 1979), vol. 1 of *The History of Sexuality*, 88–89.
17. Sandra Lee Bartky, *Femininity and Domination: Studies in the Phenomonology of Oppression* (London: Routledge, 1990) 76. Bartky concentrates on the discourses surrounding the production of the physical appearance of femininity at this point in the text.
18. Normalization also exerts pressure on men, but they are allowed greater room for autonomous behavior. Again, not all men have the same amount of room in which to

maneuver as class, age, race, and sexuality interact with gender to produce a hierarchy of masculine power.
19. Barbara Pym, *Quartet in Autumn* (London: Macmillan, 1977) 134.
20. Pym, *Quartet* 218
21. Foucault, *An Introduction* 95.
22. Foucault, *An Introduction* 96. Foucault says that there have been "radical ruptures" in history, but that the majority of resistances are more fragmented and specific than that.
23. It is worth briefly mentioning that novels will obviously not want to contest all dominant discourse. Murder, for example, is framed as an unacceptable action and a relatively small number of authors would want to change this cultural mores.
24. Bailey 115.
25. Madan Sarup, *Identity, Culture and the Postmodern World* (Edinburgh: Edinburgh University Press, 1996) 61.
26. Paoletti's research also leads her to state that "being an older woman" could "describe antithetical practices and discourses," and offers a further example of the phenomenon when considering the group's attitude toward the category "old" (xi). At times, individuals disassociated themselves from the label because of the largely negative connotations resonant in its usage. Yet, on occasions when governmental benefits aimed at senior citizens are under discussion, members of the group strategically label themselves "elderly" in order to validate their claims for various allowances. Paoletti's observations illustrate the ways in which individual subjectivity is contradictory, strategic, and under a continual process of negotiation within specific social situations. Isabella Paoletti. *Being an Older Woman: A Study in the Social Production of Identity* (London: Lawrence Erlbaum Associates, 1998).
27. For example, Woolf presents her "looking-glass" theory of the social construction of male and female roles in chapter 2 of *A Room of One's Own* (1929), and the introduction to *The Second Sex* (1949) provides a succinct summary of many of the arguments about female identity developed by later feminists.
28. Susan Bordo, *Unbearable Weight: Feminism, Western Culture and the Body* (Berkeley: University of California Press, 1993) 282.
29. Fay Weldon, *Rhode Island Blues* (London: Flamingo, 2000) 140.

30. Christine Battersby, *Gender and Genius: Towards a Female Aesthetic* (London: Women's Press, 1989) 211–213.
31. Battersby 214.
32. Robinson, *Engendering* 3.
33. Robinson, *Engendering* 7. Robinson is quoting Linda Alcoff from "Cultural Feminism Versus Poststructuralism: The Identity Crisis in Feminist Theory" (1988). It is worth pointing out that Robinson's paradigm is built on the conception of identity as strategic and the larger category of "woman" as mobile and temporary, changing its meaning in response to various historical and cultural pressures.
34. Robinson, *Engendering* 9.
35. Robinson, *Engendering* 8.
36. Foucault, *An Introduction* 21.
37. Foucault, *An Introduction* 27.
38. Neuman 15. She is quoting Nicole Brossard, *The Aerial Letter* (1988).
39. Pym, *Quartet* 3.
40. Chris Weedon, *Faminist Practice & Poststructuralist Theory* (Oxford: Blackwell, 1987) 91.

## Chapter 1

1. Alan Walker and Tony Maltby, *Ageing Europe* (Buckingham: Open University Press, 1997) 10. On a European scale, they state that at the turn of the twentieth century, one in twenty people were over the age of sixty-five; in 1966, the figure was one in seven people; and in 2020, the predicted proportion is one in five.
2. Found in a joke shop in Newquay, August 2001.
3. Margaret Laurence, *The Stone Angel* (1964; London: Virago, 1993) 3.
4. Sara Maitland, afterword, *The Stone Angel* by Margaret Laurence (1964; London: Virago, 1993) 268.
5. See Sara Arber and Jay Ginn "Choice and Constraint in the Retirement of Older Married Women," *Connecting Gender and Ageing: A Sociological Approach*, eds. Sara Arber and Jay Ginn (Buckingham: Open University Press, 1995) 85, for further information on the subject. The government is intending to raise the retirement age for women to sixty-five in the year 2010.
6. Bytheway, *Ageism* 104.
7. Working patterns are changing according to gerontologists Anne Jamieson and Christina Victor in "Theory and Con-

cepts in Social Gerontology," *Critical Approaches to Ageing and Later Life*, eds. Anne Jamieson, Sarah Harper and Christina Victor (Buckingham: Open University Press, 1997) 175–187. They argue that more people are taking early retirement or being made redundant, and factors such as gender, education, and type of employment are becoming integral to retirement decisions. Therefore, in the future, retirement age is less likely to act as an indicator of social expectations of the senescent.

8. Bytheway, *Ageism* 9.

9. Bytheway, in "Talking About Age: the Theoretical Basis of Social Gerontology," pinpoints six methods of defining age that are based on chronology, description, relations, body, pressures, and biography. For a further explanation of these terms see the essay "Talking About Age: The Theoretical Basis of Social Gerontology," Jamieson, Harper and Victor 7–15.

10. Laurence 23.

11. The differing social expectations of the effort that men and women should put into making themselves beautiful, is discussed, for example, in *The Beauty Myth* (1990) by Naomi Wolf.

12. Betty Friedan, *The Fountain of Age* (London: Vintage, 1994). Friedan analyzes the age-as-disease model fully in chapter 13 of the text.

13. Friedan 18.

14. A Foucauldian analysis of their hypothesis might also suggest that they have mistakenly read a result of ageism, the social marginalization of older subjects, as a source (in a similar way to those theorists who believe the repressive hypothesis characterizes the deployment of discourses of sexuality rather than it's being an effect of an incitement to discourse).

15. Mike Featherstone and Mike Hepworth, "The Mask of Ageing and the Postmodern Life Course," *The Body—Social Process and Cultural Theory*, eds. Mike Featherstone, Mike Hepworth and Bryan S. Turner (London: Sage, 1991) 382.

16. Simon Biggs, "Choosing Not to Be Old? Masks, Bodies and Identity Management in Later Life," *Ageing and Society* 17 (1997): 559.

17. Paul Thompson, "'I Don't Feel Old': Subjective Ageing and the Search for Meaning in Later Life," *Ageing and Society* 12 (1992): 27.

18. Barbara Macdonald and Cynthia Rich, *Look Me in the Eye* (London: Women's Press, 1983) 55–56.

19. Weldon, *Rhode Island Blues* 121.

20. Judith Butler, "Imitation and Gender Subordination," *Inside/Out*, ed. Diana Fuss (London: Routledge, 1991) 13–14.

21. Butler, "Imitation" 20.

22. Shevy Healey, "Confronting Ageism: A Must for Mental Health," *Faces of Women and Ageing*, eds. Nancy D. Davis, Esther Rothblum, et.al. (New York: Hawthorne Press, 1993) 52.

23. Walker and Maltby 122.

24. Julie McMullin, "Theorizing Age and Gender Relations," eds. Arber and Ginn, *Connecting* 40.

25. This is a similar situation to that described by Foucault in the first volume of *The History of Sexuality*, in which he explains that the belief in a repressive hypothesis of sexuality resulted in questions about sex being directed to the wrong people, thus obscuring the mechanisms of power.

26. Simone de Beauvoir, *The Second Sex*, trans. H.M. Parshley (1949; London: Picador, 1988). Her work still remains the most comprehensive feminist account of the female life cycle produced to date.

27. Jean Grimshaw successfully argues this point in her unpublished paper, "Aging, Embodiment and Identity," 2001.

28. Kathleen Woodward, "Tribute to the Older Woman: Psychoanalysis, Feminism and Ageism," *Images of Aging: Cultural Representations of Later Life*, eds. Mike Featherstone and Andrew Wernick (London: Routledge, 1995) 91.

29. Beauvoir, *Old Age* 284. Although this is probably true of many other metamorphoses that happen throughout the course of life, such as puberty and parenthood, death (and old age as a preamble to this event) is construed as too mysterious a subject to be able to discuss constructively.

30. In *Old Age*, Beauvoir does provide some examples of extraordinary individuals who have continued their projects until death but they are all male.

31. Simone de Beauvoir, "The Age of Discretion," *The Woman Destroyed*, trans. Patrick O'Brian (1967; London: Flamingo, 1984) 7.

32. Beauvoir, "The Age of Discretion" 9.

33. Beauvoir, "The Age of Discretion" 71.

34. Beauvoir, "The Age of Discretion" 17.

35. Beauvoir, *Old Age* 13.

36. Beauvoir, *Old Age* 542
37. Susan Sontag, "The Double Standard of Ageing," *The Ageing Population*, eds. Vida Carver and Penny Liddiard (London: Hodder and Stoughton, 1987) 73.
38. Naomi Wolf, in *The Beauty Myth* (1991), argues that the thinness prized by contemporary society promotes a feminine ideal that calls for a restricted diet, which supports patriarchal societies because women do not have the energy to put into political activism. If we also take into account the fact that it is not just thinness but youth that is prized, it could be suggested that the effort involved in trying to maintain its appearance contributes toward preventing older women from, among other things, campaigning for improved social status or, at the very least, feeling comfortable with themselves.
39. Fay Weldon, *Praxis* (London: Hodder and Stoughton, 1978) 157–158.
40. Weldon, *Rhode Island Blues* 70.
41. Gari Lesnoff-Caravaglia, "Double Stigmata: Female and Old," *The World of Older Women—Conflicts and Resolutions*, ed. Gari Lesnoff-Caravaglia (New York: Human Sciences Press, 1984) 11.
42. Lesnoff-Caravaglia 14.
43. Paul Higgs, "Citizenship Theory and Old Age: From Social Rights to Surveillance," Jamieson, Harper and Victor 128.
44. Beauvoir talks extensively about connections between senescence and poverty in *Old Age*.
45. Pat Barker, *Union Street* (London: Virago, 1982) 232.
46. Barker 260.
47. The Chance sisters, in Angela Carter's *Wise Children* (London: Chatto and Windus, 1991), could be described as working-class, but they are connected to a wealthy family, and as performers, seem almost a class apart.
48. Friedan 112.
49. Gail Wilson, "'I'm the Eyes and She's the Arms:' Changes in Gender Roles in Advanced Age," Arber and Ginn, *Connecting* 100.
50. See chapter 16 of *The Fountain of Age* for a more in-depth explanation of this idea.
51. Bytheway, *Ageism* 21.
52. Jenny Morris, "Feminism and Disability," *Feminist Review* 43 (1993): 66–67.
53. Morris, "Feminism" 68.
54. However, this is probably because of the effectiveness of work produced by theorists such as herself who make their points in strong enough language to make people stop and listen.
55. Maureen Cain, "Foucault, Feminism and Feeling: What Foucault Can and Cannot Contribute to Feminist Epistemology," Ramazanoglu 94.
56. Collette V. Browne, *Women, Feminism and Aging* (New York: Springer, 1998) 84.
57. Macdonald and Rich 39.
58. Macdonald and Rich 74.
59. Germaine Greer, *The Change* (London: Penguin, 1992) 270.
60. Greer 269.
61. Audre Lorde, "Age, Race, Class and Sex: Women Redefining Difference," *The Audre Lorde Companion* (London: HarperCollins, 1996) 164.
62. Kate Soper, "Productive Contradictions," Ramazanoglu 34.
63. Richard Fallis, "Grow Old Along with Me: Images of Older People in British and American Literature," *Perceptions of Aging in Literature*, eds. Dorotka Bagnell and P. Spencer Soper (New York: Greenwood Press, 1989) 42.
64. Beauvoir, *Old Age*, 210.
65. Beauvoir, *Old Age*, 89.
66. Celeste Loughman, "Novels of Senescence: A New Naturalism," *The Gerontologist* 17.1 (1977): 79.
67. Emily M. Nett, "The Naked Soul Comes Closer to the Surface: Old Age in the Gender Mirror of Contemporary Novels," *Women's Studies: An Interdisciplinary Journal* 18.2-3 (1990) 179. She credits Beauvoir in *Old Age* as providing a reading of Junichero Tanizaki's *Diary of a Mad Old Man* that stresses its obsession with sexual desire.
68. Nett 185.
69. Nett 188.
70. Barbara Frey Waxman, *From the Hearth to the Open Road: A Feminist Study of Aging in Contemporary Literature* (London: Greenwood Press, 1990) 2.
71. Waxman, *From the Hearth* 2.
72. Waxman's concept of the *Reifungsroman* arises from an engagement with the established genre of the *Bildungsroman*. Where the latter genre is a novel of youthful development, the former concerns the psychological, and sometimes more literal, journey of older protagonists.
73. Waxman, *From the Hearth* 187.

74. Kathleen Woodward, "Age-Work in American Culture," *American Literary History* 6.4 (1994): 779. She is citing Wayne Booth, *The Art of Growing Older* (n.p. : Poseidon Press, 1992).
75. Woodward, "Age-Work in America" 780.
76. Paoletti, 28.
77. Bailey 105. She is citing Michel Foucault in *Michel Foucault: Power/Knowledge* (1980).
78. Bordo, *Unbearable Weight* 298–299
79. Waxman, *To Live in the Center* 7.

## Chapter 2

1. Friedan 479.
2. Graham Stokes, *On Being Old: The Psychology of Later Life* (London: Falmer Press, 1992) 152.
3. Loughman 84.
4. Nett 182.
5. Doris Lessing's *The Diary of a Good Neighbour* (1984) can be found, with its sequel *If the Old Could...*, in one volume entitled *The Diaries of Jane Somers* (London: Michael Joseph, 1984) 13–261.
6. Waxman, *From the Hearth* 148.
7. Waxman, *From the Hearth* 148.
8. Jenny Morris, *Pride Against Prejudice: Transforming Attitudes to Disability* (London: Women's Press, 1991).
9. Morris, *Pride* 85.
10. Morris, *Pride* 88.
11. Barbara Frey Waxman, in *From the Hearth to the Open Road*, uses subtitles within her chapters that provide more information than just the title of the novel. I found this practice helpful in reading her study and so have adopted it.
12. Gayle Greene, *Doris Lessing: The Poetics of Change* (Michigan: University of Michigan Press, 1994) 194.
13. Lessing, *Diary* 39.
14. *The Canopus in Argos: Archives*—comprises of the *Shikasta* (1979), *The Marriages Between Zones Three, Four, and Five* (1980), *The Sirian Experiments* (1981), *The Making of the Representative for Planet Eight* (1982), and *The Sentimental Agents* (1983).
15. *If the Old Could...* focuses on Janna's relationship with, and eventual abandonment of, a married man.
16. Ruth Whittaker, *Doris Lessing* (London: Macmillan, 1998) 119. She quotes Jonathan Yardley in "Lessing Is More: An Unknown Author" 1985.
17. Lessing, preface, *The Diaries of Jane Somers* (London: Michael Joseph, 1984) 10.
18. For more details about the author's ideological shifts see Moira Monteith, "Doris Lessing and the Politics of Violence," *Where No Man Has Gone Before: Women and Science Fiction*, ed. Lucie Armitt (London: Routledge 1991).
19. Lessing, *Diaries* 21.
20. Lessing, *Diaries* 33.
21. Greene 193.
22. Lessing, *Diaries* 34.
23. By the end of the novel, Janna actively enjoys the company of older women to the extent that she concerns herself with two other older protagonists brought to her attention by a social worker, Vera Rogers (whom she befriends because of their shared mutual concern about Maudie).
24. Monteith 68.
25. Monteith 71.
26. Lessing, *Diaries* 123–124.
27. Lessing, *Diaries* 121.
28. Sue Scott and David Morgan, "Bodies in a Social Landscape," *Body Matters*, eds. Sue Scott and David Morgan (London: Falmer Press, 1993) 14.
29. Lessing, *Diaries* 135.
30. Mike Featherstone, "The Body in Consumer Culture," *Theory, Culture and Society* 1.2 (1982): 18.
31. Mike Featherstone and Mike Hepworth, "Ageing and Inequality: Consumer Culture and the New Middle Age," *Rethinking Social Inequality*, ed. D. Robbins, et al. (London: Gower, 1982) 113.
32. Hutter and Williams, "Controlling Women" 28.
33. Lessing, *Diaries* 163–164.
34. Lessing, *Diaries* 155.
35. Lessing, *Diaries* 63.
36. Chris Phillipson, "Women in Later Life: Patterns of Control and Subordination," *Controlling Women: The Normal and the Deviant*, eds. Bridget Hutter and Gillian Williams (London: Croom Helm, 1981) 198. As with many current theories about senescence, this connection may change in the future with a larger prevalence of women in the workplace, although this is debatable as ideologically women are still positioned as responsible for child rearing and housework (the house husband remains a cultural anomaly).
37. Laurence 64.
38. Margaret Forster, *Have the Men Had Enough?* (London: Penguin, 1989) 144.

39. Forster 144–145.
40. Morris 27.
41. Morris 29.
42. Morris 69.
43. Lessing, *Diaries* 260.
44. Sarton uses the same name for a character in the eponymously titled novel *The Education of Harriet Hatfield* (1990), which is discussed in a later chapter.
45. May Sarton, *As We Are Now* (1973; London: Women's Press, 1992) 9.
46. Sarton, *As We Are Now* 10.
47. The other texts that she mentioned alongside *As We Are Now* are *Mrs. Stevens Hears the Mermaids Singing* (1965) and *Faithful Are the Wounds* (1955).
48. Karen Saum, "The Art of Poetry XXXII: May Sarton," *Conversations with May Sarton*, ed. Earl G. Ingersol (Jackson: Mississippi UP, 1991) 113.
49. Laurence 124.
50. Sarton, *As We Are Now* 50.
51. Sarton, *As We Are Now* 70.
52. Sarton, *As We Are Now* 81.
53. Sarton, *As We Are Now* 13–14.
54. Sarton, *As We Are Now* 81.
55. Saum 113.
56. Stokes 137.
57. Stokes 142. This is useful information if only because it points to the idea that forgetfulness, for example, does not necessarily lead to a more serious type of dementia. Caro, though, begins to think that she is going mad because she occasionally forgets things. Dominant misconceptions about mental illness in senescence would encourage this reasoning, while in fact there are no certainties that the two factors are linked, as many of the causes and symptoms of Alzheimer's, for instance, remain unclear.
58. Stokes 139. These figures are collected from studies carried out in Britain, America and Japan.
59. Barbara Frey Waxman, *To Live in the Center of the Moment: Literary Autobiographies of Aging* (Charlottesville: University Press of Virginia, 1997) 2.
60. Ellen Newton, *This Bed My Centre* (London: Virago, 1980) 94.
61. For an interesting discussion on the subject, see Evelyn McEwen, "What's Special About Being Old?" Arber and Ginn, *Connecting* 89–93.
62. One nationwide study of American nursing homes, cited by Frank Glendenning, found that as many as seven percent of the sample used chemical and physical restraints. For more details see Frank Glendenning, "The Mistreatment of Elderly People in Residential Institutions," *The Abuse of Care*, ed. Roger Clough (London: Whiting and Birch, 1996) Clough 38.
63. Newton 106.
64. This move is not covered by *This Bed My Centre* but explained in notes about the author.
65. Sarton, *As We Are Now* 85.
66. Nursing the aged falls under the category of "warehousing": taking care of basic needs and prolonging lives, rather than curing illness. As such, the job has a low level of status and prestige compared with other tasks in the medical profession.
67. Helen Evers, "Care or Custody? The Experiences of Women Patients in Longstay Geriatric Wards," Hutter and Williams, *Controlling Women* 114. The three stereotypes that she identifies as most often used are the "Dear Old Gran," who does not challenge the nurses' power, is cheerful and fits in with routines; "Poor Old Nellie," who is senile but neither popular nor unpopular, although she takes up a lot of time; and "Awkward Alice," who is alert but critical. Caro is treated by Harriet and Rose as the latter sort of older woman.
68. Sarton, *As We Are Now* 16.
69. Sarton, *As We Are Now* 46.
70. Sarton, *As We Are Now* 18.
71. Charlotte Perkins Gilman, "The Yellow Wall-paper," *The Yellow Wall-paper and Other Stories*, ed. Robert Shulman (1890; London: Oxford University Press, 1998) 7.
72. Gilman, "Yellow Wall-paper" 8.
73. Gilman, "Yellow Wall-paper" 8.
74. Charlotte Perkins Gilman, "Why I Wrote 'The Yellow Wall-paper'" *The Yellow Wall-paper and Other Stories*, ed. Robert Shulman (1913; London: Oxford University Press, 1998 ) 330.
75. Forster 154.
76. Sarton, *As We Are Now* 106.
77. Saum 113.
78. Sarton, *As We Are Now* 19.
79. This extract is taken from the back of *As We Are Now*.
80. Waxman, *From the Hearth* 156.
81. Waxman, *From the Hearth* 183.
82. May Sarton, *The Reckoning* (1978; London: Women's Press, 1984) 10.
83. Saum 114.
84. Sarton, *The Reckoning* 10–11.
85. Kay Bonetti, "An Interview with May

Sarton," *Conversations with May Sarton*, ed. Earl G. Ingersol (Jackson: Mississippi UP, 1991) 86.
86. Saum 113–114.
87. Sarton, *The Reckoning* 183.
88. Sarton, *The Reckoning* 196.
89. Laurence 62.
90. Annis Pratt argues this in chapter 8 of *Archetypal Patterns in Women's Fiction* (Brighton: Harvester Press, 1982).
91. Simon J. Williams, "The Vicissitudes of Embodiment Across the Chronic Illness Trajectory," *Body and Society*, 2.2 (1996): 32.
92. Williams 33. He states that this process is common to both the chronically and the terminally ill.
93. Williams 32.
94. Pratt 136.
95. Credited to a New England tombstone.
96. Sarton, *The Reckoning* 101.
97. Laurence 216.
98. Laurence 3.
99. Sarton, *The Reckoning* 88.
100. Williams 26.
101. Sarton, *The Reckoning* 130.
102. Sarton, *The Reckoning* 130–131.
103. Sarton, *The Reckoning* 239.
104. Sarton, *The Reckoning* 254.
105. Laurence 136.
106. Laurence 264.
107. Dylan Thomas. "Do not go gentle into that good night," *The Dylan Thomas Omnibus* (1952; London: Phoenix Press, 2000) 128.
108. Lessing, *Diaries* 130.
109. Bridget Macdonald warns of the problems that will arise for women if they continue to uncomplainingly bear the responsibility for the formal care of older dependents. She writes in light of predictions about the aging population and the supposition that governments will not make the necessary provisions for this occurrence without economic recompense. She further believes that feminism, as a political movement, has not supported demands for institutional recognition of the caretaker's role. See "Exploitation by Compassion" in *Look Me in the Eye*, 43–52 for further details.

## Chapter 3

1. Peter Oberg, "The Absent Body—A Social Gerontological Paradox," *Ageing and Society* 16 (1996): 704.
2. This model is equally applicable to the same individual at different stages of their life as it is to different generations.
3. Carole S. Vance, "Pleasure and Danger: Toward a Politics of Sexuality," *Pleasure and Danger: Exploring Female Sexuality*, ed. Carole S. Vance (London: Routledge, 1984) 13.
4. Marianne Hester, *Lewd Women and Wicked Witches* (London: Routledge, 1993) 197.
5. James Sharpe, *Instruments of Darkness: Witchcraft in England 1550–1750* (London: Hamish Hamilton, 1996) 172.
6. Lois Banner, *In Full Flower—Ageing Women, Power and Sexuality* (New York: Vintage Books, 1993) 17.
7. Elizabeth Wurtzel writes eloquently about the treatment of the sexuality of the younger woman in *Bitch* (London: Quartet Books, 1988).
8. Anthony Synott, *The Body Social: Symbolism, Self and Society* (London: Routledge, 1993) 4.
9. Synott gestures to Merleau-Ponty and Beauvoir but decides their work is strictly philosophy rather than sociology. This classification can be supported but is too reductive of the influence their ideas have had upon diverse areas of cultural analysis.
10. Oberg 73.
11. Synott 1.
12. Synott 4.
13. Doris Lessing, *Love, Again* (London: Flamingo, 1996) 2.
14. Lessing, *Love, Again* 8.
15. Lessing, *Love, Again* 8.
16. Synott 4.
17. Synott 9.
18. Paradigms changed over time and according to how much importance was placed on Jesus' treatment of the body (his healing of the sick and feeding of the hungry). For a fuller summary of the body in Christian, and philosophical, thought more generally, see chapter 1 of Synott's *The Body Social*.
19. Oberg 703.
20. Lessing, *Love, Again* 41–42.
21. Bordo, *Unbearable* 5.
22. Bordo, *Unbearable* 8.
23. Lessing, *Love, Again* 136.
24. Lessing, *Love, Again* 137.
25. Lessing, *Love, Again* 137.
26. Lessing, *Love, Again* 3.
27. Lessing, *Love, Again* 136.

28. Lessing, *Love, Again* 106–107.
29. Lessing, *Love, Again* 139.
30. Oberg 707.
31. Bordo, *Unbearable* 287. She demonstrates her comprehension of the postmodern body in her reading of AIDS: "On the one hand, sex has become deadly; on the other hand, it continues to be advertised as the pre-eminent source of ecstasy, power and self-fulfilment."
32. She draws parallels with the feminist suspicion about the postmodern dissolution of the subject whereby the female subject was erased before it had a chance to speak.
33. Bordo, *Unbearable* 25.
34. Lessing, *Love, Again* 6.
35. Bordo, *Unbearable* 30.
36. Banner 324.
37. Banner 322.
38. Oberg 706.
39. Oberg 708.
40. Bordo, *Unbearable* 298.
41. Lessing, *Love, Again* 231.
42. Lessing, *Love, Again* 236.
43. Ruth Saxton, "The Female Body Veiled: From Crocus to Clitoris," published in 1994, notes Lessing's use of mirror scenes in an earlier novel, *The Summer Before the Dark*—not in itself remarkable as the mirror is a leitmotif in fictions of aging. Saxton argues, though, that its middle-aged protagonist, Kate, also demonstrates a changing attitude to her reflection as the narrative progresses. Initially, she is concerned about her appearance but learns to ignore the patriarchal "internalized voice that usually dominated the mirror." Saxton then asserts that Lessing conceives of "the sexually active body" as a "way station to female change, growth and maturity." This is a fair assessment of *The Summer Before the Dark* (1973), but *Love, Again*, which focuses on a protagonist who is ten years older, demonstrates that the subjugation of the body by the mind is not a finite or static state for the older woman. Therefore, Lessing can be read as realizing that there are no guarantees that the older sexual body can be easily quashed. See Ruth Saxton, "The Female Body Veiled: From Crocus to Clitoris," *Woolf and Lessing: Breaking the Mold*, eds. Ruth Saxton and Jean Tobin (New York: St Martin's Press, 1994).
44. Lessing, *Love, Again* 237.
45. This is also relevant, as the facial metaphor, the "mask of ageing," characterizes the older person's refusal of the whole body.
46. Synott 73.
47. Synott 75.
48. Roberta Galler, "The Myth of the Perfect Body," Vance, *Pleasure* 168.
49. Lessing, *Love, Again* 136.
50. Lessing, *Love, Again* 136–137.
51. Galler 166.
52. Lessing, *Love, Again* 298.
53. Lessing, *Love, Again* 299.
54. Lessing, *Love, Again* 329–330.
55. Saxton 121.
56. Saxton 122.
57. Greer 346.
58. Carter's text is the only one in the study that could be classed as postmodern. This was not a conscious decision, as when choosing texts my main priority was to find novels that intelligently represented the older woman, and they seem to have predominantly come from the realist or crime-fiction tradition. Nonetheless, feminist and postmodernist theory are not incompatible, and postmodernist fiction can helpfully question dominant ageist and sexist discourse. Further, Carter's unequivocal pedigree as one of the foremost feminist writers in the late twentieth-century would make trying to "prove" this issue a pointless exercise.
59. Catherine Belsey, *Desire: Love Stories in Western Culture* (Oxford: Blackwell, 1994) 7.
60. Judith Butler, *Gender Trouble* (London: Routledge, 1990) 149.
61. Lucie Armitt, *Contemporary Women's Fiction and the Fantastic* (London: Macmillan, 2000) 185.
62. Armitt 185.
63. Angela Carter, *Wise Children* (London: Chatto and Windus, 1991) 195.
64. Sarah Gamble, *Angela Carter: Writing from the Front Line* (Edinburgh: Edinburgh University Press, 1997) 180.
65. Carter, *Wise Children* 171.
66. Foucault, *An Introduction* 72.
67. This confessional urge also produces a myriad of pleasures: "What sustains our eagerness to speak in terms of repression is doubtless this opportunity to speak out against the powers that be to utter truths and promise bliss, to live together in enlightenment, liberation and manifold pleasures." Foucault, *An Introduction* 7.
68. Foucault, *An Introduction* 43.
69. Foucault, *An Introduction* 48.

70. Vance, "Pleasure" 19.
71. Colette, *The Last of Chéri*, trans. Roger Senhouse (1926; London: Penguin, 1954) 246.
72. For older men, who can potentially become fathers at any age, they could always be regarded as wasting their sexual desire on aged women.
73. Foucault, *An Introduction* 12.
74. Butler, *Gender* 140.
75. Belsey 4.
76. Belsey 5.
77. While this may be seen as a passé notion, it remains firmly ingrained in discourses of sexuality. Biological perspectives perpetuate this dualism in literature that describes sperm as swimming toward the waiting ovum (the same action could centralize the ovum and describe it as drawing in the sperm). At the other end of the spectrum, in British schools, it would still be unusual for a girl to ask a boy for a date, (and, to a lesser extent, for women to propose to men).
78. Bordo, *Unbearable* 293.
79. Carter, *Wise Children* 6.
80. Carter, *Wise Children* 192.
81. Carter, *Wise Children* 192.
82. Carter, *Wise Children* 192.
83. Angela Carter, *The Passion of New Eve* (1977; London: Virago, 1990) 5.
84. Carter, *Wise Children* 197.
85. Carter, *Wise Children* 83.
86. Gamble 182–183.
87. Carter, *Wise Children* 220.
88. There are hints in the text that Peregrine slept with her when she was thirteen, but she cannot remember if this is just memory or fantasy.
89. Carter, *Wise Children* 222.
90. Banner 314.
91. From her text *Erotic Welfare: Sexual Theory and Politics in the Age of Epidemic* (London: Routledge, 1993). It was published posthumously and edited by Judith Butler.
92. Singer 145.
93. Singer 152.
94. Singer 154.
95. Singer 153.
96. Jenny Diski, *Happily Ever After* (London: Hamish Hamilton, 1991) 18.
97. Diski 242.
98. Belsey 11.
99. Belsey 209.
100. Diski 188.
101. Belsey 3.
102. Banner 9.
103. It is worth mentioning at this point, the suggestion that the older woman/younger man partnership is one of the answers to the "man shortage" that occurs because of the disparity in numbers between older men and women. Banner, though, among others, pertinently asks in *In Full Flower* whether it is actually a problem, suggesting that it potentially could continue to divide women into those who "have a man" and those who do not. As this chapter has already stressed, it is harmful to suggest that all older women should be involved in sexual activity or that the paradigm of compulsory heterosexuality should be extended to account for the senescent. Therefore, it is inappropriate to frame the older woman/younger man relationship as a social remedy for frustrated spinsters.
104. Weldon, *Rhode Island Blues* 108.
105. Weldon, *Rhode Island Blues* 325.
106. Belsey 6–7.
107. While on the subject of the specific to the general, I want to point out that homosexuality, race, class, ethnicity and disability complicate models of sexuality in senescence. However, because these factors are rarely mentioned in fiction, I am not going to discuss them here, but believe they will, and should be, considered in future literary gerontological studies.
108. Ann Snitow, Christine Stansell, and Sharon Thompson, introduction, *Desire: The Politics of Sexuality*, eds. Ann Snitow, Christine Stansell, and Sharon Thompson (London: Virago, 1984) 31.
109. Deirdre English talks about the way in which the freedom offered by the pill has been neutralized by patriarchal discourse in her essay, tellingly entitled, "The Fear That Feminism Will Free Men First." She examines a particular strategy that Foucault recognizes in his work, whereby dominant discourse absorbs the radical aspects of reverse discourse. English suggests that the pill allowed for the ideological separation of intercourse and reproduction, but that, consequently, men felt "allowed" to break the "sex contract" that had previously existed. The implication of this social contract was that if a man had intercourse with a woman and she fell pregnant, his responsibility was as great as hers, and therefore he would provide financial and emotional support. Obviously this "con-

tract" was not always honored, but with the advent of oral contraception, a child that a man did not actively want could be defined as not his responsibility. (Perhaps this is demonstrated in the perceived need for the intervention of the Child Support Agency to attempt to locate absent fathers in order to exact financial support for their children.) See "The Fear That Feminism Will Free Men First," Snitow, Stansell, and Thompson, *Desire* 97–102.

110. Snitow, Stansell and Thompson, introduction 34.
111. Snitow, Stansell and Thompson, introduction 32.
112. Diski 7.
113. Diski 133.
114. Diski 131–132.
115. Diski 133.
116. William Wharton, *Last Lovers* (London: Penguin, 1991) 216.
117. Diski 134.
118. Diski 191.
119. Diski 157.
120. Diski 135.
121. Diski 136
122. Diski 137.
123. Elizabeth Cairns, "Echoes," *Singing in Tune with Time: Stories and Poems About Ageing* (London: Virago, 1993) 206.
124. Carter, *Wise Children* 221.
125. Carter, *Wise Children* 5.
126. Carter, *Wise Children* 38.
127. Belsey, 38.
128. Belsey, 40.
129. Diski 240.
130. Banner 331.
131. Banner 331.
132. Banner 332.
133. Snitow, Stansell and Thompson, introduction 35.
134. Lessing, *Love, Again* 4.
135. Belsey 3.
136. Maya Angelou, *Even the Stars Look Lonesome* (London: Virago, 1998) 85.

## Chapter 4

1. Nicholas Shakespeare, "Bags of Giddyap Boyo," rev. of *Time After Time* by Molly Keane, *The Times* 13 October 1983: 9. The image originally comes from comes from chapter 5 of *Time After Time* (London: Abacus, 1985).
2. Thompson, "I Don't Feel Old" 39. Thompson is one of the gerontologists who talk about the "constant reconstruction" that takes place in later life.
3. Margeret M. Baltes and Laura L. Carstensen, "The Process of Successful Ageing," *Ageing and Society* 16.4 (1996): 406.
4. Baltes and Carstensen 409.
5. Baltes and Carstensen 413. It is worth stressing that in order to challenge earlier gerontological biases toward "decline and loss," they focus on "successful" ways of aging.
6. Baltes and Carstensen 398.
7. Michel de Certeau, *The Practice of Everyday Life*, trans. Steven Rendell (1980; Berkeley: University of California Press, 1984), vol. 1 of *The Practice of Everyday Life*, xi.
8. Certeau xi.
9. Jeremy Aherne, *Michel de Certeau: Interpretation and Its Other* (London: Polity Press, 1995) 159.
10. Certeau xiv.
11. Certeau xvii.
12. Macdonald and Rich 74.
13. Kate Fullbrook, "Jane Austen and the Comic Negative," *Women Reading Women's Writing*, ed. Sue Roe (Brighton: Harvester Press Limited, 1987) 41.
14. Regina Barreca, introduction, *Last Laughs: Perspectives on Women and Comedy*, ed. Regina Barreca (New York: Gordon and Breach, 1988) 12.
15. Mary Klages, "What to Do with Helen Keller Jokes: A Feminist Act," *Women and Comedy*, ed. Regina Barreca (New York: Gordon and Breach, 1992) 19.
16. Kingsley Amis, *Ending Up* (1974; London: Penguin, 1976) 82.
17. Mark Ratcliffe, "Bleak House," rev. of *Ending Up*, by Kingsley Amis, *The Times* 30 May 1974: 10.
18. John Higgins, "Critics Choice," rev. of *Ending Up*, by Kingsley Amis, *The Times* 28 November 1974: iv.
19. Barreca, introduction 9.
20. Fullbrook 46.
21. Joy Grant, "Ascendancy in Decline," rev. of *Time After Time*, by Molly Keane, *The Times Literary Supplement* 30 September 1983: 1059.
22. Keane 14.
23. Keane 44.
24. Keane 34–35.
25. Keane 129.
26. Keane 246–247.
27. Keane 98.

28. Macdonald and Rich 56.
29. Friedan 557.
30. Keane 47.
31. Keane 9.
32. Keane 159.
33. Keane 215.
34. Keane also make humorous use of the fact that she is blackmailed by the antique dealer, who caught her stealing a figurine, into accepting her ideal job.
35. Betty Swords, "Why Women Cartoonists Are Rare, and Why That's Important," Barreca, *Women and Comedy* 80.
36. Michel de Certeau, Luce Giard and Pierre Mayol, *Living and Cooking*, trans. Timothy J. Tomasik (1994; Minneapolis: University of Minnesota Press, 1998), vol. 2 of *The Practice of Everyday Life*, 256.
37. Martin Cooley, *The Comic Art of Barbara Pym* (New York: AMS Press, 1990) 18.
38. Michael Cottsell, *Barbara Pym* (London: Macmillan, 1989) 116.
39. Hazel Holt, *A Lot to Ask: A Life of Barbara Pym* (London: Macmillan, 1990).
40. Barreca's introduction to *Last Laughs* contains an interesting discussion of the relationship between female comedy and anger.
41. Cottsell 5.
42. Cottsell 5.
43. Barbara Pym, *Some Tame Gazelle* (1950; London: Pan, 1994) 3.
44. The heroines of *Some Tame Gazelle* are in their late fifties, which is slightly younger than the other protagonists I discuss. However, they seem to belong to an older generation than women currently of the same age. In addition, the novel is based in a small village with a relatively timeless quality, and the narrative could conceivably be set in any period from the 1930s onward; therefore the sisters' behavior seems a result of their age rather than their connection to a particular era.
45. Pym, *Some Tame Gazelle* 131.
46. Pym, *Some Tame Gazelle* 131.
47. Pym, *Some Tame Gazelle* 149.
48. Pym, *Some Tame Gazelle* 208.
49. Ellen M. Tsagaris, *The Subversion of Romance in the Novels of Barbara Pym* (Bowling Green: Bowling Green State UP, 1998) 163.
50. Pym, *Some Tame Gazelle* 231.
51. Barbara Brothers, "Women Victimised by Fiction: Living and Loving in the Novels of Barbara Pym," *Twentieth Century Women Novelists*, ed. Thomas F. Staley (London: Macmillan Press, 1982) 77.
52. Barreca, introduction 16.
53. Pym, *Some Tame Gazelle* 45.
54. Daphne Watson, *Their Own Worst Enemies: Women Writers of Women's Fiction* (London: Pluto Press, 1995) 49.
55. Watson 53.
56. Pym, *Some Tame Gazelle* 12.
57. Pym, *Some Tame Gazelle* 231.
58. Niamh Baker, *Happily Ever After: Women's Fiction in Postwar Britain, 1945–60* (New York: St. Martins Press, 1989) 26.
59. Pym 85.
60. Watson 48.
61. Waxman, *From the Hearth* 116. In developing this age-conscious interpretation, it could be suggested that Pym's paradigm of love is different from the common literary model, because the common model is based on a conception of what it is to be young and "in love." While it is relatively well documented among sociologists that our ideas about what "counts" as sexual activity is based on the experience of younger people, it is not discussed that our ideas about romantic love are based on a similar demographic. Although tempestuous affairs are not exclusive to younger characters, as the previous chapter illustrated, the companionable aspects of a relationship could be labeled more "mature" and perhaps help to explain their inclusion in texts that feature older protagonists.
62. This is not as well known as her return to literary favor after Philip Larkin and Lord David Cecil named her, in a *Times Literary Supplement* article about writers of the twentieth century, one of its most underrated writers.
63. For a more detailed discussion of these events and their connection to *Some Tame Gazelle*, see Holt's *A Lot to Ask*.
64. Holt 246. This comment perhaps suggests that the youthful Pym underestimated the power of platonic relationships insofar as she could not envisage her feelings for Henry Harvey turning into something as "mundanely" comfortable as a valued friendship. Barbara Brothers writes of Pym that she "gently mocks women's naivety and their romantic susceptibilities," and yet she appears to have been as susceptible to them as anyone else. This is not to judge her behavior but to suggest that perhaps the paradigm of unrequited love (different than a "crush") could also be

tied to a younger person's outlook on relationships.
65. Waxman, *From the Hearth* 106.
66. Certeau, Giard and Mayol 171.
67. Certeau, Giard and Mayol 151.
68. Pym, *Some Tame Gazelle* 9.
69. Pym, *Some Tame Gazelle* 38–44.
70. Pym, *Some Tame Gazelle* 57.
71. Virginia Rounding, "A Charmed Circle," rev. of *The Education of Harriet Hatfield*, by May Sarton, *The Times Literary Supplement* 9 March 1990: 258.
72. May Sarton, *The Education of Harriet Hatfield* (London: Women's Press, 1989) 320.
73. Sarton, *The Education of Harriet Hatfield* 165.
74. Sarton, *The Education of Harriet Hatfield* 60.
75. Butler, "Imitation" 13.
76. Butler, "Imitation" 19.
77. Sarton, *The Education of Harriet Hatfield* 162.
78. Sarton, *The Education of Harriet Hatfield* 200.
79. Foucault discusses this in *The History of Sexuality* in relation to discourses of sexuality.
80. Sarton, *The Education of Harriet Hatfield* 162.
81. Charity V. Schoonmaker, "Aging Lesbians: Bearing the Triple Burden of Shame," *Faces of Women and Aging*, eds. Nancy D. Davis, Ellen Cole and Esther D. Rothblum (New York: Hawthorne Press, 1993) 22.
82. Schoonmaker 21.
83. Friedan 548.
84. Mary Sarton, *The Magnificent Spinster* (London: The Women's Press, 1986) 58.
85. Rounding 258.
86. Certeau, Giard and Mayol 155.
87. Certeau, Giard and Mayol 255.
88. Brothers 79.
89. Barreca, introduction 18.

## Chapter 5

1. Agatha Christie cited Green as an influence on her work.
2. Miss Silver's final appearance was in *The Girl in the Cellar* (1961) and Dame Bradley's was in *Winking at the Brim* (1974).
3. A further reason, which applies to feminist literary criticism, lies in the fact that detective fiction is generic and, as such, has only relatively recently been considered suitable for academic attention, as will be discussed in more detail later in the chapter.
4. A fact that was made clear during the five years I worked in a bookshop.
5. These categories are used by Julian Symons throughout *Bloody Murder: From the Detective Story to the Crime Novel* (1972; London: Viking, 1985).
6. Glenwood Irons, introduction, *Gender, Language and Myth: Essays on Popular Narratives*, ed. Glenwood Irons (Toronto: University of Toronto Press, 1992) xiii.
7. John G. Cawelti, *Adventure, Mystery and Romance* (Chicago: University of Chicago Press, 1976) 299.
8. Cawelti 299.
9. Irons, introduction xiv.
10. Joanna Russ, "What Can a Heroine Do? Or Why Women Can't Write," *Images of Women in Fiction: Feminist Perspectives*, ed. Susan Keppelman Cornillion (Bowling Green: Bowling Green University Popular Press, 1972) 16.
11. Russ, "What" 17.
12. Sally Munt, *Murder by the Book? Feminism and the Crime Novel* (London: Routledge, 1994) 191.
13. Marty Roth, *Foul Play and Fair: Reading Genre in Classic Detective Fiction* (Athens: University of Georgia Press, 1995) xiv.
14. Munt 5. As, too, can authors such as Christie, Mitchell, and Wentworth, who perhaps would not have described themselves as such.
15. Munt 204.
16. Munt 204. Patricia Craig, in the introduction to the *Oxford Book of English Detective Stories* (Oxford: Oxford University Press, 1990) i–xi, has also commented on the "sportive" element of the genre, although not all readers have interpreted this attitude as a means of accommodating feminine concerns in an ostensibly masculine genre. However, including questions of aging and gender foregrounds the irreverent and satirical elements of ratiocinative novels.
17. Robert Graves, *The Greek Myths: Volume 1* (1955; London: Penguin, 1960) 92.
18. Graves 239.
19. Pratt, 7.
20. Patricia Wentworth, *The Watersplash* (1954; London: Hodder and Stoughton, 1990) 100.

21. Wentworth, *The Watersplash* 262.
22. Gladys Mitchell, *The Rising of the Moon* (1945; London: Hogarth Press, 1985) 97.
23. Symons 19.
24. Graves 122.
25. Pratt 16.
26. Graves 122.
27. Craig xix.
28. Munt 5.
29. Gladys Mitchell, *Mingled with Venom* (1978; Preston: Magna Print Books, 1981) 132.
30. Graves 239.
31. Hélène Cixous, "The Laugh of the Medusa," *Feminisms*, eds. Robyn R. Warhol and Diana Price Herndl (Basingstoke: Macmillan Press, 1997) 349.
32. Mitchell, *Mingled with Venom* 363–364.
33. Roth xi.
34. Symons 143.
35. Craig i–v.
36. Tvetsky Todorov, "The Typology of Detective Fiction," *Modern Criticism and Theory*, ed. David Lodge (London: Longman, 1990) 162.
37. Symons 94.
38. Roth 31.
39. Roth 30.
40. For an interesting analysis of why readers enjoy detective fiction, see chapter 1 of Symons's *Bloody Murder*.
41. Cawelti 97.
42. Roth 30.
43. Munt 9.
44. For a more detailed discussion of this point, see Symons, chapter 12.
45. From the back cover of Dashiell Hammett, *The Four Great Novels* (London: Picador, 1983).
46. Ralph Willett, *The Naked City: Urban Crime Fiction in the USA* (Manchester: Manchester University Press, 1996) 10.
47. Willett 7.
48. For a more intricate analysis of the younger female detective, see Glenwood Irons, "New Woman Detectives: G Is for Gender Bending," *Gender, Language and Myth*, ed. Glenwood Irons (Toronto: University of Toronto Press, 1992) 127–141.
49. Beauvoir, *Old Age* 210.
50. Irons, "G Is for Gender Bending" 127.
51. Craig xiv.
52. Catherine Kenney, "Detecting a Novel Use for Spinsters in Sayers' Fiction,"
*Old Maids to Radical Spinsters*, ed. Laura L. Doan (Chicago: University of Illinois Press, 1991) 131.
53. Patricia Craig and Mary Cadogan, *The Lady Investigates* (London: Victor Gollancz, 1981) 165.
54. Craig and Cadogan 165.
55. Patricia Wentworth, *The Allington Inheritance* (1960; London: Hodder and Stoughton, 1990) 148.
56. Patricia Wentworth, *Spotlight* (1949; London: Hodder and Stoughton, 1990) 254.
57. Kenney 125.
58. Tsagaris 156.
59. The whole dynamic of "clues" can also be envisaged in terms of a marginalized epistemology. As such, it is reminiscent of knowledge produced by women that has been judged insignificant and culturally invalid. From an age-conscious perspective, this hypothesis recalls de Beauvoir's assertion that the information possessed by older women is "outdated": an assumption challenged by crime novelists.
60. Kathleen Gregory Klein, *The Woman Detective: Gender and Genre* (1988; Urbana: University of Illinois Press, 1994) 141.
61. Gladys Mitchell, *When Last I Died* (1941; London: Hogarth Press, 1985) 148.
62. As noted by Craig and Cadogan in *The Lady Investigates*, 179.
63. Wentworth 143–144.
64. Roth 45.
65. Roth 22.
66. Klein 139.
67. Klein 30.
68. Furthermore, whereas the asexual older-female detective is labeled an "honorary man," the asexual male detective, because of his relative youth and gender, is not labeled an "honorary woman" (perhaps as an aesthetes but not as effeminate).
69. Munt 199.
70. Cawelti 36.
71. The novels are *The J. Alfred Prufrock Murders, Murder in Gray and White, Murder by Owl Light, The Peanut Butter Murders* and *Murder Has No Calories*.
72. Munt 202.
73. Corinne Holt Sawyer, *Murder by Owl Light* (New York: Fawcett Crest, 1992) 21.
74. Sawyer 12.
75. Sawyer 14.
76. Sawyer 226.
77. Sawyer 240.

78. Ruth Dudley Edwards, *Matricide at Saint Martha's* (London: HarperCollins, 1994) 50.
79. Sylvia Townsend Warner, *Lolly Willowes* (1926; London: Women's Press, 1978) 237.

## Conclusion

1. Waxman, *From the Hearth* 187. *Reifungsroman* is the name she gives to texts that she believes represent older women as "ripening."
2. Vita Sackville-West, *All Passion Spent* (1931; London: Virago, 1983) 178.
3. This argument appears in chapter 17 of *The Change* and in Victoria Glendinning's introduction to *All Passion Spent*, by Vita Sackville-West (1931; London: Virago, 1983) xviii.
4. Waxman, *From the Hearth* 188.
5. It is indicative of this theoretical "gap" that I was compelled to include a rather more in-depth explanation on the epistemological and methodological underpinnings of this study than usual. As a feminist researcher, an explanation of one's starting-point is an expected part of any study. However, this process is particularly necessary when novels are being approached from, what might be, an unfamiliar angle. This also explains the diversity of theoretical material that is brought to bear on the fiction.
6. Maroula Joannou, Contemporary Women's Writing: From The Golden Notebook to The Color Purple (Manchester: Manchester University Press, 2000) 188–189.

# Selected Bibliography

## Primary Texts

Amis, Kingsley. *Ending Up*. 1974. London: Penguin, 1976.
Barker, Pat. *Union Street*. London: Virago, 1982.
Beauvoir, Simone de. *The Woman Destroyed*. Trans. Patrick O'Brian. 1967. London: Flamingo, 1984.
Bell, Nancy. *Biggie and the Mangled Mortician*. New York: St. Martin's Paperbacks, 1997.
Cairns, Elizabeth. "Echoes." *Singing in Tune with Time: Stories and Poems About Ageing*. London: Virago, 1993. 195–208.
Carter, Angela. *The Passion of New Eve*. 1977. London: Virago, 1990.
———. *Wise Children*. London: Chatto and Windus, 1991.
Christie, Agatha. *A Caribbean Mystery*. 1964. London: Fontana Books, 1971.
———. *Miss Marple Omnibus: Volume 3. Nemesis*. 1971. *At Bertrams Hotel*. 1965. *Murder at the Vicarage*. 1930. London: Harpercollins, 1997.
Colette. *Chéri*. Trans. Roger Senhouse. 1920. London: Penguin, 1954.
———. *The Last of Chéri*. Trans. Roger Senhouse. 1926. London: Penguin, 1954.
Crane, Hamilton. *Sweet Miss Seeton*. New York: Berkley Prime Crime, 1997.
Desai, Anita. *Fire on the Mountain*. 1977. London: Vintage, 2001.
Diski, Jenny. *Happily Ever After*. London: Hamish Hamilton, 1991.
Drabble, Margaret. *The Witch of Exmoor*. London: Penguin, 1997.
Edwards, Ruth Dudley. *Matricide at Saint Martha's*. London: HarperCollins, 1994.
Evanovich, Janet. *One for the Money*. London: Penguin, 1994.
———. *Two for the Dough*. London: Hamish Hamilton, 1996.
———. *Three to Get Deadly*. London: Penguin, 1997.
Forster, Margaret. *Have the Men Had Enough?* London: Penguin, 1989.
Gilman, Charlotte Perkins. "The Yellow Wall-paper." *The Yellow Wall-paper and Other Stories*. Ed. Robert Shulman. 1890. London: Oxford University Press, 1998. 3–19.
Hammett, Dashiell. *The Four Great Novels*. London: Picador, 1983.
Harris, Joanne. *Chocolat*. London: Doubleday, 1999.
Keane, Molly. *Time After Time*. London: Abacus, 1985.
Laurence, Margaret. *The Stone Angel*. 1964. London: Virago, 1993.
Lessing, Doris. *The Diary of a Good Neighbour*. *The Diaries of Jane Somers*. London: Michael Joseph. 1984. 13–261.
———. *If the Old Could.... The Diaries of Jane Somers*. London: Michael Joseph. 1984. 267–510.

\_\_\_\_. *Love, Again*. London: Flamingo, 1996.
\_\_\_\_. *The Summer Before the Dark*. London: Jonathan Cape, 1973.
Mitchell, Gladys. *Mingled with Venom*. 1978. Preston: Magna Print Books, 1981.
\_\_\_\_. *The Rising of the Moon*. 1945. London: Hogarth Press, 1985.
\_\_\_\_. *Spotted Hemlock*. London: Penguin. 1958.
\_\_\_\_. *When Last I Died*. 1941. London: Hogarth Press, 1985.
Moore, Brian. *The Lonely Passion of Miss Judith Hearne*. London: Penguin, 1959.
Naylor, Gloria. *Mama Day*. London: Vintage, 1988.
Pym, Barbara. *Quartet in Autumn*. London: Macmillan, 1977.
\_\_\_\_. *Some Tame Gazelle*. 1950. London: Pan, 1994.
Sackville-West, Vita. *All Passion Spent*. 1931. London: Virago, 1983.
Sarton, May. *As We Are Now*. 1973. London: Women's Press, 1992.
\_\_\_\_. *The Education of Harriet Hatfield*. London: Women's Press, 1989.
\_\_\_\_. *The Reckoning*. 1978. London: Women's Press, 1984.
Sawyer, Corrine Holt. *Murder by Owl Light*. New York: Fawcett Crest, 1992.
\_\_\_\_. *Murder Has No Calories*. New York: Fawcett Crest, 1994.
Spark, Muriel. *Memento Mori*. 1959. London: Penguin, 1969.
Warner, Sylvia Townsend. *Lolly Willowes*. 1926. London: Women's Press, 1978.
Weldon, Fay. *Praxis*. London: Hodder and Stoughton, 1978.
\_\_\_\_. *Rhode Island Blues*. London: Flamingo, 2000.
Wentworth, Patricia. *The Allington Inheritance*. 1960. London: Hodder and Stoughton, 1990.
\_\_\_\_. *The Clock Strikes Twelve*. 1945. London: Hodder and Stoughton, 1997.
\_\_\_\_. *Spotlight*. 1949. London: Hodder and Stoughton, 1990.
\_\_\_\_. *The Watersplash*. 1954. London: Hodder and Stoughton, 1990.
Wharton, William. *Last Lovers*. London: Penguin, 1991.
Williams, Tennessee. *The Roman Spring of Mrs. Stone*. 1950. London: Vintage, 1999.

## Secondary Texts

Aherne, Jeremy. *Michel de Certeau: Interpretation and Its Other*. London: Polity Press, 1995.
Angelou, Maya. *Even the Stars Look Lonesome*. London: Virago, 1998.
Arber, Sara, and Jay Ginn, eds. *Connecting Gender and Ageing: A Sociological Approach*. Buckingham: Open University Press, 1995.
\_\_\_\_. "Choice and Constraint in the Retirement of Older Married Women." Arber and Ginn, *Connecting* 69–86.
Armitt, Lucie. *Contemporary Women's Fiction and the Fantastic*. London: Macmillan, 2000. 184–190.
Bailey, M. E. "Foucauldian Feminism: Contesting Bodies, Sexuality and Identity." Ramazanoglu 99–123.
Baker, Niamh. *Happily Ever After: Women's Fiction in Postwar Britain, 1945–60*. New York: St. Martins Press, 1989.
Baltes, Margaret M., and Laura L. Carstensen. "The Process of Successful Ageing." *Ageing and Society*. 16.4 (1996): 397–422.
Banner, Lois. *In Full Flower—Ageing Women, Power and Sexuality*. New York: Vintage Books, 1993.
Barreca, Regina. Introduction. *Last Laughs: Perspectives on Women and Comedy*. Ed. Regina Barreca. New York: Gordon and Breach, 1988. 3–22.
\_\_\_\_, ed. *Women and Comedy*. Philadelphia: Gordon and Breach, 1992.

Bartky, Sandra Lee. *Femininity and Domination: Studies in the Phenomonology of Oppression.* London: Routledge, 1990.
Battersby, Christine. *Gender and Genius: Towards a Female Aesthetic.* London: Women's Press, 1989.
Beauvoir, Simone de. *Old Age.* Trans. Patrick O'Brian. 1970. London: André Deutsch, 1972.
_____. *The Second Sex.* Trans. H.M. Parshley. 1949. London: Picador, 1988.
Belsey, Catherine. *Desire: Love Stories in Western Culture.* Oxford: Blackwell, 1994.
Biggs, Simon. "Choosing Not to Be Old? Masks, Bodies and Identity Management in Later Life." *Ageing and Society.* 17 (1997): 536–570.
Birch, Carol. "Airbrushed Age." Rev. of *Rhode Island Blues* by Fay Weldon. *The Guardian* 23 September 2000. http://guardian.co.uk/reviews/generalfiction. 1 July 2002.
Bonetti, Kay. "An Interview with May Sarton." Ingersol 85–107.
Bordo, Susan. "Feminism, Foucault and the Politics of the Body." Ramazanoglu 179–203.
_____. Unbearable Weight: Feminism, Western Culture and the Body. Berkeley: University of California Press, 1993.
Brothers, Barbara. "Women Victimised by Fiction: Living and Loving in the Novels of Barbara Pym." *Twentieth Century Women Novelists.* Ed. Thomas F. Staley. London: Macmillan Press, 1982. 61–80.
Browne, Colette V. *Women, Feminism and Ageing.* New York: Springer, 1998.
Butler, Judith. *Gender Trouble.* London: Routledge, 1990.
_____. "Imitation and Gender Subordination." *Inside/Out.* Ed. Diana Fuss. London: Routledge, 1991. 13–31.
Bytheway, Bill. *Ageism.* Buckingham: Open University Press, 1995.
_____. "Talking About Age: The Theoretical Basis of Social Gerontology." Jamieson, Harper and Victor, 7–15.
Cain, Maureen. "Foucault, Feminism and Feeling: What Foucault Can and Cannot Contribute to Feminist Epistemology." Ramazanoglu, 73–99.
Cawelti, John G. *Adventure, Mystery and Romance.* Chicago: University of Chicago Press, 1976.
Certeau, Michel de. *The Practice of Everyday Life.* Trans. Steven Rendell. 1980; Berkeley: University of California Press, 1984. Vol. 1 of *The Practice of Everyday Life.* 2 vols. 1980–1994.
_____, Luce Giard and Pierre Mayol. *Living and Cooking.* Trans. Timothy J. Tomasik. 1994; Minneapolis: University of Minnesota Press, 1998. Vol. 2 of *The Practice of Everyday Life.* 2 vols. 1980–1994.
Cixous, Hélène. "The Laugh of the Medusa." *Feminisms.* Eds. Robyn R. Warhol and Diana Price Herndl. Basingstoke: Macmillan Press, 1997. 347–362.
Clough, Roger, ed. *The Abuse of Care.* London: Whiting and Birch, 1996.
Cooley, Martin. *The Comic Art of Barbara Pym.* New York: AMS Press, 1990.
Cottsell, Michael. *Barbara Pym.* London: Macmillan, 1989.
Craig, Patricia. Introduction. *Oxford Book of English Detective Stories.* Ed. Patricia Craig. Oxford: Oxford University Press, 1990. i–xi.
_____, and Mary Cadogan. *The Lady Investigates.* London: Victor Gollancz, 1981.
Docherty, Thomas, ed. *Postmodernism: A Reader.* London: Harvester Wheatsheaf, 1993.
Eagleton, Terry. *Literary Theory: An Introduction.* Oxford: Blackwell, 1996.
English, Deirdre. "The Fear That Feminism Will Free Men First." Snitow, Stansell, and Thompson, *Desire* 97–102.

Evers, Helen. "Care or Custody? The Experiences of Women Patients in Long-Stay Geriatric Wards." Hutter and Williams, *Controlling Women* 108–130.

Fallis, Richard. "Grow Old Along with Me: Images of Older People in British and American Literature." *Perceptions of Aging in Literature*. Eds. Dorotka Bagnell and P. Spencer Soper. New York: Greenwood Press, 1989. 35–44.

Featherstone, Mike. "The Body in Consumer Culture." *Theory, Culture and Society*. 1.2 (1982): 18–33.

_____, and Mike Hepworth. "Ageing and Inequality: Consumer Culture and the New Middle Age." *Rethinking Social Inequality*. Ed. D. Robbins, et al. London: Gower, 1982. 97–126.

_____. "The Mask of Ageing and the Postmodern Life Course." *The Body—Social Process and Cultural Theory*. Eds. Mike Featherstone, Mike Hepworth and Bryan S. Turner. London: Sage Publications, 1991. 371–389.

Foucault, Michel. *Discipline and Punish: The Birth of the Prison*. Trans. Alan Sheridan. 1975. London: Penguin, 1991.

_____. *The History of Sexuality*. Trans. Robert Hurley. 3 vols. London: Allen Lane, 1976–1984.

_____. *Madness and Civilization: A History of Insanity in the Age of Reason*. Trans. R. Howard. 1961. London: Tavistock Publications, 1977.

Fraser, Nancy and Linda Nicholson. "Social Criticism Without Philosophy: An Encounter Between Feminism and Postmodernism." Docherty 415–432.

Friedan, Betty. *The Fountain of Age*. London: Vintage, 1994.

Fullbrook, Kate. "Jane Austen and the Comic Negative." *Women Reading Women's Writing*. Ed. Sue Roe. Brighton: Harvester Press Limited, 1987. 39–57.

Galler, Roberta. "The Myth of the Perfect Body." Vance, *Pleasure* 165–172.

Gamble, Sarah. *Angela Carter: Writing from the Front Line*. Edinburgh: Edinburgh University Press, 1997.

Glendenning, Frank. "The Mistreatment of Elderly People in Residential Institutions." *The Abuse of Care*. Ed. Roger Clough. London: Whiting and Birch, 1996. 35–49.

Glendinning, Victoria. Introduction. *All Passion Spent* by Vita Sackville-West. 1931. London: Virago, 1983. vii–xviii.

Grant, Joy. "Ascendancy in Decline." Rev. of *Time After Time* by Molly Keane. *The Times Literary Supplement* 30 September 1983: 1059.

Graves, Robert. *The Greek Myths: Volume 1*. 1955. London: Penguin, 1960.

Greene, Gayle. *Doris Lessing: The Poetics of Change*. Michigan: University of Michigan Press, 1994.

Greer, Germaine. *The Change*. London: Penguin, 1992.

Grimshaw, Jean. "Aging, Embodiment and Identity." Unpublished paper, 2001.

Healey, Shevy. "Confronting Ageism: A Must for Mental Health." *Faces of Women and Ageing*. Eds. Nancy D. Davis, Esther Rothblum, et al. New York: Hawthorne Press, 1993. 41–54.

Herbert, Rosemary, ed. *The Oxford Companion to Crime and Mystery Writing*. Oxford: Oxford University Press, 1999.

Hester, Marianne. *Lewd Women and Wicked Witches*. London: Routledge, 1993.

Higgins, John. "Critics Choice." Rev. of *Ending Up* by Kingsley Amis. *The Times* 28 November 1974: iv.

Higgs, Paul. "Citizenship Theory and Old Age: From Social Rights to Surveillance." Jamieson, Harper and Victor. 101–117.

Holt, Hazel. *A Lot to Ask: A Life of Barbara Pym*. London: Macmillan, 1990.

Horrocks, Chris, and Zoran Jevtic. *Introducing Foucault*. Cambridge: Icon Books, 1999.
Hutter, Bridget, and Gillian Williams, eds. *Controlling Women: The Normal and the Deviant*. London: Croom Helm, 1984.
———. "Controlling Women: The Normal the Deviant." Hutter and Williams, *Controlling Women* 9–39.
Ingersol, Earl G., ed. *Conversations with May Sarton*. Jackson: Mississippi UP, 1991.
Irons, Glenwood, ed. *Gender, Language and Myth: Essays on Popular Narratives*. Toronto: University of Toronto Press, 1992.
———. Introduction. Irons, *Gender* xiii–xviii.
———. "New Woman Detectives: G Is for Gender Bending." Irons, *Gender* 127–141.
Jamieson, Anne, Sarah Harper and Christina Victor, eds. *Critical Approaches to Ageing and Later Life*. Buckingham: Open University Press, 1997.
Jamieson, Anne and Christina Victor. "Theory and Concepts in Social Gerontology." Jamieson, Harper and Victor 175–187.
Johannou, Maroula. *Contemporary Women's Writing: From* The Golden Notebook *to* The Color Purple. Manchester: Manchester University Press, 2000.
Kehl, D.G. "The Staff and the Distaff: Stereotypes and Archetypes of the Older Woman in Representative Modern Literature." *International Journal of Aging and Human Development* 26.1 (1988): 1–12.
Kenny, Catherine. "Detecting a Novel Use for Spinsters in Sayers' Fiction." *Old Maids to Radical Spinsters*. Ed. Laura L. Doan. Urbana: University of Illinois Press, 1991. 123–137.
Klages, Mary. "What to Do with Helen Keller Jokes: A Feminist Act." Barreca, *Women and Comedy*. 13–22.
Klein, Kathleen Gregory. *The Woman Detective: Gender and Genre*. 1988. Urbana: University of Illinois Press, 1994.
Kritzman, Lawrence, ed. Michel Foucault: Interviews and Other Writings 1977–1984. London: Routledge, 1988.
Lesnoff-Caravaglia, Gari. "Double Stigmata: Female and Old." *The World of Older Women—Conflicts and Resolutions*. Ed. Gari Lesnoff-Caravaglia. New York: Human Sciences Press, 1984. 11–21.
Lessing, Doris. Preface. *The Diaries of Jane Somers*. Lessing. London: Michael Joseph, 1984. 5–10.
Lewis, Jane, and Barbara Meredith. *Daughters Who Care*. London: Routledge, 1988.
Liddell, Robert. *A Mind at Ease: Barbara Pym and Her Novels*. London: Peter Owen, 1989.
Lorde, Audre. "Age, Race, Class and Sex: Women Redefining Difference." *The Audre Lorde Companion*. London: HarperCollins, 1996. 162–171.
Loughman, Celeste. "Novels of Senescence: A New Naturalism." *The Gerontologist* 17.1 (1977): 79–84.
Lovibond, Sabina. "Feminism and Postmodernism." Docherty 390–414.
Macdonald, Barbara, and Cynthia Rich. *Look Me in the Eye*. London: Women's Press, 1985.
Maitland, Sara. Afterword. *The Stone Angel* by Margaret Laurence. 1964; London: Virago Press, 1993. 266–271.
McEwen, Evelyn. "What's Special About Being Old?" Arber and Ginn, 89–93.
McMullin, Julie. "Theorizing Age and Gender Relations." Eds. Arber and Ginn, *Connecting* 30–41.

McNay, Lois. *Foucault and Feminism*. London: Polity Press, 1992.
_____. *Foucault: A Critical Introduction*. London: Polity Press, 1994.
Moi, Toril. *Simone de Beauvoir: The Making of an Intellectual Woman*. Oxford: Blackwell, 1994.
Monteith, Moira. "Doris Lessing and the Politics of Violence." *Where No Man Has Gone Before: Women and Science Fiction*. Ed. Lucie Armitt. London: Routledge, 1991. 67–82.
Morris, Jenny. "Feminism and Disability." *Feminist Review* 43 (1993): 57–71.
_____. *Pride Against Prejudice: Transforming Attitudes to Disability*. London: Women's Press, 1991.
Munt, Sally. *Murder by the Book? Feminism and the Crime Novel*. London: Routledge, 1994.
Nett, Emily M. "The Naked Soul Comes Closer to the Surface: Old Age in the Gender Mirror of Contemporary Novels." *Women's Studies: An Interdisciplinary Journal* 18.2–3 (1990): 170–190.
Neuman, Shirley. Introduction. *ReImagining Women: Representations of Women in Culture*. Ed. Shirley Neuman. Toronto: University of Toronto Press, 1993. 3–18.
Newton, Ellen. *This Bed My Centre*. London: Virago, 1980.
Norris, Andrew. *Reminiscence with Elderly People*. London: Winslow Press, 1986.
Oberg, Peter. "The Absent Body—A Social Gerontological Paradox." *Ageing and Society* 16 (1996) 701–719.
Palmer, Paulina. *Narrative Practice and Feminist Theory*. Hemel Hempstead: Harvester Wheatsheaf, 1989.
Paoletti, Isabella. *Being an Older Woman: A Study in the Social Production of Identity*. London: Lawrence Erlbaum Associates, 1998.
Perkins, Charlotte Gilman. "Why I Wrote 'The Yellow Wall-paper'?" *The Yellow Wall-paper and Other Stories*. Ed. Robert Shulman. 1913. London: Oxford University Press, 1998. 331–332.
Phillipson, Chris. "Women in Later Life: Patterns of Control and Subordination." Hutter and Williams, *Controlling Women* 185–202.
Pratt, Annis. *Archetypal Patterns in Women's Fiction*. Brighton: Harvester Press, 1982.
Pulling, Jenny. *The Caring Trap*. London: Fontana, 1987.
Ramazanoglu, Caroline, ed. *Up Against Foucault*. London: Routledge, 1994.
Ratcliffe, Mark. "Bleak House." Rev. of *Ending Up* by Kingsley Amis. *The Times* 30 May 1974: 10.
Robinson, Lilian S. "Consciousness Lowering." Rev. of *The Change*, by Germaine Greer. *Women's Review of Books* January 10.4 (1993): 12.
Robinson, Sally. *Engendering the Subject: Gender and Self-Representation in Contemporary Women's Fiction*. New York: University of New York Press, 1991.
Ross, Deborah, "The Voice of Experience," *The Independent Review* 17 June 2002: 4–6.
Roth, Marty. *Foul Play and Fair: Reading Genre in Classic Detective Fiction*. Athens: University of Georgia Press, 1995.
Rounding, Virginia. "A Charmed Circle." Rev. of *The Education of Harriet Hatfield* by May Sarton. *The Times Literary Supplement* 9 March 1990: 258.
Russ, Joanna. *How to Suppress Women's Writing*. London: Women's Press, 1984.
_____. "What Can a Heroine Do? Or Why Women Can't Write." *Images of Women in Fiction: Feminist Perspectives*. Ed. Susan Keppelman Cornillion. Bowling Green: Bowling Green University Popular Press, 1972. 3–20

Sartou, May. *The Magnificent Spinster.* London: The Women's Press, 1986.
Sarup, Madan. *Identity, Culture and the Postmodern World.* Edinburgh: Edinburgh University Press, 1996.
Saum, Karen. "The Art of Poetry XXXII: May Sarton." Ingersol 108–129.
Sawicki, Jana. *Disciplining Foucault: Feminism, Power and the Body.* London: Routledge, 1991.
Saxton, Ruth. "The Female Body Veiled: From Crocus to Clitoris." *Woolf and Lessing: Breaking the Mold.* Eds. Ruth Saxton and Jean Tobin. New York: St. Martin's Press, 1994. 95–122.
Schoonmaker, Charity V. "Aging Lesbians: Bearing the Triple Burden of Shame." *Faces of Women and Aging.* Eds. Nancy D. Davis, Ellen Cole and Esther D. Rothblum. New York: Hawthorne Press, 1993. 21–31.
Scott, Sue, and David Morgan. "Bodies in a Social Landscape." *Body Matters.* Eds. Sue Scott and David Morgan. London: Falmer Press, 1993. 1–21.
Seldan, Raman. *The Theory of Criticism: From Plato to the Present.* New York: Longman, 1988.
Shakespeare, Nicholas. "Bags of Giddyap Boyo." Rev. of *Time After Time* by Molly Keane. *The Times* 13 October 1983: 9.
Sharpe, James. *Instruments of Darkness: Witchcraft in England 1550–1750.* London: Hamish Hamilton, 1996.
Showalter, Elaine. "Feminist Criticism in the Wilderness." *Modern Criticism and Theory.* Ed. David Lodge. London: Longman, 1988. 351–353.
———. "Towards a Feminist Poetics." *Feminist Literary Theory: A Reader.* Ed. Mary Eagleton. London: Basil Blackwell, 1986. 188–191.
Singer, Linda. "True Confessions: Cixous and Foucault on Sexuality and Power." *Erotic Welfare: Sexual Theory and Politics in the Age of Epidemic.* London: Routledge, 1993. 145–162.
Snitow, Ann, Christine Stansell, and Sharon Thompson, eds. *Desire: The Politics of Sexuality.* London: Virago, 1984.
———. Introduction. Snitow, Stansell and Thompson, *Desire* 1–35.
Sontag, Susan. "The Double Standard of Ageing." *Ageing Population.* Eds. Vidd Carver and Penny Liddiard. London: Hodder and Stoughton, 1987. 72–80.
Soper, Kate. "Productive Contradictions." Ramazanoglu 29–51.
Stokes, Graham. *On Being Old: The Psychology of Later Life.* London: Falmer Press, 1992.
Swords, Betty. "Why Women Cartoonists Are Rare, and Why That's Important." Barreca, *Women and Comedy* 65–84.
Symons, Julian. *Bloody Murder: From the Detective Story to the Crime Novel.* 1972. London: Viking, 1985.
Synott, Anthony. *The Body Social: Symbolism, Self and Society.* London: Routledge, 1993.
Terry, Paul. *Counselling the Elderly and Their Carers.* London: Macmillan Press, 1997.
Thomas, Dylan. "Do not go gentle into that good night." *The Dylan Thomas Omnibus.* 1952. London: Phoenix Press, 2000. 128–129.
Thompson, Dorothy Perry. "African Womanist Revision in Gloria Naylor's *Mama Day* and *Baileys Café*." *Gloria Naylor's Early Novels.* Ed. Margot Anne Kelley. Gainesville: University of Florida Press, 1999. 89–111.
Thompson, Paul. "'I Don't Feel Old': Subjective Ageing and the Search for Meaning in Later Life." *Ageing and Society* 12 (1992): 27.

Todorov, Tvetsky. "The Typology of Detective Fiction." *Modern Criticism and Theory*. Ed. David Lodge. London: Longman, 1990. 157–165.
Tsagaris, Ellen M. *The Subversion of Romance in the Novels of Barbara Pym*. Bowling Green: Bowling Green State University Press, 1998.
Vance, Carole S. "Pleasure and Danger: Towards a Politics of Sexuality." Vance 1–27.
\_\_\_\_\_, ed. *Pleasure and Danger: Exploring Female Sexuality*. London: Routledge, 1984.
Walker, Alan, and Tony Maltby. *Ageing Europe*. Buckingham: Open University Press, 1997.
Watson, Daphne. *Their Own Worst Enemies: Women Writers of Women's Fiction*. London: Pluto Press, 1995.
Waxman, Barbara Frey. *From the Hearth to the Open Road: A Feminist Study of Aging in Contemporary Literature*. London: Greenwood Press, 1990.
\_\_\_\_\_. *To Live in the Center of the Moment: Literary Autobiographies of Aging*. Charlottesville: University Press of Virginia, 1997.
Weedon, Chris. *Feminist Practice and Poststructuralist Theory*. Oxford: Blackwell, 1987.
Whittaker, Ruth. *Doris Lessing*. London: Macmillan, 1988.
Willett, Ralph. *The Naked City: Urban Crime Fiction in the USA*. Manchester: Manchester University Press, 1996.
Williams, Simon J. "The Vicissitudes of Embodiment Across the Chronic Illness Trajectory." *Body and Society*. 2.2 (1996): 23–44.
Wilson, Gail. "'I'm the Eyes and She's the Arms': Changes in Gender Roles in Advanced Age." Arber 98–113.
Wolf, Naomi. *The Beauty Myth*. London: Vintage, 1991.
Woodward, Kathleen. "Age-Work in American Culture." *American Literary History*. 6.4 (1994): 779–791.
\_\_\_\_\_. "Tribute to the Older Woman: Psychoanalysis, Feminism, and Ageism." *Images of Aging: Cultural Representations of Later Life*. Eds. Mike Featherstone and Andrew Wernick. London: Routledge, 1995 79–96.
Woolf, Virginia. *A Room of One's Own*. 1929. London: Grafton Books, 1990.
Wurtzel, Elizabeth. *Bitch*. London: Quartet Books, 1988.

# Index

Ageism 1, 5–6, 15, 18, 20, 22, 24, 26, 30, 32, 36–8, 44, 76–7, 89, 98, 140, 150
Aherne, Jeremy, *Michel de Certeau* 112
Amis, Kingsley, *Ending Up* 113–118
Angelou, Maya, "Age and Sexuality" 109
Arber, Sara, and Jay Ginn 22, 32
Armitt, Lucy, *Contemporary Women's Fiction and the Fantastic* 90

Bailey, M.E., "Foucauldian Feminism" 7, 10
Baker, Niamh, *Happily Ever After* 121, 124
Baltes, Margaret M,. and Laura L. Carstensen, "The Process of Successful Ageing" 111–112
Banner, Lois W., *In Full Flower* 78, 85–6, 96, 98, 107
Barker, Pat, *Union Street* 32–33
Barreca, Regina, "Introduction" 113, 115, 123, 132–3
Bartky, Sandra, *Femininity and Domination* 8–9
Battersby, Christine, *Gender and Genius* 12
Bayley, Thomas Haynes 124
Beauvoir, Simone de 79, 131; *Old Age* 1, 28–30, 33–34, 40, 51, 111–112, 145–6; *The Second Sex* 11, 27–28, 87; *The Woman Destroyed* 28–29
Bell, Nancy, *Biggie and the Mangled Mortician* 147
Belsey, Catherine, *Desire* 89–90, 93–4, 97–9, 108–9

Biggs, Simon, "Choosing Not to Be Old?" 23
Bonneti, Kay, *Conversations with May Sarton* 68
Bordo, Susan, *Unbearable Weight* 11, 44, 82, 84–6
Brothers, Barbara, "Women Victimised by Fiction" 122–3, 132
Browne, Colette V., *Women, Feminism and Aging* 36
Butler, Judith 96; *Gender Trouble* 77, 90, 93–5; "Imitation and Gender Subordination" 25, 128–9
Bytheway, Bill, 35; *Ageism* 5, 20

Cain, Maureen, "Foucault, Feminism and Feeling" 36
Cairns, Elizabeth, 76, "Echoes" 105
Carter, Angela 15, 38; *The Passion of New Eve* 94; *Wise Children* 76–7, 79, 89–96, 99, 105–6, 109, 125, 157
Cawelti, John, *Adventure, Mystery and Romance* 137, 144, 152
Certeau, Michel de 15, 131–2; *Living and Cooking* 112, 120, 125–6; *The Practice of Everyday Life* 112
Chandler, Raymond 136, 144–5
Chaucer 78
Chesterton, G.K. 140
Christie, Agatha 6, 134, 136, 140, 147–8; *Caribbean Mystery* 141; *Murder in the Vicarage* 135; *Nemesis* 141
Cixous, Hélène 96; "The Laugh of the Medusa" 141–2
Clough, Roger, *The Abuse of Care in Residential Institutions* 62

Colette, *Cheri* 76, 92, 98–99; *The Last of Cheri* 76, 92–3, 107
Conan Doyle, Arthur 143
Cooley, Martin, *The Comic Art of Barbara Pym* 120
Cornwell, Patricia 136–7
Cottsell, Michael, *Barbara Pym* 120–1
Coupland, Douglas, *Generation X* 17
Craig, Patricia 141, 147
Craig, Patricia, and Mary Cadogan, *The Lady Investigates* 134, 148, 150
Crane, Hamilton 136

Desai, Anita, *Fire on the Mountain* 158
detective novels 15, 43, 134–156
Dine, S. S. Van 143
Diski, Jenny, *Happily Ever After* 3, 76–7, 79, 96–109, 125, 157
Drabble, Margaret, *The Witch of Exmoor* 23

Eco, Umberto, *The Name of the Rose* 136
Edwards, Ruth Dudley, *Matricide at Saint Martha's* 136, 147, 155
elder abuse 48, 58–67, 74
Evanovich, Janet: *One for the Money* 146; *Two for the Dough* 146
Evers, Helen, "Care or Custody?" 63

Fallis, Richard, "Grow Old Along with Me" 39–40
Featherstone, Mike, "The Body in Consumer Culture" 54
Featherstone, Mike, and Mike Hepworth 35, 86; "Ageing and Inequality" 54; "The Mask of Ageing and the Postmodern Life Course" 23
Fforde, Katie, *Thyme Out* 160
Fleming, Ian 136
Forster, Margaret, *Have the Men Had Enough?* 56–7, 61, 65–6, 74
Foucault, Michel 7, 9, 10, 37, 44, 96, 159; *Discipline and Punish* 8, 58–9; *The History of Sexuality* 8, 13, 77, 91–3, 119
Francis, Dick 136

Friedan, Betty 26, 32; *The Fountain of Age* 4, 21–2, 32–5, 46, 118, 130
Fullbrook, Kate, "Jane Austen and the Comic Negative" 113, 115

Galler, Roberta, "The Myth of the Perfect Body" 88
Gamble, Sarah, *Angela Carter* 91, 95
Gilman, Charlotte Perkins: "Why I Wrote the Yellow Wallpaper" 65; "The Yellow Wallpaper" 64–5
Glendinning, Victoria 158
Grafton, Sue 145, 151
Graves, Robert, *The Greek Myths* 142
Green, Anne Katherine, *The Affair Next Door* 134
Greene, Gayle, *Doris Lessing* 49
Greer, Germaine 26; *The Change* 4, 5, 21, 27–8, 37, 89, 158
Grimshaw, Jean, "Aging, Embodiment and Identity" 111

Hammett, Dashiell 144
Harper, Sarah, "Constructing Later Life/Constructing the Body" 22
Harris, Joanna, *Chocolat* 160
Healey, Shevy, "Confronting Ageism" 25–26
Hester, Marianne, *Lewd Women and Wicked Witches* 78
Higgs, Paul, "Citizen Theory and Old Age" 32
Holt, Hazel 125
humor 9, 37, 113–126, 138, 141–2, 146
Hutter, Bridget, and Gillian Williams, "Controlling Women" 3, 55

Irons, Glenwood: "G Is for Gender-Bending" 146–7; *Gender, Language and Myth* 137

Jamieson, Anne, and Christina Victor 22
Johannou, Maroula, *Contemporary Women's Writing* 159

Keane, Molly, *Time After Time* 39, 110–113, 115–119
Kenney, Catherine 147–8

Kerouac, Jack, *On the Road* 17
Klages, Mary, "What to Do with Helen Keller Jokes: A Feminist Act" 113
Klein, Kathleen Gregory, *The Woman Detective* 149–151

Laurence, Margaret, *The Stone Angel* 19, 21, 41, 55, 59, 69, 71–5, 128, 158
Lesnoff-Caravaglia, Gari, "Double Stigmata: Female and Old" 31–2
Lessing, Doris 15; *The Canopus in Argos: Archives* 50; *The Diary of a Good Neighbour* 3, 4, 33, 43, 47–58, 65, 70, 73–5, 81, 157–8; *The Grass Is Singing* 50; *If the Old Could* 50; *Love, Again* 24, 50, 76–7, 80–91, 125, 157–8; *The Summer Before the Dark* 50
Lorde, Audre, "Age, Race, Class and Sex" 38
Loughman, Celeste, "Novels of Senescence" 40–1, 47

Macdonald, Barbara, and Cynthia Rich, *Look Me in the Eye* 24, 36–7, 112, 135
Maitland, Sarah 19
Mansell, Jill, *Miranda's Big Mistake* 160
McEwen, Evelyn, "What's Special About Being Old?" 62
McMullin, Julie, "Theorising Age and Gender Relations" 27
menopause 5
middle-age 5, 20–1, 35, 37, 43, 48, 50, 53, 85, 92, 99, 135, 140, 157
Mitchell, Gladys 38, 146–8, 151–152, 154–6; *Mingled with Venom* 141–2, 149–150; *The Rising of the Moon* 139–140; *Speedy Death* 135; *Spotted Hemlock* 144
Moi, Toril, *Simone de Beauvoir* 29–30
Monteith, Moira, "Doris Lessing and the Politics of Violence" 52
Moore, Brian, *The Lonely Passion of Miss Judith Hearne* 99
Morris, Jenny: "Feminism and Disability" 35–6; *Pride Against Prejudice* 48, 57
Munt, Sally, *Murder by the Book?* 138–9, 144, 150–2

Naylor, Gloria, *Mama Day* 5
Nett, Emily M., "The Naked Sole Comes Closer to the Surface" 41–2, 47
Neuman, Shirley, *ReImagining Women* 6, 13–14
Newton, Ellen, *This Bed My Centre* 47, 61–3

Oberg, Peter, "The Absent Body" 77, 79–80, 82, 84, 86
old age: definitions of 4, 5, 25–6, 35, 159; dementia in 60–2, 154; friendships and 49–52, 55, 57–8, 63, 74, 70, 114, 121–8, 130, 158, 160; happiness and, 15, 74, 110–133; loneliness in 9, 41, 49; male characters and 2, 5, 27, 30–2, 34, 39–42, 77, 95, 98–9, 105, 114–118, 121–2, 140; physical dependency in 1, 18, 33, 35, 46–75, 114–15; sexuality in 10, 15, 29–30, 76–109, 128– 130, 157–8; spirituality in 41–2, 67–73, 158; stereotypes of 2, 17– 19, 33, 40, 63, 77–8, 88, 102, 110– 111, 134, 135, 139, 147–152, 154–5, 157–8; terminal illness and 23, 45, 49, 67–75; *see also* ageism; elder abuse; humor; menopause; middle-age; retirement homes; witches
Orbach, Susie, *Fat Is a Feminist Issue* 79

Palmer, Pauline, *Narrative Practice and Feminist Theory* 5
Paoletti, Isabella, *Being an Older Woman* 10, 43
Paretsky, Sara 3, 145, 151
Peters, Ellis 136
Poe, Edgar Allan 143
Pratt, Annis, *Archetypal Patterns in Women's Fictions* 69, 139
Pym, Barbara 38, 120, 130, 149, 157–8; *Quartet in Autumn* 6, 9, 14, 120; *Some Tame Gazelle* 6, 110–113,

120–127, 132–3, 142, 156; *The Sweet Dove Died* 120

Ratcliffe, Michael 115
retirement homes 46, 56, 58–67, 152–4
Robinson, Sally, *Engendering the Subject* 7, 12
Roth, Marty 138; *Foul and Fair Play* 143, 150–1
Rounding, Virginia, "A Charmed Circle" 127, 131
Rubin, Gayle 6
Russ, Joanna, "What Can a Heroine Do?" 137–8

Sackville-West, Vita, *All Passion Spent* 111, 158
Sarton, May 15; *As We Are Now* 39, 43, 47–8, 58–68, 70, 73–5, 107, 131, 156–8; *The Education of Harriet Hatfield* 110–113, 127–133; *Endgame* 39; *The Magnificent Spinster* 127, 130–1; *The Reckoning* 47, 67–75, 128, 131
Sarup, Madan, *Identity, Culture and the Postmodern World* 10
Saum, Karen 59, 66
Sawicki, Jana 44
Sawyer, Corinne Holt 136–137, 147; *Murder by Owl Light* 152–4
Saxton, Ruth, "The Female Body Veiled" 89
Sayers, Dorothy L. 135, 147
Schoonmaker, Charity V., "Aging Lesbians" 129–130
Scott, Sue, and David Morgan, *Body Matters* 53
Shakespeare, Nicholas 110
Sharpe, James, *Instruments of Darkness* 78
Singer, Linda, "True Confessions" 96
Snitow, Ann, Christine Stansell and Sharon Thompson, "Introduction" 100–1, 108
Sontag, Susan, "The Double Standard of Ageing" 30
Soper, Kate, "Productive Contradictions" 38
Spark, Muriel, *Memento Mori* 41

Stokes, Graham, *On Being Old* 46, 61
Swords, Betty, "Why Women Cartoonists Are Rare, and Why That's Important" 119
Symons, Julian, *Bloody Murder* 135, 140, 143
Synott, Anthony, *The Body Social* 79–82, 84, 87

Taylor, Elizabeth, *Mrs. Palfrey at the Claremont* 41
Tey, Josephine 135
Thompson, Paul, "I Don't Feel Old" 24
Tsagaris, Ellen M., *The Subversion of Romance in the Novels of Barbara Pym* 122, 149
Tuner, Bryan, *The Body and Society* 79

Vance, Carol S., "Pleasure and Danger" 77, 92

Walker, Alan, and Tony Maltby, *Ageing Europe* 26
Warner, Sylvia Townsend, *Lolly Willowes* 155
Watson, Daphne, *Their Own Worst Enemies* 123–125
Waxman, Barbara Frey 159; *From the Hearth to the Open Road* 4, 42–4, 47–8, 61, 66–7, 125, 156; *To Live in the Center of the Moment* 62
Weedon, Chris, *Feminist Practice and Poststructuralist Theory* 14
Weldon, Fay 6, 26, 38; *Praxis* 31; *Rhode Island Blues* 12, 24–5, 31, 39, 99, 157
Wentworth, Patricia 6, 146–7, 149–152, 154–5; *The Allington Inheritance* 143, 148; *The Clock Strikes Twelve* 144; *Grey Mask* 135; *Spotlight* 148; *Water Splash* 139, 143–4
Wesley, Mary, *Jumping the Queue* 39
Wharton, William, *Last Lovers* 76, 99, 103–4
Willett, Ralph, *The Naked City* 145
Williams, Simon J., "The Vicissitudes of Embodiment Across the

Chronic Illness Trajectory" 69–70, 72
Williams, Tennessee, *The Roman Spring of Mrs. Stone* 99
Wilson, Gail, "'I'm the Eyes and She's the Arms'" 34

witches 78, 139–43, 155
Woodward, Kathleen: "Age-Work in American Culture" 43; "Tribute to the Older Woman" 28
Woolf, Virginia, *A Room of One's Own* 3, 11

www.ingramcontent.com/pod-product-compliance
Lightning Source LLC
Chambersburg PA
CBHW032103300426
44116CB00007B/862